Money Matters

Essential Tips and Tools for Building Financial Peace of Mind

Money Matters

Essential Tips and Tools for Building
Financial Peace of Mind

Scott Hanson

Marketplace Books
Columbia, MD

- Publisher, Chris Myers
- VP/General Manager, John Boyer
- Senior Editor, John Probst
- Project Editor, Aphrodite Knoop
- Associate Editor, Jody Costa
- Art Director, Larry Strauss
- Production Coordinator, Chris Franks
- Design, Donna Detweiler, Indigo Ink

Library of Congress Cataloging-in-Publication Data

Hanson, Scott.
  Money matters : essential tips and tools for building financial peace of mind / by Scott Hanson.
    p. cm.
  ISBN 1-59280-252-4 (alk. paper)
  1. Finance, Personal. I. Title.
HG179.H268 2006
332.024—dc22
                            2006020662

ISBN: 1-59280-252-4

Publisher: Marketplace Books

Printed in the United States of America

CONTENT

INTRODUCTION

When I was growing up, work was for Monday through Saturday, and Sunday was the day of rest, church, family dinners, and time spent in leisure reading newspapers and recapping the week's events. Sunday was also a day when my parents discussed personal money matters and made financial decisions such as buying a car or a new piece of furniture, saving for a vacation, or paying for orthodontics or for Grandma's care. It was also the day I would hide from my creditors. I was only 12 years old and already had gotten myself into serious financial trouble.

Back then, like a lot of kids my age, I had a paper route. I used to deliver the *Daily Breeze* in Torrance, California. I'd toss papers Monday through Friday afternoons and early mornings on the weekends.

What happened to me at age 12 was probably the best financial lesson I ever had and has continued to guide me through life. In those days, paperboys had contracts with the newspaper companies for which they worked. I'd buy my papers from my supervisor Larry Rybarczyk. Larry was a friendly man who would lend me a hand on days when the newspapers were extra thick with flyers.

My job was to deliver the newspapers, collect from my customers, pay my supplier, and keep the rest. It typically amounted to about $1 per paper per month, or about $50.

My mother had always told me that I could keep only the profits that were left at the end of the month. I'd go door to door to collect the monthly subscription fee, smile wide in hopes of a tip, put the money in a jar, pay my supplier at month's end, and add my profits.

I still remember how I got into trouble. It started quite innocently when my best friend, Jerry Williams, asked me one summer day, "Hey, what are you doing today?"

"Nothing," I answered.

"Let's go get a Giant Grinder and go ride the go-carts." The Giant Grinder had the best sandwiches in the entire universe and the go-cart place was just a few blocks away.

"I can't, I'm broke," I told Jerry. "I have to wait until next month when I have some more money."

"Why don't we go collect from a couple of houses?" Jerry was also a paperboy.

"Great idea," I told him, and thus began my life of running from creditors.

I have to admit it was all based on the need for the money. (As a financial advisor 25 years later, I see these same mistakes.) Jerry and I began our summer routine of collecting payments from a couple of newspaper subscribers, chowing down Giant Grinders, and then riding the go-carts. But when the end of the month came and I didn't have the money to pay for the papers, Larry came looking for me. I had to hide from the man.

Finally, one Sunday we came home from church, and there was Larry's car in the driveway. By now, I owed him over $60 bucks and had spent all my collection money on food and entertainment. I was afraid to face Larry: not because he was bigger and could squash me like a bug, but because I was embarrassed that I didn't have his money. I knew I should have paid his bill before spending the money, but somehow I got my priorities out of whack.

I locked the door and ducked behind the back seat, hoping he wouldn't see me. Suddenly, I heard knocking on the window. I raised my head to see Larry and my dad standing there. I'll never forget the looks of utter disappointment on their faces. I wished I could just ignore my financial problem, but knew there was nowhere to hide.

My dad gave Larry $60 to bail me out, and then we had a long chat about the good things that money can buy and also all the troubles it can cause. I learned several valuable lessons that summer. It took three months to repay my dad, and by the time I was debt-free, the go-cart place had closed.

At age 12, I learned that I couldn't run from my financial problems—that they somehow always find me. Money can bring pleasures in life, but it can also cause great stress.

Today, I see people getting into the same trouble. I now have the privilege of teaching not only my kids but also regular folks—thousands of them— how to stay out of debt, how to invest, and how to manage their money. I'm happy to report that when you strip away all the baloney and learn how to reverse your debts, handling your finances can be fairly easy.

My childhood insight and 15 years of experience prompted me to write this book. I want to educate and empower everyone who desires financial independence and freedom from debt.

Each of the problems covered in this book derives from true events and has simple solutions.

Money Matters is not a textbook. It is an organized collection of ideas, examples, tips, and suggestions to awaken your creativity and encourage you to explore new ways to achieve financial peace of mind.

Who am I to help you? I am Scott Hanson, a practicing financial advisor and co-host of a weekly call-in radio program. I'm also the founder of Hanson McClain, Inc.—a registered investment advisory firm in northern California that assists in the asset management of approximately $1 billion for its clients. With my partner, Pat McClain, I also founded Hanson McClain Retirement Network, LLC, which has helped thousands of people across America to retire comfortably.

In addition, Pat and I founded Liberty Reverse Mortgage, Inc. to help seniors manage their debts and enable retirees to increase cash flow. Liberty is currently one of the top reverse mortgage consultants in the country.

I'm also a certified financial planner (CFP), a certified fund specialist (CFS) and a chartered financial consultant (ChFC). I teach several financial planning courses for Fortune 500 companies and the general public. In addition to my advisory duties, I co-host "Money Matters" each Sunday from 11 a.m. to 1 p.m. on Sacramento's largest AM station, NewsTalk 1530 KFBK.

Investment Advisor magazine has listed me as one of the Top 25 most influential people in and around the financial planning profession for 2005. *Registered Rep* and *Research* magazines listed me and Pat McClain as being among the top 40 advisors in the country in 2002, 2003, and 2004.

Over the past decade, I also wrote a weekly column for the Sacramento Bee that was nationally syndicated by Scripps Howard.

I was lucky that the paper route money disaster happened to me at such an early age because it's driven me to teach and empower people to take control of their finances. And it's probably the reason I became a financial advisor in the first place.

This book is not for the rich and famous, but for everyday people seeking to live and retire free of financial stress and worries. It's for the couple that just retired, the divorcee living on alimony and supporting three kids, the widow who needs additional income, the young couple in debt, and so on. It's for the ordinary Joe.

I've discovered that most people never receive even a basic education in finance—until it's too late—which may mean after a divorce, an improper rollover, or a death forcing a widow to deal with everything at the worst possible time. All too often the result is financial devastation.

I want to help. I want all hard-working people who find themselves making financial decisions with little or no information to have the education and tools to care for themselves financially—no matter what the circumstances.

I have designed *Money Matters* to address and recognize the financial mistakes, their root causes, and some simple strategies to give readers effective ways to achieve financial security.

We are all playing the financial game whether we want to or not. The truth is that you have no choice. Are you winning at your game? Unfortunately, most people are not. That's because they never learned the rules and never received an instruction manual, a roadmap, or a mentor to guide them along the way.

Money Matters: Essential Tips and Tools for Building Financial Peace of Mind can help readers develop the muscle they need to recognize and resist hazardous attitudes and behavior patterns, develop risk assessment skills, and evaluate the validity and effectiveness of the advice they are receiving—with the added benefit of learning how to direct their actions to achieve financial peace of mind.

Before we begin, I want to give you some basic tips on reading the book. First, it's okay to skip around. If you're looking for answers to a real estate problem, it's okay to go to that section. Please think of this book as a tool, not as a system to get rich. There are too many of those get-rich-quick books on the market, and most of them aren't worth your time.

As you read through the chapters and the real-life strategies, something interesting will happen. You'll start to feel more confident about the decisions you may have made or the ones you're about to make. You'll also be given resources for where and how to confirm that you're making the best financial decision that you can.

Finally, I want you to enjoy this book. You're embarking on an exciting adventure—one that I hope will change your financial future.

Money Matters

Chapter 1
Get Out and Stay Out of Debt

I hate seeing good people in bad debt!

Don't be one of those people who think, "I've got too much going on this month. I'll wait until next month, or next quarter, or next year to start saving." People who think like that never accumulate wealth. You always pay for your future, either today or later. People who can't commit to saving end up with the same problems later in life, but worse—and may find themselves having to decide between buying food or paying for their prescription drugs.

This chapter will motivate you to start saving today. Why don't people get themselves out of debt, even when they can't sleep, are stressed, and have to hide from creditors? Because the motivation to borrow money (they get to buy stuff) is stronger than any reason they've been given not to. That's why we keep reading about the tens of millions of Americans who keep running up their credit cards: household debts are close to $10 trillion. People need a more powerful reason to get *out* of debt—painlessly—than to stay *in* debt.

Not one individual investor has averaged better than around 10.5% for any 10- to 20-year period. If we look at the last 100 years of stock market returns, including our last great bull market of the 1990s, it still hasn't beat a 10.5% average rate of return. Yet, almost every unsecured credit card carries interest rates of 16% or 20%—after the "come-on" rate expires. A *come-on* rate is designed to lure you into using the credit card for a year or so before reverting to its underlying higher rate—which lasts forever. Clearly, it is a sucker's game.

Become a Deadbeat

Most of the time, you wouldn't want to be called a deadbeat, but that's the biggest compliment you can get from a credit card company. Most Americans carry credit card balances, but these balances carry interest and generate interest charges each month. That's what the credit card companies love. But financially smart people use credit cards for conveniences, for frequent flyer miles, or for other affinity programs. They pay off their balances each month and thus avoid interest charges. The industry has a term for those who never pay interest charge—*deadbeats*. In this case, you want to be a deadbeat.

If you're going to carry any credit card, American Express is probably the best because it requires you to pay the balance each month. American Express does not allow users to carry balances from month to month, accruing interest charges. When you use the American Express card you know you must pay that $100 purchase by next month. If you don't pay it, you'll lose the card. With Visa, MasterCard, or any other card that lets you carry a balance, it's too tempting to defer paying balances for other purchases or emergencies. Do yourself a favor and build in the full payment requirement. The American Express annual fee may cost less than the interest you would have accrued elsewhere.

Pay off One Bill at a Time

Maybe you're like the typical American—you have $8,000 in credit card debt split among nine different accounts. You may have $3,000 on your Visa card, $2,000 on MasterCard, $500 on your JC Penny's account, $100 on your Costco account, and so forth. You're getting nine bills every month. Every day you go to the mailbox, and there's another bill waiting for you. If you want to make a goal of paying them off, forget which company is charging the highest interest rate. In addition to making the minimum payments on all of them, select the one with the smallest balance and do everything you can to pay off that bill. That's one less bill you're going to get each month. You might find that you're going to pay off five of the nine creditors in a couple of months just by focusing on the smaller bills. The overall balance of your outstanding debt might not have decreased much, but from a psychological standpoint, you just eliminated five out of your eight creditors. That's invigorating and uplifting. It can empower you and provide some encouragement to continue.

Start Saving

This may sound obvious, but one of the best ways to avoid getting into debt is to have a savings plan. Many people get into debt because they feel they can't get ahead anyway, so they start spending more than they can afford, ending up with big credit card problems. Most consumer debt arises from unnecessary purchases. People shop to fill some void in their lives and make themselves feel better.

If people, in their very first job, would make an effort to save some portion of their paycheck—it doesn't matter whether it's 5%, 10%, or even 2%—they would begin to feel some financial control in their lives. Feelings of financial control lead to empowerment and to smarter decisions. These people might even find that having some money in the bank or in their 401(k) plans is far more satisfying than going to the mall and buying another pair of shoes.

Freeze Your Credit Cards

Many people have tried to get out of credit card debt but still struggle with it. Plastic leads you to spend what you don't have. There's no pain involved. You're not taking the greenbacks out of your wallet and giving them to somebody. It's just an easy transaction; you don't feel it.

The solution is to discard all credit cards and use cash for everything.

Okay, maybe keep one card for actual emergencies, and keep it where it's not easily accessible. Don't carry it with you.

Janet insisted on keeping her favorite credit card just for emergencies—except she kept using it because it was in her wallet. Today, she keeps that credit card in a jug of ice in the freezer marked, *"Open for emergencies only!"* This may sound silly, but it works for Janet. She gets to keep her card—but with an obstacle that gives her time to really consider what constitutes an emergency.

Plan Your Expenses

Some people divide their cash at the start of each month for mortgage payment or rent, insurance, groceries, and so forth. They may think, *Okay, I've* *got $34 for entertainment this month. That means I can rent a video a few times or go to the movies once. I could make dinner instead of eating out.* But at least they know at the beginning of the month what they have to work with.

When It Comes to Investing, There's No Time Like the Present

Even if you have debts, you need to start investing. When I first started as a financial planner, I thought it didn't make sense for people to start investing while paying 10% to a creditor and earning only 8% interest on their investments. But after I saw people going years and years without investing, I realized that what they need to do is to start investing regardless of their debts. So even if you're someone who has a lot of consumer or other kinds of debt, you still need to start investing for the future—for your retirement or for other needs that are going to arise. If you don't start now, there may never be a good time to start.

It's Too Easy to Buy Online

People have gotten a lot of credit card problems because the Internet makes it so easy to buy things. It used to be that you had to go to the store and walk around before you could buy something. Now, maybe you're feeling a little depressed, a little lonely, like you need something special. You can go online with a couple of clicks, and a few days later somebody's bringing you a nice package. It doesn't even feel like a financial transaction. Amazon. com even has one-click buying! If you are an impulse buyer, this is really dangerous.

A better idea for buying online is to use Paypal or a debit card so your money is deducted directly from your checking account. If the funds in the checking account are insufficient, the transaction will not clear.

Have a Cooling-Off Period

Another strategy is to set a dollar amount for spending that you won't exceed without either waiting 24 hours or first talking it over with your spouse or a designated friend. Every situation is different. The amount for you might be $200, $500, or $10,000.

People often end up with big car payments because when they go shopping for a car, they encounter a good car salesman, they drive the vehicle, and they feel good about it because the salesman pushed all their emotional buttons. Sales training is so much about getting the prospective buyer emotionally involved in the purchase. Buyers sign the papers while their emotions are seething, and only later do they think about what they have done.

Realize that emotions are sometimes more powerful than reason. If you don't have the cash, you shouldn't be spending it. Of course, if you don't have the credit card with you, it makes it a lot more difficult to buy. It's best to back away from the situation, give it some thought, and sleep on it. Make the decision only after careful consideration.

Recognize an Addiction to Buying

Just as some people are compulsive overeaters, drinkers, or gamblers, others are compulsive spenders. Typically, they're trying to fill some emotional or spiritual need in their lives. It's only when someone can actually recognize that they have a problem that they can begin to make a change. Until they do make a spending change, they will never get out of debt. They might find a short-term fix where they're paying off some credit cards, but until they get to the root of the problem, they're just going to keep getting into debt.

If you find yourself in this situation, seek support organizations such as Consumer Credit Counseling (see the Resources section at the back of this book for further information). Also, many churches and community organizations offer support groups on financial spending.

Designated Saving

A powerful way to save money for special purchases is to have separate accounts such as a Christmas Club or special car account that enable you to set a goal. These accounts provide a tangible place for savings. You can earmark money so you know it won't be spent elsewhere. This strategy helps keep you out of debt by helping you save the cash for your special purchases.

Let the Joneses Win

One of the challenges today is that so many people want to "keep up with the Joneses." Everyone has friends with greater financial means. They live in a nicer home, drive a fancier car, and take more exotic vacations. It's tough not to try to keep up with them. Unless you're Bill Gates or Oprah, you've got a friend who has more money than you do.

A lot of people get into financial trouble with vacations. They feel they've been working too hard and deserve that trip to Hawaii. The trip is fine if you can afford it. Otherwise, the pain you're going to suffer in trying to repay the money you spent is never going to be worth the trip. There's nothing wrong with going camping. If your goal is to get away from the hustle and bustle and spend some time with your family, there's an argument for sitting at a campsite where a mere $20 a night might actually provide more than cramming everyone in an airplane for 5 hours and staying at a $200 a night hotel.

Design a Personal Finance Program

Many people fail at their finances because they never take time to plan them. They take time to plan other things such as fitness, education, or vacations. It's important to devote some time to planning finances—not just to figure out how to pay this week's bills—but to see where you are. Many people have no idea how much they owe. It's just so frustrating to them that they don't even want to look at it.

But until you actually face it and sit down and plan it out, you're never going to get ahead. So even if it's 1 day a year—it doesn't matter how often it is, it's just important to do it periodically—it might make sense just to get away somewhere, bring some of your financial stuff, and map it out. When you step back and look at the long-term picture, sometimes it's a lot easier than wondering how you are going to pay the rent this month.

Don't Leverage Yourself Too High

Some people get into financial problems because they leverage themselves too high. They have some financial assets; they're in okay shape financially, but they choose to take loans against their assets as a means of purchasing other assets. In the 1990s we saw people who would take loans against their stocks to buy other stocks. We call that margin investing. When the stock market fell, they got wiped out.

Today, you see people taking money out of their primary residence and putting down as little money as possible on as many homes as possible. That's all fine if everything goes perfectly. But if they get a couple of renters who don't pay their rent or who damage the homes, or if interest rates rise and home values fall, they could find themselves in real trouble. They could find their wealth wiped out overnight. It's leverage that causes that problem.

Switch Your Focus

The more time you spend worrying about, thinking about, and borrowing money, the less time and effort you have for getting out of debt. Excessive debt limits opportunities; it doesn't increase them. It requires more effort to create the force to bring your financial life back in balance. Over the next 10 years, the consumer markets will expand at an astonishing rate. You are going to see unlimited opportunities. The bulk of spending in highly developed nations will be for products and services far above the basic necessities of food, clothing, shelter, transportation, and medical care. Imagine being in a position to take advantage of this growth period instead of worrying about debts. Now is the time to decide you want to be in this position.

Know Your Outcome; Take Action

Getting started is more a matter of behavior than of making the right investment choices. What are some correct behaviors? The first step to creating a sound financial future is to develop a positive savings *mentality*. This might require changing your internal conversation about money. Many of us feel we don't have enough money to set aside for savings. We complain that it's too late to begin, or we postpone getting started until some future event arises. And if we do have some savings, we don't want to risk it by investing.

Overcome the hurdle of getting started. Start small, but be consistent. Put money into a savings vehicle where, virtually, you *can't* spend it. You'll be encouraged by how quickly your weekly or monthly contributions add up. Challenge yourself to increase the amount frequently. From time to time, add a lump sum to your savings as if you were paying yourself a bonus or a reward. Saving that is automatic is far more successful than just hoping to have some money left over at the end of every month. Set up a plan with your bank or employer for an amount to be deducted monthly from your account and sent to your savings account automatically. Consider this as paying yourself first. You'll soon forget that it's even being deducted. Would giving up 5% of your monthly income really cramp your lifestyle?

Whether you want to save for higher education for a child, a new home, or a comfortable retirement, *paying yourself first* is a prudent layaway plan for your future.

Use liquid or short-term interest or dividend-producing savings vehicles such as savings accounts, money market funds, and certificates of deposit (CDs). Even after you've begun investing, retain a core savings vehicle for emergency funds.

A core savings vehicle will be the base on which you build overall financial security. The point is to first have a safe place to start saving, then to build outward. Think of this core vehicle as the mother ship as you explore the infinite space of investing. It's your energy source.

Saving is not the same as investing. A *saver* is someone who saves money regularly but who does *not* assume the risks of ownership. An *investor* is someone who is rewarded for assuming the risks of ownership and who has an expectation of return through appreciation in the capital value of the securities owned. I see again and again people using investment products with a savings mentality who end up disappointed when returns aren't regular or don't match advertised performance. The secret is to build your resources in a core savings vehicle and then move to investing from this base.

Turn Debt into Equity

Use the same muscles you've been using for years. You have made payments regularly on a car, on a mortgage or rent, on credit cards, or on all these and still survived. As you pay off consumer items, take the previous outgoing monthly amount and send that same amount to a mutual fund company or an investment fund. You've built up this muscle; don't lose it.

If you still buy consumer goods on credit and are reading this book, you are a fantasy investor. Let's change that now. Debt is the reverse of savings and investing, and it acts as a drag on future income. Debt breeds urgency that leads to unwise decision making and undermines investment strategy. It's why even smart people fall prey to scams. Too much debt creates fear. A decision made from fear is often a wrong decision.

Reversing Debt Strategy

Starting with $10 a day, start paying off credit cards, then—keeping this same amount—start investing into a SEP/IRA account. Assume annual returns of 10.7% in a tax-deferred account. This is an example. Returns vary depending on risk and reward.

You can be debt-free within 7 years. How? Prioritize your monthly debts based on how long it would take to pay them off paying only the minimum payment due each month. Beginning with the debt with the shortest payoff time, add some nominal amount, such as $200, to each monthly payment. Don't add a little bit to each of your debts—dump it all on just this one and continue paying only the minimum on the balance of your debts. You'll be amazed at how fast that first debt will disappear. Next, take the total monthly amount you paid to the first debt and add it to the monthly payment of the debt with the next shortest payoff time. When that one is paid off, apply the new total to the next debt, and so on. Continue with each debt until you're free and clear. Take that cumulative sum of monthly payments and build a savings account with no interruption to your lifestyle! Okay, you say, that's a great plan, but it's all you can do right now just to make the minimum monthly payment on your debts. Where are you going?

Start Now

Look at your daily spending patterns. Ever notice that no matter how much cash you start with, it disappears at the same rate? Give yourself an allowance and then stick to it! Do some obvious things like cut down or eliminate buying from vending machines and carry snack items with you, buy a regular coffee rather than the more expensive Cappuccino, buy bulk groceries, and plan meals ahead. Another sure-fire way to regularly generate a healthy lump sum by the end of the month is to dump any coin change you receive into a jar or baggie *throughout* each day. If you don't raid that "piggy bank," you'll be surprised at your month's total.

Next, do some *plastic surgery*—shred the credit cards! If you feel you really need to, keep only one credit card, preferably American Express or a similar credit plan that you have to pay off every month. Don't inadvertently accumulate more debt!

Okay then, the next step is investing.

Evaluate Future Financial Needs

Why are you saving anyway? Do you have a clear vision of what you want to achieve and how much money you will need to achieve it, or are you shooting in the dark? Charles Greenwald, past chairman of the board for General Motors, estimated that every hour of planning returns 3 hours of execution.

What are your chances of accumulating a million dollars? This is the conceptual point of no return where most people feel so overwhelmed or defeated that they lose the motivation even to begin. But if you saw that you could realistically have that much accumulated at a certain future date— and the math when double-checked actually added up—wouldn't you be highly motivated to begin? I was.

This is where the difference between saving and investing begins to make sense. You can *invest* your savings at a return rate that will accelerate accumulation and put your financial goal within your reach—without risking your base savings. The methodologies in this book will show you how. Once you see that you can reach your goal, you can start down that road by comparing what you *have* now with what you *need* to accumulate to achieve that goal. The difference between the two is called a *shortfall*. A shortfall is the amount of money needed to fill the chasm between the reality and the fantasy of reaching your goal. By identifying your shortfall, you can begin to make your dream a reality. What better motivation is there in life than that?

Organize Your Resources

Organize resources—money, time, and knowledge—to consistently get a specific result: a result that can be duplicated. "If it's stupid and it works, it ain't stupid."

Find a strategy that organizes your resources—money and time—to consistently achieve a specific result. A good approach that builds confidence is to start small and see if a certain result is repeated. The brain craves certainty and is always trying to distill the predictable from the uncertain.

The first action in the sequence is to establish a place for your money that you feel confident about and where your money will grow without your having to constantly check on it. When your money grows, your confidence grows with it.

Start by making small investments—$100, $200, or $1,000—and see the result. An index mutual fund or a favorite growth mutual fund is your best bet at this point. These reduce investment risk through diversification and offer professional money management.

Get started *now* to give your investment program as much *time* as you possibly can. Every year that you put off moving toward accomplishment of future financial goals becomes more difficult. For every year you wait, you need to increase both your monthly investment amount and the risk you take to achieve the same result. Go step by step, noting all the details. When you establish systems that work, a high degree of trust will accrue. Make improvements constantly.

Set Boundaries

Set investment boundaries. If something doesn't fit your plan, don't do it. Your personal investment policy statement can be a gauge to keep you from making inappropriate emotional decisions about your investments.

Find a Qualified Financial Advisor

Most people need some help with their investment decisions. Most of us are busy making money to invest and don't have the time or expertise to research every vehicle. Even top athletes have a coach. True, you can start investing on your own, but you will reach a point where a knowledgeable financial coach is your best guide to reaching the next level. A financial coach can be a tax or financial planner, an investment consultant, a broker, or an investment adviser. Collaborate with your business associates or friends to create an informal investment advisory board. By having influential people on your advisory board, you will gain insight into areas of investment that you may not otherwise be aware of.

Teach Your Family

Providing for family is at the heart of everyone's financial concerns. But who said it was up to you alone? Don't operate in a vacuum, leaving those you care about in the dark. There is no better way to provide for the future of your loved ones than to teach them to help themselves. Not only does this empower them as participants, but also it gives them a better appreciation of your efforts. Once you know your savings and investment strategy, and you can do it again and again, you are ready to teach it to your family.

The time to start is now!

Teaching Your Children to Invest

"Important things are always simple; simple things are always difficult."

This is one of the most important lessons you can teach your children. Children who are excluded from open discussions of family financial affairs or sheltered from the financial realities of life can sometimes develop distorted ideas about money. They may make extravagant demands, often creating unnecessary squabbles about money, simply because they are uninformed about the family's financial resources.

When these children grow up, they may be ill equipped to manage their own finances or unable to exercise good judgment in financial matters. The key is to teach your children to think about money and financial management from a positive point of view. Of course, introducing your children to money management is a very personal matter, and you as the parent must decide what is best for your child.

Be Open With Your Children About Money Matters

Many families hold regular conferences, children included, to review finances. Every family member should be encouraged to speak out freely about her or his own priorities or goals. Thus, you can illustrate that priorities need to be set and that tradeoffs are sometimes necessary for effective use of money. Even a fairly young child should be able to understand, for instance, that paying for shelter and groceries takes a higher priority than buying a new bike or taking a trip to an amusement park.

Attending these sessions can give your children a sense of involvement and a greater willingness to work toward meeting family financial goals.

Give Your Children Regular Allowance

You can begin when they reach school age, and be sure to include at least some money that they are free to spend as they like without having to account to anyone. That way your children gain experience in deciding how to spend their own money.

A recommended way to start is by giving a young child a small amount of money every day or two for little toys or treats. As the child gets older, you can spread out the payment periods and increase the size of the allowance and the purpose for which it is used. The child can have a greater voice as the years go by in determining what the allowance should be.

A teenager, for example, might receive a monthly allowance that covers school lunches and supplies, hobbies and entertainment, and clothing. This can teach the child to plan, to save for necessities and special purchases, and to shop carefully for good buys. Giving an occasional advance against an upcoming allowance may be appropriate; but if your child overspends constantly, work with him or her to bring spending in line with available income.

Teach Your Children the Value of Working for Extra Money

Children should learn at an early age that money must be earned. You do not want to pay your child for every routine household task, of course, but you might consider paying for special household chores—above and beyond the allowance.

Chapter 2
Seize Control of Your Financial Life

People continue to make the same financial mistakes for three main reasons: (1) They don't have any plan, (2) they listen to the wrong people, and (3) they make poor investment choices.

Sometimes you think you're getting objective financial advice, but don't realize you're getting what amounts to an infomercial. Too late, you find out that someone was simply trying to sell you his or her product, or maybe you decide to hire a financial planner because you assume that a planner will help you get control of your financial life. Most financial planners aren't going to do that. They're going to try to sell financial products. That's how they get paid. Some are merely insurance agents who call themselves financial planners whose goal is to sell you a big fat life insurance policy that you may or may not need. Or, if they are investment managers, they're going to want to manage your investments.

Unfortunately, many people can't separate good advice from bad. The advice you get might be bad for you and good for the financial planner. Whose retirement plan is more important—yours or his? Often an advisor, whether an investment person trying to sell an investment or a mortgage broker trying to sell a new mortgage, has something to gain from the transaction. That doesn't necessarily mean it's a bad move for you. Sometimes it's a good move for everybody, but sometimes the only person who's going to benefit is the person who facilitated the transaction. And you, as the owner of the money, might get the short end of the stick.

Finding the right financial planner isn't going to help you take control of your financial life. Only you can take control of your life.

First, you must have some basic understanding of finances. You can't rely on someone else to do it all for you. There's clearly a place for financial advisors, financial planners, or investment managers. But nobody cares about your money as much as you do—or *should*. It's up to you to understand some of the basics.

It's a great idea to follow a good financial journalist. As does anybody in business, the journalist has something to sell. The journalist's product is readership, viewership, or listenership. The journalist's job is to offer financial advice and information in such a way as to deliver an audience. Over a long period, as market cycles come and go, a good financial journalist must produce solid time-tested financial advice. That's the type of financial journalist to seek.

A Sure Thing

Suppose you've just received a $30,000 windfall. Where should you invest it? Stocks, bonds, or a down payment on a new house.? Here's an investment deal that will earn between 13% and 20%—guaranteed.

Take your $30,000 and get rid of your credit card debt. There is no better deal. Yes, you can possibly make 20% or better on a stock, but there is no guarantee. You can also lose 20% or more on a stock. Just talk to someone who bought tech stocks a few years ago.

If you have $30,000 in credit card debt at 20% interest, you are waving bye-bye to $500 a month just in interest. Think about it: you make credit card payments of $500, but the next month your balance is still the same. But if you pay off the cards, then you pay no interest because there is no balance. Over the course of a year, you will have saved $6,000! That's not chopped liver.

In addition, carrying such a large balance in consumer debt drives down your credit score. However, as a benefit of paying off your cards, your credit score will improve as financial institutions begin to report that you are eliminating your debts. A better credit score means you will qualify for lower interest when you borrow for something important.

Try to avoid frivolous purchases that leave you in hock to credit card companies—companies whose officials are delighted when you make the minimum payment and never reduce the balance. People often ask me about the best types of investments. If you're paying high interest rates to the credit card companies, there is no better investment than ending this dysfunctional relationship.

By paying off credit cards and avoiding ridiculously high interest rates, you will be saving so much money that you will have more money to buy things. And you'll do so with real money, not plastic. You will also be able to put money into savings accounts, funds, stocks, and so forth every month.

It's a sure thing.

The Bonfire of the Stocks

Perhaps you've done well in the stock market and now have a large amount invested in good stocks and funds. And, as part of the home equity loan craze of the last few years—a fad that was fueled by unusually low interest rates—you have some debt on your home.

Normally I recommend that you don't sell your stocks and funds to pay off loans unless you're unhappy with the investments and were going to sell them anyway. In the following sections are a few reasons why.

Good stocks and funds work most effectively over the long run, over several cycles of the market. Stocks in the short term can be dangerous. For example, if you started investing at the top of the market 5 years ago, then you've likely had bad returns. If you've been in good stocks or funds for 10 or 20 years, you've had some great years and should have had good returns.

Home equity loans offer you tax advantaged lending. Most or maybe all of the interest is tax deductible. And the interest rate is relatively low because—unlike a credit card loan—the home loan is secured. A home equity loan can be a good deal as long as you don't take on more debt than you need, you don't use the proceeds for frivolous purchases, and you pay down the loan over the years just as you did the mortgage. It is a kind of piggy bank. With each payment you gain more equity in the house.

Never consider taking a home equity loan to put more money in the stock market. An article in the *Wall Street Journal* in 2000 advised that the smart money was in refinancing homes to invest in the stock market. In other words, investing in what was then a hot stock market. Of course, anyone who followed that advice now has a small stock portfolio and a large mortgage balance. Never put all your money in just one thing—no matter how well it is performing. Diversified investing is the best approach for most people.

There's nothing wrong with using a mortgage to help purchase a house, but most Americans should have paid off their mortgage by the time they reach retirement. Home equity lines of credits or loans can be effective as a source of cheap money. However, unless they are paid back, they increase the amount of debt owed on a home.

It's unwise for people to use home equity loans to make an investment, but selling investments to pay off a debt is not necessarily the best move either. It really depends on what the loan is for. If it is used to buy cars and big-screen TVs, it should be paid from wages. Otherwise, the consequences of spending the money won't be noticed.

Paying off home equity loans from savings or investments may make it too easy to run up a balance in the future. Once the home equity loan has a zero balance, it may be tempting to use some of the credit to purchase additional consumer products. If you're confident that you won't run up the balance again, then paying off the line of credit may, in a limited number of cases, be a wise move.

If you sell some investments to pay off your home equity line there could be another problem: capital gains taxes. You would hate to liquidate good investments only to find yourself with a big tax bill in April.

Don't Let Housing Costs Consume Your Hard-Earned Money

Mortgage life insurance is sometimes a gimmick. It depends on what the individual is trying to insure against and how far along he or she is in a mortgage.

For example, suppose a couple were recently married, bought a home, and have an $88,000 mortgage. If either the husband or wife died, could the surviving spouse afford the mortgage payments or would he or she be forced to sell the home? If either would be forced to sell, they probably should have some life insurance on each other to pay off the home if they found themselves widowed.

Mortgage life insurance really is nothing more than life insurance tied to a mortgage and is relatively expensive. Term insurance policies may be a better option because they ensure that funds would be there if either one of the two died. Also, some people who sell mortgage insurance are just doing so because they get paid if they make a sale, regardless of whether or not the client needs the policy. However, sometimes trusted advisors, understanding the individual circumstances of a client, may believe that the client needs some kind of protection to ensure that the surviving spouse doesn't have to move from the shared home.

Mortgage-Free in Retirement

It is a commendable goal—retirement without a mortgage. But sometimes it can take ghoulish dimensions.

Jack and Abby, ages 53 and 46, would like to be rid of their mortgage by the time they retire. Their annual income exceeds $40,000. A few years ago they bought their house with a CalVet loan (30-year), which required that they have insurance to pay the loan should either of them die.

Jack and Abby had been sending an extra $100 in principal with each month's payment, thinking that it would be great to save some interest and pay the loan sooner. They recognize that the chances of both of them living another 28 years aren't especially high and reasoned that it would make more sense to do something else with the extra money rather than pay the principal on the mortgage.

Jack and Abby do plan to live in this house forever, although without a crystal ball, who knows what may actually happen?

Without meaning to, Jack and Abby have structured their financial plan so it would actually work best if one of them died—meaning that one of them will have to die for the home to be paid off. That doesn't seem like an exciting goal.

If they hope to retire, Jack and Abby should aim to eliminate their mortgage. Therefore, they should continue making the extra payments on the principal so they can be debt free at some point in their lives. They also may have the opportunity to enjoy their golden years together rather than wait for someone to die.

Paying for Wheels

There are good and bad reasons to take out a home equity loan.

Here is a good reason: Richard has two car loans, which have high rates of interest and a principal of $44,000. Let's say he decides to pay off the loans by taking a lower rate loan against his house—a home equity line at 6.5%.

This, in the right circumstances, might work. Richard plans on taking the difference in what he currently pays on the auto loans and putting it into his 401(k) for 5 years. He hopes the 401(k) will earn an annual average return of 10%. He also plans on taking the tax savings from the 401(k) and applying it toward his principal on the equity line of credit.

Richard figures that at the end of 5 years he would still owe around $30,000 on the line of credit and is planning to sell his home around that time. Thus, he would be ahead $18,000 after subtracting the cost of interest and the remaining amount on his line of credit.

Richard's plan will work well if all of his assumptions hold true. He will need to apply all of his savings to his 401(k), and he will need to earn a rate of return higher than 5.5%.

Richard's calculations show that he will be further ahead with the home equity line of credit because the cost of money is only 6.5%, whereas the rate of return assumption is 10%.

But what if he earns less than 10%, either due to a lousy market or poor investment choices? Worse yet, what if he loses money on his 401(k) over the next 5 years?

Maintaining debt while saving really is no different than borrowing money to invest—particularly if the plan is to build a portfolio without eliminating the debt. This a reasonable risk, provided Richard understands the risk.

There is good reason to avoid a home equity line for paying a car loan. The risk, of course, is earning less on your money than you are paying in interest charges. Running financial calculations can provide a starting point, but you also need to look at your savings habits. What if you lack the discipline to save the difference in your 401(k)? Perhaps you can earn a great return from your 401(k), but what if you don't maintain your contributions?

Quite frankly, auto loans exist because most people lack the discipline to save for cars.

Only you know if you have the discipline to make this plan work. If you believe you have it, go forward with your plan. If you are in doubt, work on paying the car loans and forget about the home equity line.

Refinancing Debates

Lois and her husband Sal have lived in their house for 5 years and expect to move to another state within the next 4. They have a mortgage with an 8.5% interest rate, but wonder whether they should go through the bother and expense of refinancing.

Many mortgage lenders charge numerous fees to refinance a loan. Those fees mean it could take months to recoup the costs. In some circumstances, it may take as long as 5 years before the lower interest rate offsets the fees. However, some lenders will refinance the mortgage with no fees if the loan is large enough ($150,000 or more).

The process works like this: the lending institution will pick up all miscellaneous fees incurred during a refinance. The lender will typically earn a smaller than normal fee in this type of transaction. Lois and Sal may pay a higher interest rate, but they will not incur costs for the transaction. If they refinance and then sell their home a few months later, their only cost would be the hassle of completing all the paperwork.

The Blank Check

Has this happened to you? You receive an offer from a credit card company claiming it has a better deal than your current company: a significantly lower interest rate than the card you are using. You're now paying somewhere between 13% and 21% on your card, and they offer you 6% interest—on a trial basis.

To get started, all you have to do is use the blank checks the company has sent to you to transfer your balances from your original card. Seems like a good deal, doesn't it? Most times it is a worse deal than the one that got you in the red in the first place. Run, don't walk, away from blank checks sent to you by credit card companies. Unlike credit card purchases that have a grace period, these checks immediately start to generate interest charges.

Credit card companies have been chasing debt aggressively by offering low-interest teaser rates. They'll offer cash advances or payoffs of existing balances at incredibly low rates. However, they usually have an agenda of making money in other areas, such as charging higher rates on new purchases and existing balances. In your case, you probably would have been better off had you not transferred your balance.

Ouch! Your credit card company is taking you to the cleaners. What's happening to you is happening to tens of thousands (if not millions) of other Americans right now.

Unfortunately, what the credit card company is doing to you is legal, as long as it is properly disclosed to you. Whether or not it was disclosed is debatable. I'm sure this bait-and-switch tactic was spelled out in the offering, but reading the fine print on credit card disclosures ranks right up there with reading a foreign language you don't understand. You can read the printed word, but you cannot decipher its meaning.

Never transfer your balance without fully reading and understanding the fine print. Too many companies have devised clever tactics to sock it to you once the transfer is complete. Realize that there is no easy way to get out of debt other than spending less and learning to do with less for a while. Adopt a practice of paying off credit card balances each month and never carrying credit balances. If you do this, you will save thousands—maybe tens of thousands of dollars—over the course of 20 or 30 years. Saving this much sounds much better than signing a blank check.

Paying Down the Mortgage

Does it make sense to pay down a mortgage early? Sometimes. Let's look at one case. Jeffrey and his wife Carol own a rental unit. They want to accelerate the pay-down of the principal balance.

They have 29 years and $75,000 left on a 30-year, 7.25% fixed-interest mortgage. Their dilemma is whether they should pay it down early or maybe refinance with a 15-year mortgage, assuming the rate is as good or better than their current rate.

They are also confused about whether the extra principal payment simply reduces the principal balance, or whether it also decreases the portion of subsequent mortgage payments that go to interest and increases the portion that goes to principal.

Home mortgages are simple interest loans. That means that the interest charged is based on the outstanding loan balance. It is not based on the length of the original loan or on how many payments are left on the loan. Any extra principal payments Jeffrey and Carol make will reduce the outstanding loan balance as well as their total interest charges.

For example, with a $100,000 loan at 7%, interest charges for a year would be $7,000 (100,000 multiplied by .07). If $10,000 were paid toward the principal, the outstanding loan balance would drop to $90,000. Now the total interest charges would only be $6,300 (90,000 multiplied by .07). In subsequent monthly payments, less of the mortgage payments would go to interest and more would go to principal.

Paying extra may be a good idea for Jeffrey and Carol. But refinancing is probably even better. If they cannot get a rate much lower on a rental, Jeffrey and Carol might consider refinancing their home and paying off their rental loan. Rates on owner-occupied homes are much lower than rates on rentals.

The Mortgage-Burning Party in Your Future?

America has one of the highest rates of home ownership in the world. That's a good thing because owning property gives a person a stake in a community. However, many Americans carry mortgages on their dream houses and dream of the day when the bank no longer owns any part of their home.

Let's say you want to finance or refinance a home. The first thing you want to consider—along with your advisor—is where interest rates are and where they are expected to go.

There are several ways to look at the big loan against your home. You can view refinancing as, "Look how much money I can save each month on my payments," or you can view it as, "Look how quickly I'll be able to pay off my mortgage with rates this low." Here's a hypothetical situation: Suppose 4 years ago you took out a 30-year mortgage at 7.5% for $100,000. Your monthly payments for the past 4 years have been $699. Today, your mortgage balance is down to $95,860. If you refinance your mortgage into a new, 30-

year mortgage at 6.5%, your payments will drop to $605 per month. Paying the minimum of $605 per month will result in 4 additional years before your home is paid off. However, if you continue paying the same payment as your previous mortgage ($699 per month), your home will be paid off in 21 years. The refinancing will save you 5 years of mortgage payments.

Interest rates are typically lower on 15-year mortgages. Obviously, the lower the interest rate, the better. If you took out a 15-year mortgage at 6.25%, your payments would increase to $821 per month. If you can afford to increase your monthly payments to that amount, your home will be paid off in just 15 years.

A 30-year mortgage will give you more flexibility because your monthly mortgage requirement will be less, but it won't give you any assurance of paying off your home in less than 30 years. If you can afford the payments on a 15-year loan, get one. Not only will you save on interest charges, but you can also be assured your home will be paid off in 15 years.

The Mortgage or the Taxman?

Many Americans in their late 50s nearing retirement are about to gain access to the largest amount of cash they will receive in their lifetime. They're making some of the most important financial decisions of their lives because for the first time in their lives they have the opportunity to do so.

For example, Jerry and Joan will soon be able to take money from their IRAs, which have approximately $300,000, without a penalty. They also have a 401(k) with $60,000. They're thinking about various options. Should they take the money from their qualified plans all at once and settle the big tax bill? Or should they do it gradually and pay the taxes slowly over time? With the first option, they would take a big chunk of the funds and pay off their mortgage.

Most people want the security of having a home free of any debt when they quit working. But determining whether it makes sense to pull cash from retirement accounts to pay off a mortgage can be tricky.

Be aware that $1 in an IRA is not equal to $1 in cash. The reason? The taxman wants a portion of what is in your retirement plans and, if you have any gains in accounts outside of retirement plans, he wants a portion of those gains as well.

If Jerry and Joan were to cash in $300,000 worth of IRAs, they'd be killed by taxes. They'd pay 35% to the Feds and 9.3% to the state. Obviously, if they have a low interest rate on their mortgage, it would take years of interest payments to equal what they had paid the taxman.

However, if they had that same $300,000 sitting in cash or a savings account, there would be no taxes due on the withdrawal. They could take the entire balance and pay off the mortgage and pay nothing in taxes.

It's not advisable to withdraw large chunks from retirement accounts to pay off the mortgage, but taking low-yielding savings accounts to pay down the mortgage is.

If the goal were to be debt free, spreading withdrawals from the IRAs over several years would greatly reduce the tax burden and accomplish your goal of paying off your mortgage, just not immediately.

Eliminating Private Mortgage Insurance (PMI)

Kate and John purchased a house 2 1/2 years ago for $155,000. They have a 30-year FHA loan fixed at 7.5%. They owe about $147,500 on the house. They plan to stay at least another 3 to 5 years in this house. The same model home in their neighborhood recently sold for $185,000. Now Kate and John—along with millions of other American homeowners who see low interest rate—are trying to figure out if they should refinance.

Every situation is different, and refinancing may be worthwhile even if there is a minor difference in rates. What they need to examine is the PMI they are currently paying. PMI is levied on mortgages that exceed 80% of the value of a home.

Because their down payment was very small, they're being hit with expensive PMI. If they calculated the cost of PMI as an interest expense, they'd find that they're actually paying over 12% interest on the money that was borrowed above the 80% level.

Since home values have increased in their area, and it appears that their loan is now about 80% of their home's value, it would be wise for them to get rid of the PMI. Kate and John can contact their existing lender and ask for a reappraisal of the home, or they can contact a new lender and refinance their home. There are some lenders that will refinance a loan of this size with no cost whatsoever.

If they can find one that will refinance the loan with no cost at a 7.5% rate and eliminate PMI, it'll be well worth their time.

Borrowing Against Insurance

Lana's husband, Tony, has a paid-in-full life insurance policy, with a $6,000 outstanding loan against it. Lana and Tony are now in a position to start paying down the loan amount in order to avoid yearly interest charges.

They are exploring several options: pay a minimum amount to the life insurance company each month, or deposit that same amount in a savings account each month to earn interest, paying down the loan when a sizeable amount has been saved.

The earlier they pay down the loan balance, the more money will be saved. Interest charges are typically calculated on a daily basis. If Lana and Tony save up their money until they can make a sizable payment, they will incur greater interest charges.

Before Lana and Tony pay off the loan, they should check with the insurance company to see what the effective loan rate is. Some policies have zero-cost loans. If the policy is charging more than one can earn elsewhere, Lana and Tony's best bet is to pay whatever they can to the insurance company each month.

Is Wall Street on Your Side? You Could Be the Next Victim

Be afraid. Be very afraid when dealing with national full service brokerages, otherwise known as wire houses. This is not to say that some people who work for them aren't good. However, they work in a brokerage system that often pressures them and gives them maximum compensation for selling things that often are not in the best interests of the average individual investor.

Bob, in his late 70s, questioned whether he had cause to sue one of these giant firms. He had invested with this firm for retirement over several years. Bob was assigned to the vice president of the firm. He had hopes of getting advice on his investments, but those hopes came to nothing. The only contact he received were phone calls from the vice president asking Bob to let him sell two stocks. One of the stocks was Bob's major investment for retirement, which at one time had zoomed up to about $1,750,000. It now was worth about $77,000.

Remember, no one can watch your money or property the way you can. Bob now realizes that he should have kept a better eye on this stock's action, as it was his major investment. He also believes that his broker should have cautioned him to take some action when he noticed the drop in price.

Watching your stock position fall from almost $2 million to less than $100,000 has got to hurt. Whether the broker is partially responsible has to do with a number of factors.

What type of relationship did Bob have with the broker? Did the broker have discretionary authority over the account, or did he merely place Bob's orders? Did commission or fees pay him? Did he ever warn Bob of the considerable risks of having a highly concentrated portfolio?

There have been countless burned investors over the past few years, and there is plenty of blame to go around. In this person's situation, the broker should not be blamed for not warning Bob when the stock began to fall. Maybe he thought it would come back up.

However, he should be blamed for not warning Bob about the risks of having such a large position in just one stock. As we've all heard countless times, the key to a successful retirement is having a diversified portfolio.

To learn more about whether one may have a legal claim against a broker or his employer, check out www.investorrecovery.com. This Web site helps investors determine whether broker misconduct has occurred, and whether there is a viable claim.

By the way, one shouldn't let the "vice president" title impress too much. In the investment business, it seems almost everyone is a vice president. Most don't earn the title based on responsibility; they earn it based on how much business they generate.

Beware of Forecasts and Prepare for the Unexpected

Denny Foreman works for a software company in Silicon Valley. Recently he received a lump sum of $250,000 from a stock option and doesn't want to take any chances with his windfall. He doesn't want to take the risk of investing in the stock market and instead wants to buy bonds, but with all the disparate economic forecasts he's not sure what to do.

How does one prepare for the unexpected? By using flexible investment strategies that react to changing conditions and deliver good results in all market conditions.

Denny should talk to a few investment advisors before making any decisions. Stick with the advisor who spends more time focusing on the risks of your investment strategy than on any potential returns one could make.

College Savings

It's never too soon to start saving for your child's education. Given the persistence of inflation—especially higher education inflation—the cost of putting your child through college in 10 or 15 years will likely be huge. There are many ways to save for a higher education, but 529 plans are considered the best college savings plans around.

The plans allow you to save in a variety of investments, and your money grows tax-deferred. That's provided the money is used for college. Then the money comes out tax-free.

Many mutual fund and investment companies offer 529 plans. Shop around to find a plan that has low fees and good investment options.

When it comes to applying for grants, loans, and financial aid, money in the 529 plan will come into play. Money in a 529 won't count against your child as much as money outside a 529 plan, but it could still reduce financial aid. Even so, a young person would be much better off entering college with funds in a 529 plan than entering college with no money whatsoever.

IRA Withdrawals for the Divorced Person

Pat is confused about IRA withdrawal rules. She understands that there are certain ways one can withdraw funds from an IRA before age 59.9 without penalty. One example is for a first-home purchase. Pat is wondering whether that would apply to a newly divorced person who has purchased homes jointly with an ex-spouse in the past but who now wants to make a first purchase as a single individual.

Who qualifies as a first-time homebuyer? Those who have either never purchased a home or have not owned a home for at least 2 years. If someone hasn't owned a primary residence for 2 years, then he or she can qualify as a first-time homeowner.

Pat should keep in mind that if she withdraws money from an IRA to purchase a house, the withdrawal would still be subject to ordinary income taxes. The first-time homebuyer exclusion only avoids the penalties. Pat is happy; she's on her way to buying her first home on her own.

Saving for a Child's Education

Be careful how you save for a child's education. Not all savings vehicles are the same.

Tom established a tax-free account for his son at birth under the Uniform Transfer to Minor's Act. The fund now has a balance of $58,000.

The purpose of the fund was to be used for a college education. Unfortunately, Tom's son, now 17 1/2 years old, does not have the grades to attend a 4-year college. So the revised plan is for Tom's teenage son to first attend a community college.

There is always the possibility that he won't continue his higher education. Therefore, Tom wants to transfer the money into another type of college savings plan, such as a 529 plan, so that he and his wife can still be in charge of the money when their son turns 18. They're worried that the boy could go crazy with the money.

The bad news is that there is not much the parents can do at this point. Money that has been deposited into a child's account was money that was gifted to the child. Tom may be able to change the age to 21 with the financial institution that holds the account, but most companies require age 21 to be listed on the account when it is established.

Furthermore, in some instances a parent was able to persuade a judge to move the age to 24, but Tom would need to go through some legal wrangling to get that accomplished.

Tom can transfer the account to a 529 plan, but it won't help to keep the money out of his child's hands. Any Uniform Transfer to Minor's Act account that is transferred to a 529 plan retains all of the provisions of the Uniform Transfers to Minors Act (UTMA).

Consider Tom's predicament before you put any money in your child's name (under a UTMA). Many teenagers are more interested in car catalogs than they are in college catalogs.

Getting Pop to Invest

Karl's father is retired. He has money sitting in the bank earning next to no interest. He would like to invest the money to bring in extra income for him. The money needs to be liquid, yet at the same time his risk has to be low, as this is his retirement fund.

The fact is that some people shouldn't invest. If Karl's dad has never invested in anything other than a bank account, he may be a little apprehensive about doing anything new—particularly if he is using the money to provide living expenses.

Karl should take his father to a qualified financial planner or investment advisor to discuss the pros and cons of the various options available. And he should make sure the planner is certified or the investment advisor is registered.

If Karl's father can develop a relationship with a financial planning professional he trusts, he may find more comfort in making a change with his investments.

To find competent financial planners in your area, contact the Financial Planning Association http://www.fpanet.org/.

Is Your Broker-Advisor on Your Side?

Brokers' bosses too often want them to move product—stocks, bonds, mutual funds—especially funds originated by the company. Brokers usually get paid through commissions or transaction fees, regardless of whether the investment works out for the investor.

Here, in essence, is the potential conflict of interest that leads many investors to question the quality of service that Wall Street offers through its big national, full-service firms. But some brokers are switching to new compensation methods. Sometimes, instead of commissions, brokers will agree to a fee to manage your portfolio, assuming you keep a large account with the firm.

For example, the fees charged for investment management can run anywhere from as low as 0.25% to as high as 3% per year. Typically, the larger the account, the lower the fee.

Over the past several years, many brokers and financial advisors have moved away from charging transaction fees or commissions and switched to asset management fees based on a percentage of the money being managed. This can reduce the inherent conflicts that arise when a broker gets paid only when a transaction occurs. When you have a fee-based arrangement with a financial advisor, you don't have to question the motive behind a recommended transaction. Because your advisor is not getting paid as a result of a transaction, you know a recommendation didn't occur simply because your broker's BMW lease payment was due.

Life Begins at Age 55

What is retirement? Unfortunately, many people have been sold on the idea of just sitting around and "taking it easy" once they reach age 55 or 60. Some retired people watch television all the time or play limitless rounds of golf. And many of these people believe they have achieved utopia. However, just as constant work can wear a person out, so, too, can constant rest. Neither extreme is a good thing. And for millions of well-heeled Americans who have a lifetime of knowledge and skills, retirement can be the antithesis of utopia. It can be a big bore.

But for an increasing number of Americans retirement is no longer traditional retirement. Some are using their financial independence to embark on second careers. Some are even returning to school.

Jack will turn 54 years of age soon and is seriously thinking about attending law school next year. He's already looking into an academic scholarship that might waive most of his tuition. And for 3 years, he can live on his pension. His pension would be about $1,900, and he will be covered by his company's health plan for life. He also has about $180,000 in IRAs and 403(b) plans. He's single and his only debt is his mortgage.

Jack has no plans for a rocking-chair, sports-centered life. He wants to practice law part time and plans to do so well into his 70s. Jack wants a second career to fend off boredom and to make him more useful.

How will he pay for his education? Jack hopes to pull some money out of his retirement accounts. He also hopes to obtain a tuition waiver. Any money Jack pulls out of his IRA to cover educational expenses will not be hit with an early withdrawal penalty, but will be subject to taxes. However Jack's 403(b) will be treated differently. He cannot pull money from his 403(b) for educational expenses and avoid an early withdrawal penalty. Jack would need to move his 403(b) to an IRA prior to a withdrawal to avoid the penalty. He can transfer his 403(b) to an IRA once he retires.

Jack has an excellent plan. A career change is daring and exciting. With modern medicine helping us to live longer, healthier lives, it will be necessary for many Americans to have a career they can pursue well into their golden years. Jack is in a great position to make his dream happen.

Don't let anyone talk you out of following your dreams. You may or may not be further ahead financially than Jack, but doing what you love is worth much more than money.

Nightmare on Wall Street

Lucy and her husband have a simplified employer pension (SEP) IRA invested in B-shares mutual funds. They have just hit the $100,000 mark. Their advisor suggests that they now move their money to a managed account. By the way, many Wall Street brokerages are pushing their brokers to put their client assets into managed accounts because it would be good for the firm—although it is not always the best for the client.

The penalty imposed by the B share mutual fund plan to move these assets now is $3,000 for the clients. But if they wait 2 years, it will not cost them anything. It will also cost the client 2% in fees to set up the managed account at the brokerage.

Clients, after hearing these managed money spiels, often wonder if they can recover the $3,000 after it is moved to the managed account.

Here is a case in which the financial advisor is very concerned about growing wealth. Unfortunately, I believe his concern is more for his wealth than for yours.

Unless the fund owned by this couple is a bow-wow—and I mean a shaggy dog of funds—it probably won't perform much differently from a managed account with a similar objective. After all, isn't a mutual fund a managed account? When you buy a mutual fund, you turn your assets over to a fund manager so he or she can make daily investment decisions for you.

In my opinion, most "managed accounts" aren't much different from mutual fund accounts. Typically, the only real difference is that a managed account is set up separately from other investments, giving you your own cost basis in the underlying securities. This can sometimes be helpful for taxable accounts, but it is of no value for money held inside retirement accounts.

If your mutual fund performance is in the toilet, you can exchange the fund with a different fund within the same mutual fund family and avoid paying the $3,000 surrender penalty.

A decent investment advisor would recommend this before having you pay a hefty surrender charge to get out of a fund. Furthermore, your annual management fee on the mutual fund would probably be less than what you'd pay for a managed account. Quite frankly, the advisor's recommendation would likely be considered unethical. But that won't stop some people who have production quotas and aren't too particular about how they obtain them.

Capital Gains and IRAs

Greg wants to buy a new pickup truck. He plans on selling some stock he's owned for many years. However, the stock is in his IRA, and he worries about triggering a big capital gains bill.

Buying or selling securities inside an IRA does not trigger a taxable event. You can sell a stock for many times over its purchase price without having to pay any income taxes. However, it's pulling money out of an IRA that triggers a taxable event. Any money withdrawn is taxed as ordinary income, even if the money is a result of a capital gain.

Many financial advisors recommend holding individual stocks outside of retirement plans to receive favorable tax treatment. If the stock Greg sold was not held in an IRA, Greg could have used the more favorable capital gains tax rates.

Special Needs Trust

Planning for your special-needs child presents unique problems. For instance, some parents start education funds for a child with Down's syndrome or a severe Autism Spectrum Disorder. But this may not be a good move. Children with these conditions have a wide range of development possibilities. The child, the parents hope, could become self-sufficient and might someday be able to go to college. However, traditional savings and education plans may not work too well for the child. There are a number of governmental benefits that will be available to the child as an adult; however, many of these are based on financial need. If the child has any assets at all, he or she will not qualify for the program.

An account in your child's name can spell trouble in other ways as well. If he or she does not have the ability to make sound financial decisions, the child may spend the money unwisely. Worse yet, people with disabilities tend to be a target for swindlers and con artists.

What these parents should do instead is establish a special-needs trust. These trusts are designed for special-needs children who may need help with financial decisions. With a properly structured special-needs trust, the child—when he or she becomes an adult—can have money to help with his or her living expenses, such as rent, mortgage payments, entertainment, and educational expenses, and still qualify for other benefits.

In this case, the parents need to meet with a good estate-planning attorney who has had experience with special-needs trusts. Not only do they need to plan for the child's future as an adult, but also they should make plans today in the event one or both of the parents die before the child reaches adulthood.

A 401(k) All-Points Bulletin

A 401(k) is a defined contribution plan. You decide how much to put in the plan, and your employer will often match your contributions to a certain point. Generally, you are in control of the assets. You determine how much of your contributions will go into the various investment options that are set up by your employer.

This contrasts with defined benefit plans in which the employer tells the employee how much to put in a plan and controls the assets.

However, there are times when an alarm bell should sound for someone who is part of a 401(k) plan. Let's say the employees have recently found out that the funds have not been sent to the plan administrator on a regular basis. Let's say they suspect that the employer is pocketing this money or using it for other things. This, if true, is a serious offense—an offense that could land an employer in jail for many years. The employer has both a legal and a moral obligation to see that the funds are deposited into the 401(k) account within a reasonable period of time.

All 401(k) plans are governed by strict Employee Retirement Income Security Act (ERISA) guidelines that place a fiduciary responsibility on your employer. The employer must see to it that your funds are deposited in a timely manner. Failing to do so could put the employer in a position where both civil and criminal penalties are imposed.

The best plan of action for employees at this point is to contact the U.S. Department of Labor (DOL) and file an official complaint. The DOL will then contact your employer and investigate the situation. If funds have been diverted, the 401(k) participants will be among the first to be repaid in the event of bankruptcy or liquidation.

Brother-in-Law Partnership

It may sound like a great idea when a longtime friend, relative, or business associate proposes becoming business partners. But stop and think about it. No matter how good the partnership seems—and partnerships, like major league baseball teams in spring training, all seem to be great enterprises before one actually starts to compete—serious questions must be settled before one starts.

Which is the best way to finance your portion of the deal? Savings, or equity from your home? If you finance it from savings, it will not totally drain the home equity bucket.

Another consideration is the best way to deal with taxes on potential profit resulting from the partnership. There are other issues to be aware of when going in on a partnership with someone. The following example highlights these issues.

"In the beginning it was fine; we both took out second mortgages on our homes to fund our new enterprise, but nine months after we signed our partnership agreement my brother-in-law left his wife—my sister—and I'm angry at him," Dave says regretfully.

There are many factors to consider before forming a partnership. The most important issue is having a clearly defined, legal partnership agreement. This agreement should spell out each partner's responsibilities and how to handle any disputes that may arise.

In addition, the agreement should make it clear how to unwind the partnership if someone either neglects his or her duties or wants out of the partnership. Furthermore, all partners need to agree on the objectives of the partnership. Is it managed for current income, or is long-term appreciation more important?

The best way to reduce your tax liability is for the partnership to be managed for tax efficiency. This may mean exchanging one property for another to defer capital gains taxes. This is one of those areas that the partners need to consider before forming the partnership. Any tax planning should be done within the LLC. Interest income, capital gains, business income, and so forth, will pass through to your personal income tax return.

When it comes to funding the deal, if you have the cash in the bank, don't bother with a home equity loan. The interest you'll pay on a home equity loan will be more than the money you're currently making on your savings.

Proceed with caution. Partnerships are easy to get into but can be a real pain in the "asset" to unwind.

Saving for College

Joanne has a 4-month-old baby. She wants to start a college fund for the baby.

There are two decisions Joanne needs to make before she starts saving for the child's college: (1) Should the account be set up in a college savings program, or should the money be accessible for other expenditures? (2) Which types of investments should be used?

There are a number of ways Joanne can establish a savings fund for her child. She can establish an account in her own name and earmark it for her child.

In this situation, Joanne maintains full control over the money, but she would need to report all interest and dividends on her income tax return. She also can set up an account under the UTMA. With an UTMA, a portion of the interest escapes taxes each year. The funds are fully accessible to the child at age 21.

If the funds were designated solely for college, a 529 plan or Coverdell IRA would be advantageous. With both the 529 plan and the Coverdell IRA, all funds grow tax-deferred and come out tax-free as long as the money is used to cover college expenses.

529 plans offer greater flexibility with deposits, whereas the Coverdell IRA can be used for primary education expenses as well as for college costs. There are a few other minor differences, but 9 times out of 10, the 529 plan is preferable over the Coverdell.

Regardless of which method Joanne chooses, there are a number of investment options available. Given that the child has 18 years before the money is needed, the best solution may be a well-diversified portfolio of stocks of quality companies. These can be held directly or in an UTMA, 529 plan, or Coverdell.

Social Security

Who planning for retirement doesn't worry about it?

The surpluses from the Social Security Trust Fund are paid out to beneficiaries and spent on anything and everything the government wants to do with the money. The government spends now and lets the government of 20 years from now worry about how the bills will be paid then.

Jim, a young man who sees a large part of his salary eaten up by payroll taxes, wonders what will be there for him in 30 or 40 years. He wonders if he should even plan for any retirement income from Social Security.

That is a question that most Generation X-ers are asking. The fact is there are already too many people receiving benefits compared to the number of workers paying into the system. There will need to be some changes in Social Security for the system to survive. That is, if we want this system to survive.

We will probably see Social Security become more "needs based." Those who need the benefits will receive them; those who do not, won't. We have already seen the taxation of benefits for higher income retirees. There is even talk in Washington that if someone is extremely wealthy in retirement (whatever that means), they shouldn't receive benefits.

Perhaps the most prudent thing for Jim to do is to plan to do without it. If he saves enough money to be financially independent without Social Security, his standard of living won't be jeopardized in the event he doesn't receive it.

The Roth Road

With the multiple advantages of a Roth IRA, many people about to move their 401(k) accounts want to move their money into this retirement savings account.

Unfortunately, you cannot immediately convert a 401(k) directly to a Roth IRA. Even if your adjusted gross income is $100,000 or less, tax rules don't allow this. Still, your ultimate goal can be achieved. Tax laws do permit rolling a 401(k) to a traditional or rollover IRA and, once the funds are in the IRA, convert the account to a Roth IRA.

You may run into a problem with your 401(k) provider. Prior to 1993, a person could not roll over a 401(k) to an IRA unless that person terminated his or her employment. Today, tax law allows for any 401(k) balance to be rolled over to an IRA regardless of employment status. But 401(k) plans are governed by both tax law and sponsors' plan documents. Because many of the 401(k) plans were set up prior to 1993, some older plans have not modified their documents to allow current employees to withdraw funds from their 401(k) plans.

The tax law that President Bush signed a few years ago requires that employers begin offering Roth 401(k) plans in 2006. Whether that ever happens will be dependent on future changes in the tax code. And, remember, the tax code is changed virtually every year, so you—or your advisor—need to stay on top of what is happening.

Unless your employer will allow you to transfer your 401(k) to an IRA, you will be unable to convert any 401(k) monies until the Roth 401(k) is introduced.

Think Before You Collect

Don't blow it. In many cases, you may only get one chance.

You've spent many, many years accumulating those precious retirement dollars. But the work isn't finished. Indeed, some may see this as the tough part: How will you take your assets?

Let's say you're 55. You and your wife are looking forward to retirement. You are preparing to retire from a job and qualify for a pension. Now comes the difficult part, the part that makes you realize that retirement planning isn't all beer and skittles—you have to select from two options in taking your pension benefits.

Option one pays $1,000 more per month during your lifetime, but upon your death will provide your wife (now age 50) only 60% of the pension amount until her death. Option two would pay you $1,000 less per month but would provide your wife with the full amount until her death. Let's assume that you are in good health, and as people are living longer and longer today, it could be another 30 years or longer before your Maker summons you to meet the saints.

The problem is that there is often no easy answer. However, you must make an irrevocable decision on your pension the day you leave the company. For many people this choice will be the most important financial decision of their lifetime.

There are many factors to consider before making your choice, such as your current health; financial obligations such as mortgages; health care needs for your wife, should you die early; and financial needs for your wife if you go first. The latter is statistically the most likely scenario.

In our hypothetical situation, taking the higher payout may provide both you and your wife with the greatest benefit. This way you can enjoy the extra dollars today, but if you were to predecease your wife, she would still receive 60% of the pension.

These are difficult issues. And they can change as quickly as a politician changes issues in the midst of a heated campaign. It pays to have a trusted advisor go over the various scenarios and run the numbers. He or she should be someone who has known you for years and understands the unique needs of both you and your wife.

Time to Play Defense

Bobbitt Brock and her husband Curt are both retired. They have adequate income and have savings of $75,000. They don't want to take any chances with this money. They want to protect their principal and see if they can get it to generate an extra $300 a month and not get whipped around by interest rates.

Their goal is to generate $3,600 per year from a $75,000 investment. That requires a yield of only 4.8%. Although that might sound high in comparison to current bank savings rates, that yield is achievable if they are willing to invest in a long-term portfolio.

There are a number of options available to them. Long-term corporate bonds from quality companies offer yields in the 4% to 6% range; possibly a real estate security (REIT) will provide that sort of yield; many stock dividends of many companies currently approach that range or could grow into that yield over time.

Rather than invest in one type of security, they could also buy a laddered bond portfolio.

The Brocks should talk to a few investment advisors before making any decisions. Stick with the advisor who spends more time focusing on the risks of various investment strategies than on potential returns.

The Beneficiaries of Your 401(k) Plan

What happens to my 401(k) assets when I die, Vince asked. He was concerned for his children. He wondered if they would be able to spread the withdrawals over the rest of their lives or if they could do a "stretch 401(k)." If not, were there any special rules that could reduce the amount of income tax that must be paid?

The answers to Vince's questions are that, unfortunately, beneficiaries have limited options when they receive a 401(k), 403(b), 457 or other company retirement plan. Unlike with IRAs, they do not have the ability to stretch the retirement account for the rest of their lives.

Spouses listed as beneficiaries of qualified retirement accounts can roll the money into their IRAs. Once it's in the IRA, the spouse has all of the rights and privileges available with any other IRA. He or she can receive income from it right away or defer any distributions until age 70½.

Non-spouse beneficiaries, such as children, do not have the same rights as spouses. When a child or other person receives a 401(k) or other retirement plan, that individual cannot roll the money into an IRA. Most 401(k) administrators require that the account be distributed within 1 year of the account holder's death. When the funds are received, the money is fully taxable as ordinary income to the child. Depending on the account size and other income the child may have, the income tax bite could be more than 40%.

From an estate-planning standpoint, it is always better to leave a child an IRA rather than a 401(k). If you are retired and you want your children to avoid paying as much tax as possible, you ought to consider rolling your 401(k) into an IRA. Once the funds are in an IRA, the children will have a multitude of options when you pass on.

Who Should Manage Your Money?

The first question to ask yourself is: Do I want someone to manage my account?

You may have an account that requires little activity, and you may be fine with paying a commission when you buy or sell a security. On the other hand, you may want someone to monitor your holdings and make changes when appropriate. If this is the case, switching to a managed account may be a great move for you, provided your broker has a long history of managing these accounts and has the educational background that goes beyond sales.

Beware of stockbrokers, especially those with little experience and few educational designations.

Some stockbrokers are little more than glorified salesmen who would try to sell iceboxes to Eskimos if their bosses told them to do so. Others are experienced, sage advisors, many with certified financial planner or law degrees. It is critical to separate the former from the latter.

Once you have found a qualified stockbroker, other questions are how much power he or she should have over your account and how your broker should be compensated.

The brokerage industry is in the process of moving away from charging commissions based on transactions to charging annual fees to monitor accounts. This is a step in the right direction. Removing transaction fees and commissions can take away many of the inherent conflicts that exist in today's stockbroker relationships.

Keep in mind that you can have more than one account with your broker. You may choose to keep a portion in a traditional account where little activity is required. Too often investors hold cash and low-yielding bonds in expensive managed accounts.

Brokers today are often pushing their clients to try managed accounts. The broker is pushing the managed account by telling the client it yields a much higher return. Why does it have higher returns? Is it because the broker's security selections have been poor, and he or she now wants to outsource that job to someone else? If that's the case, you may want to find another financial advisor.

On the whole, I like a model whereby an investor pays for advice not based on transactions, but on results. That way, when a recommendation is made to buy or sell a security, you don't have to ask yourself, "Is this move in my best interest, or does my broker need the commission to make the lease payment on his BMW?"

Consider the Best Time to Start Social Security

Harry will be 63 years old in a couple of months. He is retired and has a pension. Harry is debating whether he should start his Social Security.

Harry's wife still works, so he doesn't need the money immediately. If he received Social Security, he would just save the money. He's trying to decide whether he should wait until age 66 before collecting his full retirement payment. He could also wait until age 70 and get bigger payments.

The decision to start Social Security should never be taken lightly. Once retirement benefits begin, there is no turning them off.

When one starts Social Security before a normal retirement age, one will take a cut in benefits. Benefits can start as early as age 62, but the reduction can be as great as 30%. If Harry started benefits at his present age, he would face a hit of about 20%. If Harry were to die young, taking the cash at age 62 would net him the most money. But if he lives well into his 80s and beyond, waiting until later will net him the most.

There are other factors to consider. One is the taxation of benefits. That depends on any other income. With a spouse still working, Harry's income could be high enough so that 85% of his benefits would be taxable. That's right. He paid the Social Security tax for years. And, if he started working in the 1960s or 1970s, the payroll tax then was a whopper of a tax. Now that he's finally going to get his payments, he's likely going to pay taxes on it *de nuevo*. In other words, he'll pay the same tax for a second time.

The bottom line is this: if you are healthy and won't spend the money right now, delay the start of your benefits. Wait until you reach your normal retirement age, and you won't take a hit for the rest of your life. If you find you won't need the money at that time, you could wait until age 70. At that point, you'd receive a raise of greater than 30%.

Our Social Security system forces you to make a ghoulish bet on how many years you're going to live.

Now that you're motivated, the next step is to think like a saver. But first you need to overcome any remaining resistance. A hockey puck sliding on a sheet of ice can travel great distances, and the smoother the ice, the farther it goes. Debt is the friction in most people's saving strategies. Remove the friction, and the puck can travel unlimited distances. With no friction, the puck can continue indefinitely in the same direction and with the same velocity with which it started. This is Newton's law of motion—an object ("body") at rest stays at rest, and an object in motion tends to stay in motion.

Chapter 3
Accumulate Wealth

The secret of accumulation of wealth is to begin with a pay-down plan that you can follow that will expand into saving, then investing, without changing the principles of your plan. In this section, you will discover what other ordinary people have done to start building wealth using the strategies covered in Chapter 1. If your goal is to change your spending and saving behavior, this section will be most important to you.

Sometimes people don't start saving because they are afraid to make a decision. Ordinary people can accumulate riches. This chapter will show you how.

Ordinary People Can Get Rich

Many people with good jobs and fat incomes never accumulate any significant wealth. How is this possible? They have no roadmap, no idea how they are going to get from point A to point B, from zero assets to financial independence. Indeed, many people don't even take the time to think about why wealth is important to them, what they want, and how much they need to achieve their dreams.

Without a plan for the future, they're unlikely ever to achieve their goals even though they have great incomes. They don't have a system for spending, saving, or investing.

Buying Lottery Tickets Is Not a Retirement Plan

Many poor souls believe they're going to get lucky and get a financial windfall; they hope to invest in the next Microsoft or win the lottery. The definition of insanity is doing the same thing over and over and expecting different results. And many people do insane things with their finances. In order to accumulate some wealth and have financial independence, you must take control of your finances.

Start Small

If you have a company-sponsored 401(k), start by contributing just 1% or 2% of your pay. People get discouraged sometimes because they're so far behind that they just feel like throwing in the towel. If you suddenly go from saving nothing to putting 15% in your 401(k), you might find that you can no longer afford even McDonald's. You're going to give up and quit saving altogether. But starting gradually is much less painful. When you go from nothing saved to even just a couple of hundred dollars, you feel encouraged and want to continue. Then every time you get a pay raise, bump the amount up. Even if you only get a 2% pay raise each year, add another 1% to your 401(k).

Stop Looking at Your Retirement Portfolio Every Day

Does it matter what your portfolio balance is if you're only 45 years old? No. In fact, if you're still working and saving for retirement, you should pray for tremendous bear markets. You want a huge bull market to happen *during* your retirement, not *before*. It's insane for a young person to get excited because the market is up and their 401(k) is going up. That person doesn't understand markets.

Stop Buying Investments When They're Expensive

People are illogical when it comes to investments. When the price goes up, they buy more. And when the price drops, they buy less or even sell what they've got. It's the same with real estate. Real estate prices double and people buy more properties. When the market's soft, they don't want anything to do with it. But with consumer goods, it's just the opposite. If you go to the grocery store and find that milk is on sale, you might buy two gallons instead of one. And if there's a shortage of milk and the price goes up, you might cut back on it because it's too expensive. You should think of investments the same way. You want to buy when everyone else is selling and sell when everyone else is buying.

The Best Investment of All

There are times—a precious few times—when one must spend money to make money.

An example of this is education. Education is actually much more than how many years were spent in school. But, to prospective employers, how many and what kind of degrees one has is often the most crucial factor in hiring. Indeed, one can't even obtain an interview for many jobs without a certain degree. So spending money on your children's education—or your own—is key to determining one's career earnings.

The difference between the career earnings of a high school graduate and a college graduate over an average lifetime is dramatic.

Suppose you are stuck in a job you don't like. You want to obtain a degree, or an additional degree, so you qualify for a better, or more satisfying, job. You are in your 30s or 40s. What's the best way to do this?

There are several factors to consider: personal, tax, and economic. First, it might be a good idea to keep your day job and go to school at night for a while. This will do two things: It will let you experience university life without making a complete commitment to it. Second, by going part time, you can string out the payments for college over a longer period, reducing the need for or the extent of borrowing.

University night students, typically adults with full-time jobs, are more responsible than daytime students. They're paying for their education, and they realize how precious it is.

Now let's talk a little about the financing. There's a few ways to go. You can probably obtain low-interest student loans, borrowing only what you need. The student loans, also, can provide some deductions. Some people choose to sell or mortgage their house to pay for higher education. Unless you've decided to attend Harvard University full time, the sale of a house is probably too extreme. Some form of mortgaging should be enough. You can also get a home equity loan at a low interest rate that will likely be tax deductible. However, you shouldn't do something just to obtain a tax deduction (enjoyable as it is to send less money to our Washington wizards). Not spending money is always better than obtaining a deduction.

Obtaining a degree can be a very smart move for you in a number of ways; but as with all actions that have tax consequences, you should discuss it beforehand with your tax advisor.

What Should You Pay Your Financial Advisor?

Millions of Americans, many who do not have substantial stock holdings, are looking for help managing their portfolios. They are in the dark as to how to find an advisor and what to pay for financial advice.

Francis needed an advisor and he also needed a benchmark. He didn't know what a fair fee for a financial advisor was. One advisor had quoted Francis a 1.25% quarterly management fee with an initial minimum investment of $115,000. An investment less than that would incur a charge of $350 a quarter.

The part that Francis found distressing was that he would have to pay these fees even if the portfolio were to underperform. However, the advisor also told Francis that he would credit him toward the $115,000 minimum for an annuity and an IRA account that Francis already has with his firm (total of both is approximately $33,000).

The fee Francis was quoted is probably about average for that size account, assuming the 1.25% fee is an annual rate, with payments made quarterly. The fees charged for investment management can run anywhere from a low of 0.25% to as high as 3% per year. Typically, the larger the account, the lower the fee.

Unfortunately, most advisors receive their fee whether the account goes up or down in value. They want to grow the account, however, because as your account grows, so do their revenues.

Over the past several years, many brokers and financial advisors have moved away from charging transaction fees and switched to asset management fees based on a percentage of the money being managed.

This is an excellent move because it can reduce the inherent conflicts that arise when a broker gets paid only when a transaction occurs. When you have a fee-based arrangement with a financial advisor, you don't have to question the motive behind a recommended transaction. Because your advisor is not getting paid as a result of a transaction, you know a recommendation didn't occur simply because your broker's BMW lease payment was due.

Given the fact that Francis has already done business with the financial advisor, the advisor should give Francis credit for the accounts he already manages. After all, Francis's advisor probably received a commission when he invested Francis's money.

If the firm chooses not to give Francis some sort of credit for his existing investments, he can always choose to find another advisor. There are plenty of them.

Stocks or Bonds?

Many investors are the unwitting victims of short-term thinking. It is a myopia that affects almost anyone in every aspect of life. Either too optimistic or too pessimistic about a current style of investing, they let the events of the day or week change their thinking. In the game of investing as in the game of life, victory almost always goes to the patient ones who have a big-picture, long-term outlook.

Here is an example of how short-term thinking can distort investment realities. Lydia started investing early in the year 2000, just as stocks had gone through one of the best decades in history. Her portfolio investment alternatives were stocks and bonds. Like many Americans who got carried away during that time period, she put all of her assets into stocks. Five years passed. During that period through March 30, 2005, Lydia's stocks had an annualized return of minus -3.16% as measured by the S&P 500 index, a well-known benchmark of stocks. In other words, she had an average loss of a little over 3% in each of the 5 years. Incidentally, bonds during this 5-year period averaged about 6% a year.

Therefore, someone suffering from investment myopia would conclude that stocks are no good and they should put all their money in bonds. But if Lydia's money had been in the Standard & Poor's 500 for 10 years instead of 5 (from 1995 to 2005), something very different would have happened. She would have had an annual return of 10.79% on her stocks.

And how did bonds do in this same period? They trailed stocks by about 4% per year, recording 6.05% on an annualized basis.

Select good stocks and bonds for the long periods, ignoring short-term woes and media noise. And remember, stocks tend to beat bonds over extended periods, but bonds do have periods in which they are better than stocks—such as during the past 5 years. Will it continue this way? The truth is, no one knows.

So, invest based on long-term goals and your individual needs. Are you an aggressive investor with many years ahead of you? Then you can have a big portion of your money in stocks and a small portion in bonds. Are you a conservative investor who has accumulated a big portfolio and expects to retire in just a few years? Then you should have a smaller stock and a bigger bond stake.

To balance risk with time horizons, also consider partitioning your money into two pots. One pot would be for money that will be needed within the next 5 years. These dollars should be invested conservatively, with guaranteed investments and short-term bonds.

The second pot would be earmarked for long-term needs, such as retirement. This pot should be invested for maximum growth. What the value of the portfolio is over the next year or two should be irrelevant. Your goal should be to get the pot as large as possible by the time you reach retirement.

Currently, many published articles talk about the benefits of bonds and the risks of stocks. Go back and read some of the articles written 5 years ago (they're easy to find on the Internet). You'll read just the opposite. And 5 years from now we'll probably be reading about how lousy bonds are and how great stocks are.

Why You Need to Understand Investing!

This is a true story of Mary, an advisor who at 11 years of age learned one of the best financial lessons of her life. She had a babysitting job during summer break and planned to save all her earnings over the summer for next fall's school clothes.

Mary made a cute piggybank by coating a balloon with *papier mâchè*. Then once the *papier mâchè* hardened, she cut a hole in the top and painted her do-it-herself piggybank in beautiful colors of red, green, and yellow.

Mary was disciplined in her saving, cramming all her hard-earned dollars into her bank every week. She had calculated she would have just enough money to buy her school clothes by the end of summer. Finally, the big day arrived. Mary invited all her girlfriends to a little celebration of the big "opening." Her mother even baked a cake. "It was like a birthday party— until we cut open the piggybank," said Mary. "At first I thought some- one had played a cruel joke on me. The inside was a goopy mess—and no dollars."

Unfortunately, inside the rubber balloon the paste had stayed moist and wet, causing the paper dollars to turn to soup.

This story doesn't have a happy ending, but it demonstrates the need to un- derstand what's going on inside your retirement accounts. You can't afford to cut open your 401(k) plan and discover 30 years later your investments have turned to soup!

Living Large on the Stock Market

Walter is a schoolteacher who invests in the stock market. Because interest rates are still relatively low and because his house is paid off, Walter wants to dive deeper into the stock market. Walter is only 5 years from retirement and, although he now appears financially secure, he believes that he can make monster profits within a short time period. He says he's discovered the Holy Grail of investing. He wants to mortgage his house and put the proceeds into the market, using the same stocks that have just made him tons of money.

Walter should beware. With relatively low interest rates (even though they're now starting to rise), it can be tempting to pull equity out of your home to invest. It is a tempting idea when stocks are rising or when the segment of the market you are in is doing well. But think about it. Banks, insurance companies, pension plans, and even individual investors are willing to lend money for 30 years at low rates. Do they not see how great stocks are performing? Are they stupid? Or do they realize that having some money invested in secure investments at lower rates is prudent? They understand what veteran investors know: No matter how well the stock market is doing, there are years that bonds do better than stocks. Pulling equity out of your home (a secure investment) when you're 5 years away from retirement would not be prudent. Walter should think twice before making such a drastic move.

Investing at Stock Market's Peak Proves Costly

Michael inherited about $400,000 and invested about $390,000 in three annuities. The plan was to let them be and, hopefully, grow. However, the $390,000 dwindled to about $260,000 some 3 years later. Each month they kept going down. Finally, Michael couldn't take it anymore. He pulled his funds out of the stock market and put the money into annuity money market funds. Now he is even thinking of terminating the annuity contract. But if Michael withdraws from the annuity, he will have to pay $12,000 in early withdrawal fees.

Unfortunately, Michael invested in what appeared to be a fairly aggressive portfolio at the height of the stock market. Obviously, he had no idea that a big bear market was just around the corner.

Keeping Michael's money in the money market fund within the annuity is a losing strategy. With rates so low right now, Michael's accounts could actually be declining each month after the insurance company deducts its fees. Many variable annuities offer a fixed interest fund. If Michael has that option within his annuities, transferring the money to the fixed account would at least stop the bleeding.

Most variable annuities have some sort of a death benefit. This is a guaranteed minimum amount that is payable upon the death of the contract owner. Typically, the death benefit is at least equal to the initial deposits minus any withdrawals.

If Michael withdraws all the funds from the annuities, he'll be able to claim a loss on his income taxes, but he'll be forfeiting the death benefits.

However, if Michael withdraws most of his money from the annuities but leaves enough to keep the contracts in force, his heirs will be guaranteed to receive all the money Michael lost. For example, if Michael withdraws $259,000 from his annuities and leaves $1,000 in the policies, the annuities will maintain a death benefit of $131,000 ($390,000 minus $259,000).

Michael's annuity policies carry early surrender charges, so he should keep in mind that any strategy that results in withdrawing money from the annuities will cost him.

Shifting Michael's funds within the annuities to a balanced approach might be the best bet. But without knowing more about his situation, no financial advisor can tell Michael what he should do unless he spends many hours going over his situation. Michael should talk with a few financial planners to devise a strategy that can best accomplish his goals and objectives.

A Fool and His Money

Market mountebanks are always coming up with new schemes to separate you from your money. Market timing—the idea that someone can consistently pick market lows and highs, getting clients in or out at precisely the optimum time—is such an old scheme that it's almost new. But whenever and wherever the charlatans offer this crackpot idea, you must disdain it just as you would a politician who promises to cut your taxes while expanding government spending.

The case for market timing is that it can work. And indeed it can over short periods. However, the problem with market timing is that you have to be right all of the time. No investment professional is right all the time.

Market timing cannot reduce risk. On the contrary, market timing will increase risk. Risk is reduced through diversification. Moving in and out of investments is wonderful if you make the right decisions, but what happens if you make the wrong decisions?

Most pension plans, foundations, endowments, and the like use an investment strategy that stresses diversification among a broad array of investments. There may be minor adjustments to their allocations from time to time, but they don't manage money by moving in and out of different investments. It is expensive to move in and out of investments. You're charged commissions and other transaction costs whenever you jump in or out of markets.

Diversified portfolios may not get you rich, but they'll keep you from becoming poor.

From Employee to Entrepreneur

Tim likes to plan many years in advance. Tim is a 39-year-old, single, state employee. He plans to retire with a pension in about 17 years. Additionally, Tim contributed to a 457 deferred compensation plan and has a Roth IRA. For some time, he has planned to start a sole proprietorship. Tim has been thinking about a new business for years and plans to start soon.

Tim estimates that $35,000 per year is a reasonable earning estimate initially. He wonders which self-employed savings options would work best for a small business owner.

Tim will have several options available to him once he has self-employment income. But there are a couple of things Tim must remember. First of all, Tim can only contribute a portion of his net income, not his gross income. If Tim has many startup expenses, he may find he has little or no net income his first year. Second, Tim must contribute to any employee's retirement fund the same percentage that he would contribute for himself.

As a self-employed individual, Tim will have the ability to contribute to a SEP-IRA, a Simple IRA, a Uni-K, a Keogh, or a traditional IRA. Each plan has its own nuances. Depending on the plan that Tim selects, he could contribute as much as 25% of his pay.

Most of the plans must be established by December 31. But Tim will have until the time he files his income taxes to make the contribution. Once Tim's business is up and running, he should talk with a financial advisor who specializes in small business retirement plans. Together Tim and the advisor can determine which type will work best for the business.

Teaching Your Kids How to Get Rich

How do you get rich? You do it slowly. You invest on a regular basis for an extended period. The earlier you start, the better your chances. Therefore, start early to educate your child about money.

Just as you want your children to have library cards and start borrowing books as soon as they are ready, so, too, should you help them to save by opening a savings account as soon as possible.

As your children become teenagers and start earning money from part-time jobs, you can start explaining to them how stocks work. And, with small contributions, you can buy them their first stocks. It's wise to begin with some of the more conservative stocks. Your kids might become more interested in the process if they start by investing in some of the companies they patronize.

Let's say your 16-year-old son could afford to put about $50 a month in stocks; and your 14-year-old daughter, between $10 and $20. They would reinvest any dividends they earn. You could encourage them by matching the money they save for stocks. Explain why it's important to invest in stocks, and that if the next 50 years are anything like the past, owning stock in quality American companies should provide returns that far exceed savings accounts.

The main advantage your children will receive by investing in corporate stock will not be the money they accumulate, but the lessons they will learn. Many people don't comprehend investments until they are in their 30s or 40s. Sometimes, they don't learn about why stocks are necessary in most portfolios until it is too late to accumulate a healthy retirement account. It's much better to learn these lessons while children are young and can afford to lose some money than when they retire and invest their life savings in things they know nothing about.

Most companies offer plans to purchase their stock directly rather than through a broker. The best place to start is on a company's own Web site. Typically, this will take you to an investor-relations department, which will explain how the company's investment plan works. If you want to invest in a company that does not offer a direct purchase plan, you will have to use a broker. An online discount broker may be your best bet to keep fees low.

The Bypass Trust—Another Mixed Blessing

The government gives tax breaks. And it also taketh away. This is another reason why you need a good tax advisor. The breaks and the penalties change practically every year. And the way these rules are interpreted and implemented changes endlessly.

For instance, let's look at the bypass trust, which can be a way of avoiding, or reducing, estate taxes. The downside is that it can also lead to potential capital gains.

Let's say a husband and wife bought a home in 1977 and lived in it until each of them died. They had created a bypass trust in 1990 and put the house in the Dad's side when he died in 1991. The Mom continued to live there until her death in 2002.

When the house is sold, the heirs, the children, hope to use their Mom's $250,000 tax exemption against any capital gains. Sorry. Can't do. The heirs are stuck in a place where it will be very difficult to avoid paying capital gains taxes when the home is sold.

A/B trusts, sometimes known as bypass trusts, can be effective in reducing estate taxes, but they can create other tax problems down the road. These trusts are used when a couple's estate is worth more than the amount one person can pass on without estate taxes.

When the Dad died, the home was not transferred to the Mom, but was instead put in a bypass trust. The Mom had the right to live in the home the rest of her life, but the home was not part of the Mom's estate. She had no ownership interest in the home.

Now that the Mom has died, the heirs will pay capital gains taxes on whatever they net from the home above the home's cost basis. The cost basis of the home is most likely not what the Mom and Dad paid for the house, but what the home was worth when the Dad died.

Typically, when a person inherits an asset, the asset's cost basis is "stepped-up" to the current market value—thus eliminating any capital gains. But when an asset transfers years after a person's death, as in this situation, the stepped-up cost basis reverts to the time when the individual died, not when the asset was transferred.

For families with estates greater than the exemption amounts ($2 million), it makes sense to use an A/B trust to reduce estate taxes. However, keep in mind that the portion that remains from the one who died will not receive a second stepped-up basis when the surviving spouse dies.

The government gave you a break. Now it wants that break back.

The Pluses and Minuses of Custodial Accounts

Jerry is a proud grandfather. Indeed, he is already planning to set up a college fund for his new grandson. He plans to buy stocks direct from the companies through dividend reinvestment plans. That part is fine. But he's not sure the stocks should be in a custodial account or in the name of the mother, his daughter.

Jerry has many options. Basically, in beginning a college fund, Jerry must decide how much control he wants. For example, a custodial account would provide Jerry with some tax relief, but the money would be the grandson's when he becomes an adult regardless of whether he plans to attend college.

But if this isn't a major issue for Jerry, then titling the account as a custodial account may be a good option. Having the account in the daughter's name can be a benefit for Jerry because he won't have to worry about paying any income taxes on the stock dividends each year. That responsibility will be the daughter's. The daughter can also determine when and how the grandson will receive the funds when he becomes an adult.

One problem with having the daughter own the account is that the college fund will be reviewed when applying for any college aid. The fund could potentially reduce the amount of aid the grandson would have otherwise received.

A third option is for Jerry to own and hold the account, earmarking it for the grandson. Jerry will be responsible for taxes on any income the account generates, but if he invests in low-yielding stocks, this really won't be an issue. When the grandson goes to college, Jerry can gift the stocks to him. The grandson can sell the stocks and pay capital gains at his tax rate, which would presumably be lower than Jerry's.

Neither a Borrower Nor a Lender Be

A good goal for this year is to not borrow a dime from anybody. Avoid car loans, credit cards, store charge cards, and even home equity loans. If you can manage to stay out of debt, you'll have fewer financial obligations each month and the peace of mind of knowing that you don't owe anything to anyone.

There is no correlation between income and net worth. Some people earning hundreds of thousands of dollars per year have nothing saved for the future, and others on modest incomes have enormous sums set aside for retirement. It's not how much you make that counts; it's how much you keep.

Most of us have a hard time saving each month. We enjoy spending money so much that we confuse our wants with our needs. That's okay as long as it doesn't cause financial problems. And the best way to ensure that your spending doesn't cause financial ruin in the future is to save first and spend second.

Save 10%

A good rule of thumb is to save 10% of your paycheck. Before you buy groceries, pay the rent, and so forth, and put a portion of your income into a long-term savings or investment plan. If your company offers a 401(k) or 403(b), that's great, because the money will be yanked out of your check before you have a chance to spend it. If it does not, set up a monthly withdrawal from your checking account so that your savings is taken out of your account the day your paycheck is deposited.

Focus on Long-Term Results

There are people who do a great job saving and avoiding debt but still have financial disasters. Why? Because they ignore long-term trends and instead focus on the latest investment fads. They truly believe that it is possible to get rich quick by picking the right investment.

In 1999 Jake was so enamored with technology stocks that he wanted to dump his real estate investment trust (REIT) holdings. REITs were in a slump at the time, and he felt his money would be doing better in technology stocks. He sold his real estate to buy tech stocks. And we all know what happened to tech stocks.

If you would like less stress when it comes to investing, stay diversified. If there are some ways to get rich quick, you're not going to find them. By the time you hear about them, you're too late. You'll wind up buying high and selling low.

Obviously there are many more financial goals that can help you in the years to come. Using a couple of the ones just listed won't make you rich, but they should keep you from going broke. And they may even help you sleep better at night.

Time, the Most Valuable Element in Investing

Give me enough time and I can accomplish anything. The only problem with that truism is that each of us has a limited amount of time.

Kurt, a teen, wanted to know when would be the best time to begin investing. He said his business teacher had recently announced that now is the best time to begin.

Kurt's business teacher gave the class wise advice. That's because the earlier you start investing, the better. There are two great reasons for beginning to invest at Kurt's age: (1) Investments will have many years to grow, and (2) you'll be starting a good habit of investing.

If you contribute $2,000 to a Roth IRA at age 20 and do so for the next 35 years, by the time you're 55 years old, you will have accumulated over $542,000, assuming you earned an average of 10% per year on your investments. If you wait until you reach the age of 30 to begin investing, you will have accumulated less than $200,000 by the age of 55.

That's a $342,000 difference. For Trump, Buffett, or Oprah, $342,000 may not mean much. For the average American, that is a heck of a lot of money.

Investment success is mainly based on time—the more time you have, the better the compounding effect—and rate of return. Let's say you put $300 a month away in an investing program. You do it for 30 years. You earn 9 percent a year.

That means you will have some $553,342 before taxes after 30 years. But let's say you get the same rate of return, but do it for 40 instead of 30 years. The difference? About $900,000! You end up with $1,414,929 before taxes. Boy, that extra 10 years changed everything.

But let's take the same investment program—$300 a month over 40 years—but let's say you found better investments and, instead of earning 9% a year, you earned 12%. The difference? About $2.1 million! At the end of the period you have $3,564,726. Time and returns can make a tremendous difference.

Unfortunately, most people at age 20 do not feel they have enough money to begin investing. The same is true for people at age 30. And age 40. And age 50. And age … In fact, most people never have "excess money."

The key is to develop a habit of saving and investing regularly, regardless of how much money you are making. If you can develop this pattern while you're young, before you're married with kids, you'll be well on your way to financial freedom.

And remember, even small amounts over long periods generally are much better than large amounts over small periods.

Mortgage Freedom or 401(k) Contributions?

You can't wait to have a mortgage-burning party. Homeowners will go to great lengths to start the bonfire of the mortgage. In some cases, they think that putting off paying into retirement accounts such as 401(k)s makes sense if they're getting rid of the mortgage.

This attitude is going too far. There are opportunities to save for retirement here and now that must not be passed up because you won't get them tomorrow, especially if you switch jobs. There are matching contributions your employer will give you and reduced taxes you can get just by putting money into a 401(k) account.

You need to find a balance between these two worthwhile goals—saving for retirement now—and retiring a mortgage as soon as possible. If you stop contributing to your retirement accounts, you run the risk of not having enough to fund your retirement. Remember, inflation will eat away at today's dollars so you will need many more of them to maintain your lifestyle 20 or 30 years from now. I don't think it is necessary for you to take an either/or approach.

Here are some other things for you to consider: Are you still raising children? Could you save more once they're grown and gone? Do you plan on staying in your home until you die, or might you downsize when you retire? Are you in a high tax bracket today where a current 401(k) deduction might be worth a lot? Is there a chance that your income will increase so that you can save more in the future? Do projections with your financial advisor of what you would have in assets if you stopped contributing to your 401(k) right now.

Planning a home payoff to coincide with retirement is a great goal. However, you want to make sure you'll have enough money so you could afford to live in your home during retirement. Rather than discontinue your 401(k) deposits altogether, perhaps you should find some compromise.

By the way, the sagacious Coolidge, who high tailed it out of the presidency because he saw the stock market crash of 1929 coming, died a very wealthy man.

When Company Stock Is a Good Deal

You should never invest most of your wealth in your employer's stock. This means almost all of your economic fortunes—your earnings and investments—are tied to your employer's. That's too big a risk. What if you end up working for the next Enron?

Yet there are times when company stock—bought on a limited basis and held for a short period of time—can be a very good deal. For example, at one time, MCI (formerly WorldCom) had a stock purchase program for its employees. It was designed to enable workers to buy shares of MCI at a 15% discount to the market. Employees, who participated in the program and sold the shares every 6 months, received a minimum of a 15% return. That's less any commission. But the future return for those who hold on to the shares will be based on the value of MCI stock.

Many companies have similar programs available to employees. If you take advantage of the program, play your cards right and don't get carried away; it could be quite profitable for you.

When Should You Cash Out of Company Stock?

Suzanne purchased common stock through a company where she formerly worked. The shares are older than 5 years and have performed well. Now she wants to cash in the stock and use the proceeds for a down payment on her dream house.

Cashing in some stocks for a down payment on a house is an excellent idea. Taking profits is almost always a good idea.

Although nobody knows how the real estate market will perform over the next several years, owning your own home is sound financial planning. As long as Suzanne doesn't refinance her home every few years, she will one day have her home paid for and will be able to enjoy a retirement with no house payment.

Where Should Your Money Be Invested?

Many financial planners say that the most important investment decision you will make is how you divvy up your assets among investments. The industry term for this is "asset allocation," a process by which the investor determines what part of his or her money should be in stocks, bonds, cash—and possibly other investments such as real estate. Asset allocation is key because the proper mix can ensure that you get good returns, which, in turn, determines whether you can do everything you want to in those golden years.

And, over long periods of time, just a percentage or two more in returns makes a tremendous difference. Here's an example. Two people put $200 away a month for 35 years. One allocates his assets effectively and receives 9% a year. The other doesn't do quite so well. She invests over the same number of years, but her returns are only 7%. How much difference is the 2%? Mucho dinero! The difference is $230,000! ($592,000 vs. $362,000) But to get that extra money, you must allocate your assets properly.

Determining how your investments should be allocated is based not only on your age and income needs but also on how much risk you can stomach without losing too much sleep. If market gyrations don't cause you to panic, the majority of your portfolio should be in stocks. History tells us that over long periods of time, stocks have outperformed just about every other type of investment.

One method of determining how much stock you should own is to look at what the large pension funds own (after all, their job is to pay monthly income to retirees like yourself). The typical pension plan in the United States has about 65% of its dollars in stocks with the remaining in bonds, cash, and real estate. If you manage your portfolio similarly to the big pension funds, your retirement should work out just fine. Again, this might be an instance in which you want to obtain the advice of a planner.

Who Gets Paid First?

Steve and Marcy are in their late 30s and have two children. They owe $240,000 on their home mortgage and have no credit card or auto loans. However, they owe a family member $40,000. And, rightly, they want to pay him back ASAP for their peace of mind and because he was "so generous in helping us out," according to Marcy. But as they would also like to increase their savings toward retirement and college they are looking at putting off paying off the relative for a year and a half. After that, they would pay the debt by cinching up their budget or taking out a home equity loan.

Steve and Marcy's first instinct is the best one. That's because there is only one thing worse than owing a bank. And that is owing money to a friend or family member.

The bank is impersonal and really doesn't care what you do with your money so long as you make your payments on time. But family members can be a different matter. They can have a tendency to judge every financial decision until they receive their money back.

Steve and Marcy should take the home equity loan and pay off the family member who loaned them the money.

The relative would probably be pleased and quite proud to have the money paid back early.

What this married couple wants to avoid is keeping the $40,000 home equity balance on their home for the next decade. Just as they have a plan now to pay off the loan to their family member, so they should also have a plan in place to get the home equity loan paid off. But rather than doing it in 18 months, they may decide to take 5 years or so to give them the opportunity to invest in their employer's retirement plans and college savings plans.

Chapter 4
Balance What You Want and What You Have

Very few people have as much money as they want. Judy has a seven-figure portfolio, a size that makes most people envious; yet, she's always worried about money. She's worried about the markets, worried about outliving her money—always worried. She said, "I'd feel so much better if there was more." But the truth is it would not matter. She could add another zero to her net worth and she would still have the same worries.

Of course, more money can always provide additional things, whether it's another house or paying for the grandkids' education. There's nothing wrong with wanting more money, but you need to be realistic.

Most Americans don't have enough money saved for retirement, particularly the baby boomers. Baby boomers historically spend everything they make and in many cases, more. Most baby boomers are used to instant gratification and have little patience for deferring purchases until they can more easily afford them. They spend money frivolously; for instance, they buy a new car for $50,000 when they can buy a comparable used car for $15,000. That used car is still going to get them from point A to point B. Sure, the new car is fun to drive—for a few weeks. But soon the new car smell wears off and the new excitement wears off, leaving only the hefty payment.

People who are behind on their savings goals should determine what is it they're trying to accomplish financially. Why are they delaying saving or ignoring other financial goals? Maybe they don't plan on retiring, but not everyone will be able to work for their entire lifetime. Some will become incapacitated by physical problems and not be able to work even if they want to. It's imperative to have some savings set up for that eventuality.

A Hopeless Situation?

What happens if you're 55 years old and you've saved nothing for retirement? Is your situation hopeless?

It's difficult, yes. But it's not hopeless. Here are several things you can do to catch up over the next decade.

Maximize contributions to qualified plans. You never signed up for the 401(k) plan at work? Sign up immediately and make the maximum contributions. You have no IRA? Open one up and make the maximum contributions every year, regardless of whether the contributions are deductible or not.

Cut spending. Do something that our massive federal government never does. Adopt a zero-based budgeting system. For the next 10 years buy only what you absolutely need. Any money you don't spend should be swept into a money market account each month. Be sure the money market account has a dirt-cheap expense ratio.

Try to find some extra income. Do you have a hobby or something that might earn you extra money? Take any of this extra money you earn and put it into another savings/investment account.

Consider selling your house and moving to another state. You can take the proceeds from the first house and buy another one for half the price. The profits get plowed into a savings/investment account.

Set up automatic saving/investing plans. Don't count on yourself to save and invest each month. That's what got you into this fix. Have large amounts taken out of your checking account and sent to your mutual fund company each month.

Still coming up short? Seriously consider working past the age of 65. Maybe you could take a part-time job or do some consulting. This solves two problems. Many retirees are bored. You won't be. And the additional income will ease your retirement problems.

An IRA Escape

In general, one should stay away from breaking into an IRA or almost any qualified account before the age of 59½. That's because an early withdrawal can trigger a penalty and taxes. However, Carol, who is 53 years old and recently qualified for Social Security disability payments, wonders if she qualifies for an exception to the early penalty rule.

The tax code clearly permits penalty-free withdrawals from retirement accounts (including IRAs) prior to the age of 59½ if a person is totally disabled. The code does not specify how to determine whether someone is totally disabled, but most tax experts agree that qualifying for Social Security disability is about the best proof.

Still, not everyone who is disabled will qualify for disability benefits. Therefore, there may be other methods to verify disability, such as a letter from one or more qualified medical doctors.

More information regarding penalty-free withdrawals from IRAs can be found in Internal Revenue Code 72(t).

Balance What You Have and What You Want

Brice, a United Airlines pilot, retired 2 years ago at age 62. Brice had been receiving a $12,000 a month pension, but not anymore. A recent federal court ruling allowed United to terminate its dramatically under-funded pension plan. Brice's monthly check was reduced to $2000 a month.

His situation is becoming commonplace. Although the United pension default is the largest to date in U.S. history, it comes on top of a string of bankruptcies and retirement plan meltdowns in industries over the last several years, which directly reflects the retirement security of millions of Americans. Bradley Belt, executive director of the federal pension benefit guarantee corporation, which is funded through corporate premiums, has moved from a $10 billion surplus in 1998 to a $20 billion deficit in its insurance program. The agency had $39 billion in assets and 62 billion in long-term liabilities. Belt estimates that the underfunded pension system could reach a record half-trillion dollars with the auto, airline, and retail industries at risk.

College Saving—The Sooner the Better

Time is critical in achieving a financial planning goal. That's because the more time you save for a goal, the more the compounding effect takes place. And the better the chance that you will achieve your goal.

In the case of college saving, the task is made more difficult by the persistence of higher education inflation, which almost always seems to outpace general inflation.

Peter, who has two children, ages 6 and 4, wants to start saving for their future college costs. He was motivated by a workbook on planning for college costs. The accompanying worksheet told Peter that he needed to save $600 per month per child. That got Peter's attention.

Calculating the cost of college for a child can be a sobering experience. The cost of an education has been accelerating. Providing children with a full ride to college will not be possible for many Americans in the future.

Instead of focusing on saving $600 per month for each child, Peter should consider starting with a much smaller figure that he can afford. Although a smaller monthly investment may not be able to send the kids to an Ivy League school, the money will help with some of their costs.

Whatever Peter is going to do, he should get started right now. If you don't start with something now, no matter how small, you may find you'll never start. Peter is a little behind now. It would have been better if he had started college savings plans at the birth of his children. But the problem will only worsen if he doesn't start immediately.

Your Employer Can Put Your Child Through College

Many companies have generous employee stock purchase as well as 401(k) plans. Some parents figure they can use one or both of these plans to build up a nest egg for their children's college education.

Employee stock purchase plans can be an excellent way to acquire shares at a discounted price. If your company offers you a plan that guarantees you can sell the stock for a profit each 6 months, that's even better.

Nevertheless, the employee stock purchase plan is not the best way to save for a college education. There is one big drawback: The stock purchase plan lacks diversification. It is only one company. Some people have their entire savings tied up with one company. That's never a good idea, regardless of how well the company has been doing. But as long as you can maintain a diversified portfolio—in other words the company stock is only one of a number of investments—than the company stock purchase plan can be a part of a successful wealth-building program that may put your children through college.

Assuming all of your college savings are in the stock purchase plan, you can simply give your children a portion of the shares when they are ready for school. That way, any capital gains due would be taxed at the child's tax rate, not the adult's rate, which will be higher.

The gamble you are taking with the employee stock purchase plan is that the employer's stock will be high when your children enter college. The stock may be a jewel today, but it could have also turned into a bow-wow.

It's best to stay with the stock purchase plan. But rather than continuing to accumulate the shares, sell their newly purchased shares every 6 months (to lock in your profit) and place the proceeds in a 529 plan. By doing that, you remove the risk from the employer's stock and use a tax-favored college savings program.

Get Going!

Gene, who has done very well in his profession, is 38 years old and has a confession to make. He doesn't have anything saved for retirement. He has heard repeatedly about the importance of starting savings early, so he figures it's about time to start. Gene is self-employed and makes good money. He wants to know where and how he should start.

Many people don't start saving for retirement until some years past his age. Therefore, he shouldn't feel too bad. It would have been great if he started a decade ago. But he still has plenty of savings years ahead of him.

The best types of retirement vehicles are the ones that have tax advantages and adverse consequences if you withdraw funds prior to retirement. Since Gene is self-employed, he can establish a retirement plan known as a SEP-IRA. This plan allows Gene to contribute 15% of his income to the plan, receive a tax deduction for his deposits, and then have his money grow tax-deferred.

It may also be wise for Gene to contribute to a Roth IRA in addition to the SEP. Gene has many investment options available to him with both the SEP and Roth IRAs. And because Gene is relatively young, he should consider investing his money somewhat aggressively.

Here's a Piece of Cake. Don't Eat It

James has opened seven 529 plan accounts for his grandchildren, who range in age from 9 to 14. Yet James thinks he has spotted a flaw: What happens if one of his grandchildren ends up not going to college?

When a child does not need the money for college expenses, taxes and penalties apply. Money that is contributed to a 529 plan grows tax-deferred and comes out tax-free as long as the money is used for qualified education expenses.

When a parent or grandparent makes the contribution, the 529 plan is excluded from the donor's estate, thereby providing additional estate tax benefits. Furthermore, money in a 529 plan doesn't count against a student too much when applying for financial aid. Such plans are a great deal.

If you want to set aside money for your grandchildren that can be used for anything, you could set up a custodial account under an UTMA or UGMA. A portion of the interest generated each year will be tax-free, but you'll lose total control of the money.

Once the child reaches the age of majority, the money is the child's and can be spent however he or she chooses. Obviously, not all young adults make wise choices with their money.

One thing James might consider is setting up four or five accounts rather than seven. He must list just one beneficiary per account, but he can change the beneficiary. By reducing the number of accounts he establishes, he'll be reducing the odds of having to pull money out that is not used for college costs.

IRA Withdrawal Rules

Joan and Peter have $147,000 in IRAs and 401(k)s. They plan to continue contributing to the 401(k) at the maximum amount for the next 23 years until Peter retires at age 65. But they wonder if they will be tying up too much money in their retirement funds. They have two children, ages 6 and 3, and they wonder, if they come up short on their children's college money, whether they will be able pull money out of their retirement funds before they reach the age of 59½. The answer to Peter and Joan's question is yes. Until a few years ago, withdrawals from IRA plans prior to age 59½ were hit with early withdrawal penalties even if the funds were used for educational purposes. However, the tax code changed in the late 1990s. This created a provision that enables a family to withdraw monies from IRAs to pay for college costs without any tax penalties.

As long as the proceeds are used for the costs associated with higher education, the withdrawal will not be subject to the penalties, just ordinary income taxes. This exception only applies to IRAs, not 401(k)s or other pension plans. You could borrow the funds from your 401(k) if your plan allows, but the money must be repaid.

401(k) Homebuyer

Tony thought he might have been given the wrong advice when he was told he might not qualify for a penalty-free $10,000 withdrawal from his 401(k). Tony has done some research on the topic and recently had several discussions with a 401(k) plan trustee about it. He is employed with the company that sponsors his 401(k) and is in the process of purchasing his first home. In all of the discussions Tony had with the plan trustee, he was told that he could not roll over a portion of his 401(k) into an IRA so that he could withdraw from the IRA for the home purchase. Tony was told this was an IRS stipulation, and that he would have to no longer be employed with the company to roll over any of the 401(k) into an IRA.

Prior to 1992, a person could not roll money into an IRA unless that person had severed employment and had rolled over at least 50% of his or her employer's retirement balance. But those rules were liberalized over 10 years ago. They now allow people to transfer money from a 401(k) to an IRA in any denomination without terminating employment.

The Economic Growth and Tax Relief Reconciliation Act of 2001 made the rollover rules even more liberal. Essentially, a person can now transfer money among various types of retirement plans, regardless of whether the money comes from an IRA, 401(k), 403(b), and so forth.

There is no IRS stipulation stating that you cannot roll over a portion of your 401(k) while you are still employed by the company. These rollovers are called "in-service rollovers," and a number of people have done them.

There is a way Tony can accomplish his objective even if his employer doesn't allow for an IRA transfer. Request a $10,000 early withdrawal. The company will withhold 20% for federal taxes and Tony will receive a taxable check for $8,000.

Once Tony receives the check, he will have 60 days to deposit the check into an IRA to avoid any taxes. If Tony adds to his deposit an additional $2,000, he will have successfully completed a tax-free IRA rollover. The IRS will refund the $2,000, and he can now withdraw the $10,000 penalty-free from the IRA for the purchase of his first home.

Maxed Out at Work? Don't Stop

Some people make the maximum contributions to their 401(k) plans at work and then want to find other ways to save for retirement. Good for them for maxing out their 401(k) deposits. Most people end up at retirement age with far too little in their retirement accounts. Regardless of income, people tend to find other "needs" that require money before they ever max out their 401(k) contributions.

You can contribute to a Roth IRA as long as your income falls below $95,000 if you're single or $150,000 if you're married. The Roth won't help reduce your current income taxes, but the money will grow tax-deferred until retirement and come out tax-free as long as you wait until age 59½.

If you want to save more than the Roth IRA will allow, or if your income is such that you do not qualify, you'll have to save money outside of retirement accounts. In that case, make sure you invest tax-efficiently, owning investments that do not spin off much in the way of taxable dividends or capital gains.

And finally, thanks for not being part of an expanding majority of people in America who are taking the nation's savings rate down to horrific levels.

When you have it, don't take chances with it.

More 401(k) or More Capital Gains?

Two of the great advantages of 401(k) contributions are that they're made with pretax dollars (dollars that are taken off of your taxable income) and taxes on what you earned are deferred until you start taking distributions at age 59½.

However, what you earn outside of a 401(k) is taxed every year. These capital gains have, until recently, been taxed at a very high rate. Hence there is an advantage in putting as much money as possible into a 401(k) or some other retirement plan that qualifies for special tax treatment.

Recently the tax rate on dividends and capital gains was lowered to 15%. However, the 401(k) distribution will be still taxed as ordinary income.

Let's say someone's current marginal tax rate is 25%. If this person invests his or her money outside a retirement account instead of on a 401(k), any capital gain and dividend will be taxed at a lower rate now rather than at a higher rate as ordinary income when the person retired. Once again, a tax change has changed the strategies of the game of tax reduction—a game that must be played by every overtaxed American who wants to achieve financial independence.

Again, remember that one of the primary benefits of the 401(k) is the tax-deductibility of the deposits. Every dollar that is saved is a dollar that is reduced from your taxable income, thereby reducing your tax bill. Because of this tax savings, people are able to save more per paycheck than they could otherwise.

Consider the following example. Suppose someone was putting $1,000 per year into his or her 401(k). If that person chose to take that money and invest it somewhere else, the $1,000 would be taxed. It would be added to his or her W-2 at the end of the year. At a 25% marginal tax rate, that person would have to pay $250 in taxes and would be left with only $750 to save.

The 401(k) investor saving $1,000 a year would have an account balance of $14,486 after 10 years, assuming an 8% growth rate. The 401(k) account would be taxable, and after a 25% tax reduction, the after-tax balance would be $10,865.

The non-401(k) investor only has $750 per year to save, so after 10 years, that investor's account balance is $10,865—the exact amount the 401(k) investor has remaining. However, the non-401(k) investor still has capital gains and dividend taxes to worry about. Assuming a 15% tax on capital gains, the tax bill would be $505, leaving the investor with $10,360.

As you can see from the previous example, it's typically a good idea to use an employer's 401(k), regardless of whether or not there is a match. The one time it does not make sense is if an investor is in a lower tax bracket today but believes he or she will be in a higher tax bracket in the future.

More Roth Contributions?

Thomas is a 67-year-old retiree with sufficient retirement assets to support his lifestyle. He wants to add a Roth. His motivation is to make investments where income would be tax free, with no mandatory age-related withdrawal.

There is bad news for Thomas. To qualify for a Roth IRA contribution, Thomas or his spouse must have earned income. Required minimum distributions from retirement accounts are not considered earned income. Neither are pension income, dividend and interest income, rental income, and so forth.

Earned income is income derived from wages or self-employment income. If you are fully retired, you probably don't have any earned income. Thomas could come out of retirement, but the Roth IRA hardly sounds worth it.

No Money to Contribute to Retirement?
Keep Looking

So many young people make this mistake. They put off saving for retirement for years. They turn a small problem into a huge problem that—neglected long enough—cannot be solved. But the problem is not nearly as daunting as most young people think it is. That's provided they start as early as possible with small amounts.

Very few people say they can comfortably afford to save for retirement. The fact is that the immediate satisfaction we receive from a purchase can be much more stimulating than the delayed gratification of saving for the future. The key is saving even when you apparently cannot afford to do so.

The earlier a person starts saving for retirement, the better. Let's say one starts saving $100 per month in a deferred compensation plan at age 26. Most people can handle that amount.

If one starts early, he or she can accumulate $342,000 in a deferred compensation plan by age 60. But, if one delays just by 9 years, then he or she will accumulate only $132,000 (both calculations assume a 10% long-term growth rate). The trick of wealth creation is using the compounding effect—dividends throwing off dividends. The longer this magical process can take place, the richer a person can become.

That's why if a worker just starting out could save a little more—say $200 a month for 40 instead of 35 years—the net increase would be mind-boggling. Indeed, let's use that as an example. And let's say the person only got 9% return. Then, after 40 years, our person has $943,000! Is $200 a month into a deferred compensation really so much? For some people the answer is yes. But for many other young people, the answer is no.

Indeed, every young person should have a goal of saving 10% of his or her income. Not only is it a good habit to start early, but also it's much easier to save before there are house payments, child-care expenses, braces, college tuition, and so forth. If people can't save when they're young, odds are they will never be able to save.

And remember these examples are all good—whether we're talking about contributing to a 401(k) plan at work or an IRA that you set up for yourself. These plans are an excellent way to save for the future. And they will give you a tax break now in exchange for staying away from the funds until age 59½.

Transferring a 401(k) to an IRA

Transferring a 401(k) to an IRA after you quit a job makes a lot of sense. People change jobs frequently, and there is no reason to leave a 401(k) balance at each previous employer. An IRA is an account that you can control, and you can roll over funds from just about any type of retirement plan.

A recent study stated that a person entering the workplace will have 11 different employers by the time he or she retires. By rolling over 401(k) balances to an IRA after each job change, that person can enter retirement with just one IRA, rather than multiple 401(k) accounts to track.

Pension Decisions Depend on Individual Situation

There has been a lot of news recently on under-funded pension plans. Carl questions whether he should choose to take a pension amount versus rolling over a lump sum into an IRA.

Carl is married and will turn 70 years old this year. He and his wife live comfortably on their current income from investments and Social Security. They are very conservative investors and are not willing to take many risks.

They have a pension plan with Georgia Pacific and need to make a choice on whether to take $735 a month for life, $655 a month for life with refund, or a $92,900 lump sum rolled into an IRA. Carl and his wife are lucky in more ways than one. They do not need the income currently. They have plenty of other assets. And, unlike most of their fellow Americans, they have no debt.

There is no question that the majority of pension plans of established corporations are under-funded. However, because the pension plans are insured under the Pension Benefit Guarantee Corp. (PBGC), Carl and his wife shouldn't let this issue cloud a decision. Their pension would continue regardless of what happens to Georgia Pacific.

Their decision should be based on three factors: health, the internal rate of return on the lump sum, and income needs.

If Carl is in poor health and does not have a normal life expectancy, obviously the lump sum is a good deal. On the other hand, if Carl is in perfect health and plans to live to 103, the guaranteed monthly income looks more attractive.

Once Carl has examined the life expectancy issues, he needs to determine what rate of return is required on $92,900 to generate $735 per month. Based on a normal life expectancy of 17 years, the internal return is about 6.2%. If he has a normal life expectancy and can earn greater than 6.2%, the lump sum is attractive. On the other hand, if he cannot earn greater than 6.2%, the pension has more appeal.

Finally, Carl and his wife need to determine their income needs. If they have no need for the monthly income, the lump sum can be invested for compound growth.

As you can see, there is no clear-cut answer. Carl and his wife need to make the decision based on what works best for their situation.

Profits Versus Nonprofits

Patricia just joined a nonprofit organization after having always worked for a for-profit company and contributing to a 401(k) plan. Now she has access to a 403(b) plan. However, she isn't sure if she should take her 401(k) assets and roll them into her 403(b) plan.

This is an issue facing tens of millions of Americans, who typically will switch jobs far more times in their lifetimes than their fathers and mothers did.

401(k) plans and 403(b) plans are very similar. Both are retirement plans, and both are sponsored by the employer and provide tax benefits for retirement savings.

The main difference between a 401(k) and a 403(b) is who controls the account. With a 401(k), the employer contracts with a 401(k) provider, and the participant's investment choices are limited to the options provided by the employer.

With a 403(b), the employer merely acts as a conduit for a portion of an employee's salary that is directed to a retirement plan. The employee chooses the 403(b) provider in addition to choosing the investment options.

When you leave an employer with a 401(k), you can either leave your money with your previous employer or transfer it to another retirement plan. You cannot add any new deposits to the plan, nor can you borrow from the account. When you leave an employer with a 403(b), your 403(b) remains intact. You can continue depositing money into the plan as long as your new employer offers a 403(b). Furthermore, you can borrow from your account regardless of whether or not you are employed. It is an individual choice. If Patricia is pleased with her previous employer's 401(k), then there is no reason to transfer it to a 403(b) at this time. Unless Patricia is planning on taking a loan from the account, she will not benefit by rolling her money to a 403(b).

Close the Gap with Your Home

Reverse mortgages can be a good way to turn your home into retirement income!

If your savings aren't big enough to support the retirement lifestyle to which you aspire, you may be sitting on a valuable asset that can help you bridge the financial gap: your house.

With a 65% increase in home prices over the past 5 years, a growing number of retirees are tapping the home equity wealth they've accumulated by taking out reverse mortgages.

In 2004, there were more than 40,000 such borrowers, nearly five times the number there were in 1999, says Walter Updegrave, columnist for *Money* magazine.

Reverse mortgages are essentially mirror images of regular mortgages. You don't make payments to the lender; instead, the lender makes payments to you based on your home's value. You can take the cash as a lump sum, monthly installments, a line of credit, or some combination of these. The money you receive is tax-free and does not affect your Social Security payments. And you do not have to repay the loan as long as you live in your home; the loan is repaid using the proceeds from the sale of your house after you move or die. If its value at that time doesn't cover the balance, well, that's the lender's problem.

But reverse mortgages can be an expensive way to generate income, particularly compared with options like a home equity line of credit or trading down to a smaller home. And the complex features of reverse mortgages can make them tricky to evaluate. If you understand how reverse mortgages work, you can decide whether one is right for you.

Reverse mortgages generally make the most sense if you're looking for an ongoing source of income throughout retirement or you need a large lump sum. A reverse mortgage doesn't make sense if you might move in a few years or just need cash for some relatively small bill. That's because the stiff up-front expenses on these loans—origination fees, closing costs, and mortgage insurance— drive the effective short-term loan rate into the stratosphere.

The amount you receive through a reverse mortgage depends primarily on your age (you must be at least 62 years old to qualify), your home's market value, prevailing interest rates, and any other home loans you have. Generally, the older you are, the more your house is worth; and the lower interest rates are, the larger the loan you'll be able to get.

But the size of the loan will also depend on the specific reverse-mortgage program you select. Most homeowners qualify for the biggest cash advances under the Department of Housing and Urban Development's home-equity conversion mortgage (HECM) program. But if the market value of your home is well above the average house price in your area, you may get a larger loan from a private lender

Reverse Mortgages Have Benefits, Drawbacks

Reverse mortgages can ease retirement for some people who don't have much in financial assets. They can also guarantee that someone will live in a house for the rest of his or her days. However, there are also drawbacks to reverse mortgages.

Currently, only a small number of seniors are informed about reverse mortgages, but we'll likely see the use of these products explode as baby boomers enter retirement.

Unlike a traditional mortgage, a reverse mortgage requires no monthly payments. Equity in a home can be paid out as monthly income, taken as a lump sum, or withdrawn as needed. Interest is charged each month and deducted from the home equity balance.

The most common reverse mortgage is the federally insured Home Equity Conversion Mortgage. This mortgage guarantees a retiree can remain in his or her home until he or she passes away or moves out. Any remaining equity in the home belongs to the retiree's heirs. The lender gets nothing.

Reverse mortgages do have some drawbacks. First of all, they are not cheap. The interest charged is comparable to a traditional mortgage. But the start-up costs are steep. This is in part to insure the loan. In addition, all persons on the title must be at least age 62 or older.

To learn more, contact AARP at (800) 209-8085 and request the booklet "Home Made Money." You can also access information online at <u>www.aarp.org/money/revmort</u>.

Roth Puzzle

A Roth IRA can be a great bargain.

If you convert from a regular IRA, you have to pay the taxes. But once you want to start withdrawing from the account at age 59½, the savings can be considerable. However, there are limitless questions about how to withdraw from the account and how contributions can be made before age 59½.

To contribute to a Roth IRA, you must have wage or self-employment income of at least the amount you contribute to a Roth IRA. Self-employment income must be determined after all legitimate business expenses. If your business has expenses greater than its income, that business is operating at a loss, and you would not have any self-employment income.

Both spouses do not have to be working to contribute to two Roth IRAs. As long as one spouse's income is at least equal to or greater than the amount contributed, Roth contributions are allowable.

You have until April 15 of the next tax year to make an IRA contribution for the previous year. Contribution limits once were only $2,000 a year. But now they have been going up over the past few years. And there is a catch-up provision that allows people age 50 and over to contribute a bit more each year.

Don't Stop Saving for Tomorrow

Many older people are healthier today than ever before. They could spend more years in "retirement"—a word that many people could debate—than in the years of full-time work. In addition, some people begin taking Social Security payments at age 62.

Charlie, who starting taking Social Security at age 62, is in excellent health. He is worried that he and his wife might outlive his assets. His wife is still working and plans to for some time.

Charlie wants to contribute to his spousal IRA and receive a deduction for 2005. This is a good move. He can contribute to an IRA and receive a full tax deduction as long as his family income is below $150,000 per year. The only requirement is that Charlie's spouse has earned income equal to or greater than Charlie's IRA contribution.

If this situation applies to you, you should try to make the maximum contributions to qualified accounts because they will have tax-deferred treatment. That means they will grow faster than nonqualified accounts, which generally incur taxes that must be paid each year. That slows the account buildup. And you want all accounts to buildup as much as possible because retirement will not be cheap.

What Charlie and his wife are doing makes sense. They want to make their golden years the best years of their lives. They plan to travel and will be buying a second house. With some luck, they will be able to do almost all the things they want.

Short on College Savings? Consider Another Source

Kim has not saved enough for her daughter's coming college education, and now she is scrambling to find funding sources. Kim should consider her IRA. The rules governing this retirement allow for penalty-free withdrawals. That is if the money is used for educational purposes. It does not allow for tax-free withdrawals, merely penalty-free.

Kim has also built up a big stash in her 401(k) plan at work. But money distributed from a 401(k) does not qualify for penalty-free treatment. However, there may be a way to avoid the 401(k) plan penalty with some careful planning.

Because the law is favorable toward IRAs, Kim will need to shift some funds from her 401(k) to an IRA. This can be done by electing an "in-service distribution" of her 401(k) and having those dollars transferred directly to an IRA rollover account. Once the funds are in the IRA, she can then withdraw money for educational expenses penalty-free.

This transfer is permitted by law. Unfortunately, not all employers allow a plan participant to transfer money out of the 401(k) while someone is still with the company.

Social Security Woes

Let's assume you're reaching retirement age. You've paid into the Social Security system for 35, or maybe 45, years. Sometimes your Social Security payroll tax was higher than your income tax. Now it's time for the government to start paying you for all the years you were forced to "contribute" to this system. Guess what? Adding insult to injury, you're probably going to have to pay taxes on your Social Security payments.

It's time to get the most out of your Social Security. Many people just don't know if they should take early Social Security at age 62 or wait to a later age. Social Security ages are slowly being raised. Prospective retirees also worry that if they don't want to sit around doing nothing and decide to make a little money at a part-time job, this will reduce their payments.

Social Security benefits are not based on the previous 10 years of working, nor are they based on the past 1 or 5 years. They are based on the considerable taxes paid over one's entire working career.

The longer one works, whether full time or part time, the greater the benefits will be. Every year you wait to begin receiving your retirement benefits will result in a larger monthly check. Additional working can increase that benefit, but lack of work will not reduce it.

So turn off the reruns of Seinfeld. Go out and do a little work, if that is your pleasure. You have a lifetime of experience and knowledge. The world desperately needs people like you.

Stretch That IRA

Joyce and Fred, an elderly couple, have a plan to help avoid estate taxes. They have named their daughters, who are, respectively, 49 and 47 years of age, as their IRA beneficiaries. This is a very smart move. Listing an adult child as a beneficiary of an IRA can provide significant tax benefits to heirs.

If, God forbid, Joyce and Fred were to die today, their daughters could stretch their withdrawals over the next 35 to 40 years (their life expectancy).

The first year they would be required to withdraw at least 1/35.9 of the total; the second year, 1/34.9; and so on. They could withdraw more if need be. And taxes would be due only on the amount withdrawn.

This "stretch IRA" strategy can be one of the best ways to pass money down to children. They can receive a substantial tax-deferred account that can help them with their retirement.

The Social Security Enigma

Now or later? That's the conundrum some people face who are trying to figure out if they should take Social Security at age 62, or wait to a later age and receive a higher payout.

It's not an easy decision. Obviously, you should take your own projected life span into consideration. You should also think about how long your parents and grandparents lived. Also, another factor is how much you have in retirement savings such as your 401(k) account and how the investments in that account have grown. Should you use your money first or your Social Security payments? Again, you should talk it over with your financial advisor.

However, as a general principle, between the choice of spending one's own money and taking Social Security, Social Security is the better option. If you waited until a later date, you could receive a greater benefit, but what's the point of waiting if it means drawing on your 401(k)? Any money you pull from your 401(k) will be fully taxable, whereas only a maximum of 85% of your Social Security benefits will be taxable.

Statistically, you would need to live until your mid-80s before it would pay to defer benefits until your full retirement age. But there's no guarantee you will receive what you're entitled to down the road. Congress can always apply a "means" test and reduce your benefits.

Take the money today and hope the 401(k) grows.

Time for Retirement Account Drawback

Some retirees use a contrary strategy with their qualified accounts that adds tens of thousands of dollars to their assets. They take an extra decade or so before they start to pull money out of their qualified accounts, which can add greatly to the tax-deferred benefits.

In general, one has the right to start pulling money out of qualified retirement at age 59½ without any tax penalties. However, one is not required to do so. So some sage retirees, with multiple sources of incomes, will leave their qualified accounts alone and begin their retirement years by living on taxable accounts that are not qualified accounts. In some cases, they even put more in the qualified accounts, adding to the advantages of tax deferral. However, this tax break is not unlimited. The government does force the smart investor using this strategy to start taking money at some point.

Required minimum distributions must begin from IRAs, 401(k)s, 403(b)s, and so forth, no later than April 1 following the year in which you reach age 70½. And one must account for all of qualified retirement plans when determining your withdrawal, excluding one's Roth IRAs.

Unfortunately, money that is withdrawn from an IRA to satisfy the required distribution cannot be converted to a Roth IRA. One can, however, withdraw additional dollars to convert to a Roth IRA.

To Rent or to Own?

Cora and John recently sold a house for a decent profit. They want to use the money for a down payment on a house but have run into a dilemma.

They pay only $540 in rent, so buying a house for $200,000 would more than double what they pay for housing. Cora's father said that whenever annual rent payments are less than a year's worth of interest on a house, one is better off renting. So his advice is to invest the money and continue saving. Is this good advice?

Cora and John would like to reevaluate their position in 1 year. They used less than half of the money to pay off their car and credit cards, and they can easily save $1,000 per month. They are first-time investors and nervous about maintaining their principal.

It's anyone's guess how much homes will be selling for 1 year from today. If you asked 10 local economists what they thought, you would receive 10 different answers.

Obviously, home prices have skyrocketed over the past few years, with many homes doubling in value. But real estate prices tend to move in unpredictable cycles.

If Cora and John plan to buy a home and live in it for several years, it probably doesn't make much difference when they buy. But if they might need to sell in the next few years, then they should be a little more cautious about buying right now.

Money that Cora and John have saved for a home should not be invested in anything that fluctuates in value. They should stay away from the stock market and park the cash in a safe, boring account at the bank. That way Cora and John will know the money will be there in the future when it's time to buy a home.

To Roth or Not to Roth

Do you need a tax deduction this year, or would you prefer to receive big tax savings when you are retired? That's one of the issues before tens of millions who are trying to save for retirement.

The traditional IRA could provide some tax deductibility to millions of middle-class Americans each year, but you pay taxes on the account when you start pulling money out in retirement. The Roth IRA offers no immediate deductibility. But, once you are in retirement, you pull money out of it tax-free.

So how do you decide? You look at your individual circumstance and you discuss it with your tax or financial advisor. If you can afford to put the maximum into a Roth IRA, the Roth would be better. However, if you are looking at your tax bill coming due in April, you'll see that you'll owe more if you contribute to a Roth IRA instead of to a traditional IRA.

If you're in a situation where you could afford to put $3,000 into a traditional IRA, but could not put that much into a Roth due to the increased tax bite, it doesn't matter which IRA you choose.

For example, if you were in the 25% tax bracket, your tax bill would increase $750 if you did not contribute to a traditional IRA. That increase in taxes would leave you with only $2,250 to put in a Roth. The traditional IRA would have a greater account balance at retirement, but after paying taxes at 25%, it would be worth the same as the Roth.

On the other hand, if you have a set amount of money that you are planning to put into an IRA, use the Roth. You'll end up paying more taxes next April, but you won't have to worry about those taxing authorities during retirement.

Uncle Whiskers Is Famished; Beware of Tax Hit on Large 401(k) Withdrawals

It will take the average investor 30 or 35 years to accumulate the large amounts in his or her qualified retirement plans. It takes the government a very short time to eat up a large part of it.

Remember to be very careful as you pull money out of these accounts. The taxman is waiting for you to make just one mistake. That one mistake could be very costly.

John and Susan, who are both about to turn 62 years of age, are eyeing their qualified retirement money and thinking this would be a great time to use 401(k) money to pay off the mortgage. John and Susan must be careful, very careful.

Having a home paid off for retirement should be a top goal for everyone. When there's no mortgage payment due each month, it's much easier to get by on a fixed income.

If John and Susan had a large stash of cash that was not tied up in a retirement account, they should pay off the home as quickly as possible. But, having money in a 401(k) is not the same as having a chunk of cash. The reason? You have a silent partner in your 401(k)—Uncle Whiskers.

The taxman has an interesting set of rules resulting in the fact that the more money you make in any one year, the larger the percentage of your 401(k) your ravenous uncle wants.

Federal income tax rates range from 10% to 35%. That means a withdrawal could be taxed as little as 10% or could be taxed as high as 35%.

Depending on John and Susan's income and the size of their mortgage balance, it may be best for them to pay their home off over the next few years.

Let's say they take a large withdrawal from their 401(k) in 1 year. They may be paying 10% or more in unnecessary taxes. Before making a decision, they can run some tax projections to see how a 401(k) withdrawal will impact their taxes. They can purchase an inexpensive software program to run the calculations. They could also have a session with a good tax planner.

Once they can determine the tax hit, they can then make a wise decision as to the timing of their home payoff.

You'll Be on Easy Street

You're close to retirement. You are 64 years old, but believe you have many good years ahead. You can see financial independence just ahead. You're around the corner from Easy Street. You're about to pay off a 30-year mortgage. You're a very happy person.

Then your advisor tells you not to pay off the house. No, he says, borrow against the house and put $100,000 of your hard-earned money into a real estate investment that will easily earn you 10% to 15% a year and you won't have to take any risks.

Really?

If there were guaranteed investments that paid 10% to 15%, everybody should borrow as much money as possible and buy those investments. But the fact is that there is nothing in the marketplace that guarantees anything close to 10%.

When things are heading in a certain direction, people have a tendency to believe they will continue that way. Five years ago, when the stock market was booming, people were borrowing like crazy to invest in stocks. After all, it seemed so easy to make 10% to 15% while everything was heading higher.

Now that the real estate market has been skyrocketing, there are those who are advocating borrowing like crazy to invest in real estate. Although there may or may not be a major decline in the real estate market, there's no reason to believe it will continue at the pace it has been going.

What happens if you take out a mortgage and your investment doesn't pan out? What if you don't receive enough return to pay the mortgage payment? What if the property remains vacant for several months while you repair the damages made by the previous tenant? What if ... ?

On the other hand, if you can eliminate your mortgage and still purchase another real estate investment, it would certainly make it easier to retire. You would have the assurance of knowing that whatever happened in the world, you would have a place to lay your head at night.

If you have the cash to purchase investments, fine. Just don't go into debt to invest in something that may or may not work out, particularly at a stage in life when you should not have to worry about money. You worked many years to reach this point. Don't blow it.

And one more thing: Get another advisor.

Chapter 5
Make Your Money Outlast You

The key is not to spend your principal. Most of us would love to die broke—maybe have our last check bounce. But the reality is we don't know the day we're going to die. Every year you live you've got to figure you're going to keep on living. If you're 70 years old, you've got to figure you might be around to 95 or 100 of age. Who knows? You hate to plan on living to age 85, survive that long and be out of money. You need to plan for a long life expectancy; otherwise, you're going to run out of money. If you have a balanced portfolio, you might have some years your portfolio is up and some years it's down. But then you need to take a withdrawal that's based on some realistic projections.

The Savings/Investment Dilemma

Ken, a popular professional artist who makes good money, is 45 years old. Recently, he made a painful disclosure: "I have nothing saved and almost nothing invested. How the hell am I going to retire when I turn 65?"

Ken says he could write a book on all the money he's blown on ridiculous things. If only a fraction of that "mad money" (Ken's phrase) had gone into savings and investments, Ken would now be living on Easy Street. However, the issue is what can Ken do now?

Ken's plight is not an unusual one. There are millions of Americans with good jobs and comfortable lifestyles, who have little or nothing in financial assets.

Most financial planners say you should count on Social Security for no more than 10% of your retirement income. Some skeptical advisors don't even include projected Social Security payments in their retirement planning.

It's not too late for Ken. If he starts to impose a bit of spending and saving discipline on himself, and if he commits to a 20-year plan, than he will be in good (not great) financial shape by age 65.

Commit to Automatic Saving

Your employer has a 401(k) plan and you're not part of it? You're probably making a big mistake. The idea is money gets taken out of your pay before you see it so you can't spend it. It is put aside for your future and, in the meantime, the deduction reduces your taxable liability.

What if you don't have a 401(k) at work? In that case, you can set up your own automatic savings or investment plan. Most mutual funds will let you set up an account with a small initial amount if you commit to putting at least $100 a month in a fund. Most people can do that. In fact, most people can do much more than that.

A Company Man?

You've come this far, so you probably agree that thrift is not an obscure branch of voodoo. Most likely, you now believe that saving and investing are critical to achieving financial independence in the near future or 20 years from now.

So, what should you do with the money you're putting aside? If you work for a company that offers stock, take advantage of the plan, but do not put the bulk of your retirement savings in company stock. This can be dangerous.

An employee stock ownership plan (ESOP) is a special type of retirement plan whereby a corporation transfers a portion of its ownership to the employees. Each employee has an account that holds stock in the corporation. For tax purposes, the ESOP is treated similarly to a 401(k) or 403(b).

If you are in this situation, move some of your ESOP money to other investments rather than count too much on the company from which you earn a living. As a rule, never put the bulk of your money in any one place. Remember, many people were Enron millionaires on paper.

The most important thing you can do to protect your retirement savings is to diversify your money.

Transferring the funds into an IRA may be your best alternative, as you will avoid current income taxes while having the ability to invest in a multitude of investments. You can allocate your funds so that you have diversification while still having a chance for growth of your investments.

Getting the Most Out of a Roth

Jim's wife, Toni, worked until the birth of their daughter. Toni made approximately $500 before leaving her job. Both Toni and Jim want to make the maximum contributions to their IRAs, which has been $4,000 for each person, or $8,000 for a couple (these amounts will increase in the next few years).

Here is a case in which the earnings of one person can make up for those of the other.

Both Toni and Jim can contribute the maximum $4,000 to either a traditional IRA or a Roth IRA, regardless of Toni's income. That's provided they have collectively earned income in excess of their total IRA contributions ($8,000), as Jim did.

Their joint adjusted gross income can be as much as $150,000 before they lose the ability to contribute to a Roth IRA. The $100,000 limit is for Roth conversions, not for Roth contributions. By the way, these numbers often change, so check with your tax advisor before contributing to your IRA.

How Should You Invest? Think About the Long Term

Henry wants to retire in 5 years. He is 54 years old. And now—like many investors—he is concerned about the stock market and worried that it is about to tank. He has a little over 50% of his 401(k) in stocks, but is thinking of switching all his stock money into stable, or money market, accounts.

The uncertainty of the stock market today (or tomorrow or the day after) can lead even veteran investors to become panicky at times. However, the long-term investor shouldn't pay too much attention to market dips and corrections. After all, the United States has ridden out many financial crises over its history, and the odds are a few years from now we'll all wonder what the panic was about.

Henry will be only 59 years old when he retires, and odds are that he'll live another 20 plus years. Therefore, he should invest his 401(k) not only for when he is 59 years of age but also for when he is 69, 79, and 89 years of age.

As long as you have a long-term time horizon, are working and contributing to your 401(k), and are well diversified, having 50% por so of your portfolio in stocks is not too high. In fact, you should welcome market corrections as opportunities to buy more stocks at lower prices.

Henry should reconsider putting everything in money markets.

How to Make a Million—To Thine Own Self Be True

The advice of Polonius in the Bard's great play *Hamlet* still rings true 5 centuries later. If you want to succeed, if you want to make money and obtain success—do what you do best.

Kitty is well on her way to financial independence. That's because she invests in plain vanilla domestic equity stock funds and has been doing so for about 15 years. Why is she doing well? For the same reason that Warren Buffett is a fabulous investor. He puts money only in vehicles he understands. Kitty and Warren Buffett share this characteristic.

In the late 1990s, when investors were going gaga for tech companies (that never showed any profits and proclaimed that the business cycle didn't apply anymore), neither Buffett nor Kitty was investing in tech.

Kitty said she didn't understand tech stocks. She understood average run-of-the-mill companies that showed consistent growth. She put her money in funds that invested in meat-and-potato companies that showed consistent profits. Result? Kitty never experienced the huge losses of others in the bear market of 2000 to 2002. Kitty lost some money during that period, but it was a relatively inconsequential amount compared to those who had flipped over tech even though they had little idea how that style of investing worked.

Some investors were so discouraged by the bear market of 2000 to 2002 that they have stopped investing. They are confused about how to go about achieving financial independence.

Know thyself.

Moving? Read This First

For many Americans, their home is their prime asset. This is partly deliberate and partly inadvertent. Due to zooming real estate prices over the last few years combined with sluggish stock prices, suddenly many people have more money in the family house than they could have imagined.

Many of these people, closing in on retirement, are planning on selling the home for a big profit and taking the proceeds to a less costly place, where the money will go a long way.

But what about capital gains? Fortunately, in these circumstances capital gains are not a factor. As long as you have lived in your home 2 or more of the prior 5 years, you won't pay any capital gains taxes on the sale of your home. It doesn't matter how much you spend on a new home in another, less taxing, state.

The tax law lets a couple exclude up to $500,000 worth of gain from the sale of their primary residence no matter what they do with the money. The exclusion amount is $250,000 for a single person.

Let's say that you use this tax reduction strategy and the sale of the old homestead leaves you with a $100,000 profit, no part of which Uncle Whiskers can eat up. Then regardless of what you pay for a new home, you can apply the full $100,000 as your down payment and take the money you will save on your reduced mortgage payments and put it into a combination of Roth IRAs and 401(k)s to help you prepare for retirement.

Overemphasizing Tax Breaks

Rarely, if ever, should one buy something solely for a tax deduction. Barry purchased a home 9 months ago and took out a $100,000 mortgage just for that purpose, based on advice from his tax preparer (who, by the way, is not a certified public accountant).

Barry is paying 7% interest on the house, but he also has about $70,000 in bonds that are earning about 5%. His tax preparer stressed to Barry that the tax deduction for the mortgage was the best thing for him.

The truth is that paying out $1 in interest to save 35 cents in taxes is never a good deal. You're still out 65 cents. That is essentially the extent of the "tax savings" Barry is receiving by having such a large mortgage. The "tax savings" may be even less if you are in a lower tax bracket.

Because of Barry's age and the fact that he has such a large bond balance, he should probably apply the bulk of the bond portfolio against his mortgage balance. He is currently earning less money on his bonds than he is paying in interest charges. He would be further ahead if he owed less money on his home.

The problem is simple: The tax preparer was looking at the small picture. He was neither equipped nor inclined to consider Barry's total financial picture before he offered his advice. If he had looked at his entire financial picture, not just the tax return, the tax preparer would have seen the fallacy of taking out a large mortgage when Barry had cash in the bank.

Many financial professionals are trained in only a few areas. If they give advice outside of their area of expertise, disaster may follow.

Roth Conversions

Sara is a smart young woman who became interested in investing as a teenager. She made nondeductible IRA contributions in 2001 and 2002 while she was employed. But she became a full-time student in January 2003 and has no earnings for 2003 and 2004. Now she is thinking of converting her traditional IRA to a Roth IRA.

Sara's course is clear. If anyone should convert money to a Roth IRA, it's Sara! If she converts this year, she will probably avoid all taxes because she has no earnings. And by the time Sara retires, the Roth IRA should be tax-free. However, if she does nothing, the majority of her IRA will be taxable.

Sara's situation raises an issue that comes up often. Roth IRAs are an excellent deal for most people. This is due to the changes in the Roth that Congress approved in 1997. But many clients who want to convert their traditional IRAs to Roths ask the same question: What happens if Congress changes its mind on the Roth? Will Congress tax me on my money in the future?

The Roth IRA that became available to us back in the late 1990s promises tax-deferred growth of investments and tax-free withdrawals upon retirement. Still, no one knows what tax law will look like several years from now.

It is wise to diversify tax strategies as well as investment strategies. Don't invest all of your money in the Roth IRA, 401(k), or any other vehicle. Spread your investments among tax-deductible, tax-deferred, tax-free, and taxable accounts.

That way, if Congress changes the tax laws, your life savings won't be hung out to dry.

Starting Over at Midlife

It's likely happened to someone you know. Or it will likely happen to someone you know. Or, God forbid, it could even happen to you.

You could be one of the millions of Americans who get divorced each year. Divorce is usually a financial disaster as well as an emotional disaster. The woman, who usually has a smaller income, can be especially vulnerable.

No matter one's state, here are some commonsense steps you should take to try to minimize the trauma as you start over again financially.

1. Try to get over your emotional baggage. Yes, it's easier said than done. But unless you can dispassionately review your financial situation, there is a danger of financial disaster. You may need to get psychological/financial counseling. Don't resist it. Everyone needs help from time to time.

2. Face financial facts. Many people don't want to know their financial circumstances. But how can you ever hope to get control of your life if you don't know your situation in detail? A person who is deep in debt and doesn't want to discuss it is usually someone who will never get out of it. So draw up a statement of your bills and your income. Start to figure out where you money is going, now that you are in charge and no longer sharing your finances with a spouse.

3. Search for ways to cut expenses. It's up to you to find creative ways to make your budget work. You can do it. There are many possibilities to save money for a creative, imaginative person like you.

4. Look for work. Don't depend on a divorce settlement to take care of you for the rest of your life. It probably won't. Extra income will help you solve or ease some of your problems. Also, having a job will keep you busy and probably lead to a new group of friends. These are things that may help you overcome this period of emotional and psychological stress.

Take Stock in America?

Sandra and her husband have been buying savings bonds since they were first married. Indeed, Sandra's mother still sends them $50 bonds for birthdays. Many have matured; some have not. They don't know what to do with them.

U.S. savings bonds were originally introduced to help finance our wars. In fact, the North would not have been able to win the Civil War without the selling efforts of financier Jay Cooke. Some even believe that the South lost the war because the North had better financing schemes.

Traditionally, purchasing a savings bond was considered one's civic duty. Certainly, that was true in World War II when FDR pushed the sale of government bonds. However, savings bonds were marketed not as great investments, but as a patriotic duty.

Today, there is very little reason to purchase a savings bond as an investment, but it may be worthwhile to hold on to any that you have. Savings bonds do not pay interest; instead, they are issued at 50% of the maturity value. For example, a $50 savings bond costs $25. The gain on the bonds over the years is tax-deferred and becomes taxable when the bonds are sold. Once a bond has matured, you can continue to hold the bond, and the bond will continue increasing tax-deferred until 30 years after the purchase date. After 30 years, they no longer appreciate in value.

Some of the older bonds pay competitive rates and may be worth holding. If Sandra and her husband cash them in today, they'll have to realize taxable income on their income tax return.

The Automatic Pilot that Could Be a Shipwreck

It took years and years, but Walter made it to financial independence. He got there because he maximized his contributions to various tax-advantaged retirement vehicles, which can probably take care of Walter and his family for the rest of their lives.

Now what? Walter would like to leave assets in his 401(k)s, annuities and other tax-advantaged plans, draw the money down from there, and forget about any further investment planning.

Walter, that's not going to work! The financial world is becoming a more complex place every day. It would be fantastic if financial planning and investment planning were as simple as setting up a program and forgetting about it. But the fact of the matter is that the world of finances is ever changing.

What may have been a great investment in the past may be a lousy investment today. It wasn't very long ago that fixed-income investments were paying near 20% and real estate partnerships were the hot investments.

Obviously, things are quite different today. Any prudent investor should constantly evaluate his or her investment program and make adjustments according to market conditions and changing tax laws.

Ignoring his investment program may be the easiest thing for Walter to do. But it certainly won't be the most profitable. Indeed, it may be dangerous to his financial health.

You Can't Eat Cheesecake Every Night and Be Slim

Life is not "a cabaret, old chum." Instead, life is a series of hard choices.

Economists call this an opportunity cost. One selects one thing over another. You can't spend the same money on more than one thing.

Take Tom. He is 72 years old, retired, and looking for ways to increase his income. Tom currently owns several stocks and two bonds. He was considering purchasing preferred stocks because of the high yields they provide. However, Tom faced the either/or choice that we all face in various forms. He would have to sell one investment to buy a preferred stock.

Preferred stocks are investments that have characteristics of both stocks and bonds. Like a bond, they provide a consistent stream of income. Like a stock, they provide ownership in a company. Preferred stocks typically pay higher yields than bonds do but also carry additional risk.

The dividends of preferred stocks are not a liability of a company and are paid only if the company earns a profit. The dividend is paid before any dividends are paid to common-stock shareholders, but in return for that "preferred status," preferred stocks carry no voting rights and shareholders have little claim in the event that a company folds.

A major downside of preferred stocks is interest rate risk. If interest rates rise, the value of the preferred stock could fall. And because preferred stocks have no maturity date, the value could fall dramatically. Preferred stocks could be a great complement to a portfolio, but they certainly shouldn't make up the lion's share. As with any portfolio, diversification among different types of investments is key.

A good financial planner can only explain these choices, and then leave it to intelligent clients like Tom to make the decision.

If You're into Bonds, Watch This Index

Like many retired families, John's family has a large portion of investment assets in bond funds, ranging from short-term to long-term bond funds. But John understands that if the insider investment community becomes convinced that interest rates are about to increase, his family will almost certainly begin to see a decline in the net asset value of the longer term bond funds.

John's strategy is to observe what the insiders are doing. He is being very prudent in trying to assess the risk he may have in the bonds and bond funds. Bonds—like stocks—also carry plenty of risk. For example, a few years ago bond prices were at 45-year highs, and many investors are still being lured into them because of the high return bonds realized during those few years. Although there's no question that bonds can play an important role in one's portfolio, understanding their limitations is important.

The horrendous stock market of 2000 to 2002 caused many investors to look for safe havens. A great deal of money moved out of stocks and into bonds. As the demand for bonds became greater, the prices of bonds increased (supply vs. demand).

Investors became willing to accept lower and lower returns. Bonds that had commanded double-digit returns several years ago were paying in the 4% to 5% range, as the bear market was about to end.

The benchmark rate that institutions and traders pay attention to is the 10-year U.S. Treasury Bond. Other high-grade bonds move in step with this benchmark. As this rate falls, the value of bonds rises. Inversely, as this rate rises, the value of bonds declines. The longer the maturity of the bonds, the greater the price fluctuation.

Obviously, it is impossible to predict where rates are headed. Rates will rise if investors (1) move money out of bonds and into stocks, (2) believe inflation is heating up, or (3) simply demand a higher return on their money.

If John believes rates have a greater chance of heading higher than they do of falling, he should keep bond maturities toward the short-term range. Any additional yield John will receive from the long-term bonds could easily by wiped away in price declines.

To see what can happen to bond prices, review what occurred in 1994 and 1999. Both were awful years for bonds. No investing or asset class is 100% safe.

Chapter 6
Build Real Estate Wealth

If you own your home, your goal should be pay it off. For those who are still working, the goal should be to pay off the mortgage by retirement. In the meantime, how much free cash flow do you have in the house? Can you afford to go out to dinner? Can you afford some trips? Or are you going to be stuck at home watching TV and eating frozen dinners or take-out pizza? Or are you going to have to sell your house?

Once you retire, it might not be your goal to pay off the house because now your goal is cash flow. Maybe the goal at retirement is to take whatever mortgage you have and stretch it out for the next 30 years. Or maybe even use a reverse mortgage. Then you don't have to make any more payments, or maybe even get some cash flow out of the house because it's now an asset for you. These are different strategies. After you're retired, let's make sure that house is going to cost as little as possible. I've seen people who are 65 years of age, working like dogs to have their house paid off by the time they're 75 years old, only to die at the age of 76. I guess the kids like it. They inherit a little more.

Adjustable Rate Mortgages Are for the Birds!

And they're too dangerous for most people. Suppose you wanted to lease a car today and the dealer said, "Well, this month your car payment is $500 and we guarantee it will be $500 for the next 6 months, but after that it becomes adjustable based on the market. Six months from now the payment might be $450 or it might be $600. We don't know. But the maximum it could ever be is $900 a month." Who would buy a car? That's exactly what homebuyers are doing by taking adjustable rate mortgages. With a fixed-rate mortgage your interest rate might be slightly higher than the market in some periods. You can look at that as simply insurance. You can live in your house forever.

An Advantage of a Community Property State

Jill, a widow, owns a vacation rental, which she acquired 28 years ago as a 1031 exchange. She is fed up with being a landlord. She wants to sell the property, which is now worth about four times what she and her husband originally paid for it.

Jill feared a huge capital gains bill because the property would suddenly be valued at its current worth. But the good news was that because Jill lives in a community property state, the cost basis on the rental is now equal to its current market value. Jill no longer has any embedded gains.

Tax law is such that when you receive an asset through an inheritance, you receive that asset with a cost basis "stepped-up" to the fair market value, basically eliminating any capital gains. Although Jill owned the home with her husband, the community property rules treat it as though she received the entire property through an inheritance.

To determine its new cost basis, Jill must get an appraisal for the value on the date that her husband passed away. The only gain (or loss) Jill might have to report is the difference between the appraised value and what she receives for the home.

A Cognitive Bias and Investing

Jim, a quasi-retired real estate agent, and his wife decided to move to Florida to buy property because the market was so hot. Prices had gone up so much they planned to buy a property, stay in it for 2 years to avoid paying capital gains, and then sell it. When asked why he expected the property to appreciate, Jim responded, "The market in Florida is just going crazy. Besides, real estate always goes up. The thing we don't want is any more stocks. We're done with the stock market."

In 1999, Jim and his wife had sold all their real estate and put their money into stocks. And, of course, the market crashed right after that.

But wait a minute. When no one wanted real estate and everyone wanted stocks because the stock market was on fire, that's when Jim thought it was a good time to sell his real estate holdings and buy stocks. Where are we currently? No one wants stocks and everyone wants real estate. Aren't they doing the same thing they did 6 years ago? They don't want to hear that.

A cognitive bias is a process of thinking that causes us to leap to the wrong conclusion. Hindsight is a cognitive bias in that it is a process where you look at the past, and because you know the past, you think that nothing could have happened other than what actually happened, which leads you to believe that the future is as predictable as the past. This method of thinking is common, normal, and nevertheless wrong. Investing based on past performance is like trying to drive somewhere by looking through the rear-view mirror to see where you're going. You do get somewhere, just not where you want to go.

A House Gift

Many Americans will be inheriting a house from a relative. And this can trigger all sorts of difficult tax issues that stem from the value of the house skyrocketing in value because of improvements or simply because inflation has driven house values sky high in some choice urban areas. The homeowner may want to sell the house but worries about a potentially huge capital gains bill.

Here are some general principles to remember if you inherit a house. Property and other assets that you receive from an inheritance are typically passed with a cost basis "stepped-up" to the current fair market value. The cost basis is determined by the fair market value of the property on either the date of death or an alternative date 9 months from time of death.

Your capital gain in the property is determined by taking your net sales price (after commissions and other selling costs) and subtracting your cost basis. Any capital improvements you put into the property would increase your cost basis, whereas commissions and other selling costs would reduce your net sales price.

Also, remember, there is an excellent way to get around most capital gains on the sale of a house. Make it your primary residence for 2 years or more and you can avoid up to $500,000 in capital gains if you are married. That break is $250,000 for a single person.

An Apartment Is Not a Home

When Sam was growing up, his family lived in various apartments, some of which had expensive rents. Sam's parents, who always wanted to buy a house in the suburbs, could afford high rents. But they could never afford a house, which was their dream. They never got a home in the city because the apartments they rented had no permanence. Once a lease expired, they could be told to move, or possibly see their rent skyrocket.

They, like millions of Americans before them and millions of Americans today, could never afford the down payment on a house. They could never reach their dream home. Currently, there is an additional resource for many Americans who want their first home. It is in your qualified retirement savings.

You can withdraw up to $10,000 from either a traditional IRA or a Roth IRA and avoid early withdrawal penalties as long as the funds are used toward the purchase of your first home. Money withdrawn from a traditional IRA will be subject to ordinary income taxes, but money withdrawn from a Roth IRA will be tax-free.

As strange as it may be, the IRS considers anyone who hasn't owned a home for the past 2 years to be a first-time homebuyer. This doesn't have to be your first home to qualify for the exemption. As long as you haven't owned a home in 2 years, you qualify as a first-time homebuyer (according to the IRS).

Once you've withdrawn the funds from your IRA, you have up to 120 days to complete a home purchase. Anything can happen when a home is in escrow, so it's a good idea to wait until you've identified a house and are well into escrow before you withdraw money from your IRA.

Buying a Home in Another State

Here's a portrait of a typical restless American. He sells his home and makes a big profit. Then he takes the money and moves to another less costly state. He buys another home there.

A business associate, Larry, recently did this. He netted $150,000 on the sale of his old home. Now he's headed for another state and wondering what his tax bill will be for the gains from the old house.

Larry's tax bill will not be dependent on how much he spends on his next home. We are no longer required to purchase another home to avoid paying capital gains taxes. In fact, whether one buys a residence will have no bearing on determining how much tax one owes.

The current tax rule lets people like Larry exclude from gain up to $250,000 if single or $500,000 if married. To qualify for the exclusion, you must have owned and lived in your residence for at least 2 of the last 5 years. Any gain that exceeds the exclusion amount will be taxed as capital gain.

Larry, by the way, is moving from California to Texas. He is joining the mass migration of retirees leaving California. With home prices as high as they are, thousands of retirees are selling the old homestead and moving to states where they can cut their housing costs by 50% or more.

Gains Good, Losses Bad

It's almost never wrong to take profits, even if it can sometimes result in a capital gains bill. Indeed, some people—for unexpected reasons—must sell a primary residence even though it will result in a big tax bill.

A primary residence sold less than 2 years after owning and occupying it will result in capital gains taxes. The only time a portion of the taxes can be avoided is if the homeowner was forced to move due to health reasons or a change of employment.

Short-term capital gains taxes, for homes sold within 1 year, are taxed at the same rate as ordinary income tax, which ranges from 10% to 35%. Long-term capital gains, for homes held longer than 1 year, are taxed from 5% to 15%.

You may feel bad having to give still more money to Uncle Whiskers. On the other hand, you may have a sound reason for selling in less than 2 years and not obtaining the tax break.

Keep in mind that a capital gain is always better than a capital loss. It is rare to be able to sell a home after owning it for only 1 year and make a profit. The past few years in the residential real estate market have been nothing short of phenomenal. There's nothing wrong with selling in this market and pocketing a nice gain. And also remember that real estate—like the price of stocks or commodities—never goes up—or down—forever.

Helping an Adult Son

Many young adults just starting out in their first full-time jobs are having problems making a decent living.

Ron and Jane have a 22-year-old son who was out of work for 6 months. He recently returned to work. Their son and his wife and 2-year-old daughter live in a cramped one-bedroom apartment.

Ron and Jane have a family trust and would like to buy a home for their son and his family with the trust money. But they are considering various options: buying a home in the trust name and rent it to him, giving him money for a down payment on the house to let him buy his own, or jointly buying a home with him and the trust.

With home prices skyrocketing in many parts of the country, they are not alone in feeling a need to help a child purchase a home. Many incomes will simply not support the house payments required on the typical home. The avenue they should take with their son depends on what they are trying to accomplish. Obviously, they'd like to see their son, daughter-in-law, and granddaughter living in a larger place than a one-bedroom apartment. But are there other things they should want to encourage by this transaction, such as a change in career or better financial management. Assuming the son is a healthy, competent man, they should structure the deal so that he has some responsibility.

If Ron and Jane simply buy a home for him and rent it to him, this could create a wedge between the two if he has trouble paying the rent. If they jointly purchase a home together, and Ron has trouble making the mort-gage payments, this could create a bigger headache.

It might be best just to give him money for a down payment. Then let him be responsible for the house payments. Any money they give their son in excess of $11,000 annually will be considered a taxable gift; they won't have to pay a gift tax until their total gifts exceed $1 million.

Helping the Neighbor Kid While Turning Down Your Own

Our tax code is sometimes meshuginah. It's full of contradiction, chaos, and craziness. Just ask a CPA about the Alternative Minimum Tax (AMT), which is soon coming to a middle-class household near you. Here's another bit of tax code loony tunes.

The bulk of wealth and financial assets in this country are held by those age 50 or over. Much of the money of these over 50 folks, most of whom own their homes, is tied up in qualified accounts. These are IRAs, 401(k)s, and other retirement accounts that "qualify" for special treatment.

By contrast, many young people have little or no financial assets. They often are hard-pressed to find the money for their credit card payments, no less a down payment on a first house. Just starting in their careers, young people frequently have small incomes and must rent, which (under our tax code) is usually a bad deal. (Owners who tend to be wealthier than renters are, in effect, subsidized by renters.) Homeowners can usually deduct property taxes and any mortgage interest. Renters can't deduct anything under the tax code.

So, given these inequities, it should be simple, right? Older folks help their children get started in their first house. Well, not exactly.

Many parents—with brimming 401(k) accounts and fat IRAs—want to buy houses within their self-directed IRAs as an investment. That's fine according to the taxing authorities, provided one's sons, daughters, or immediate family does not use the house for personal benefit. In other words, you can help your neighbor's kid buy a house, but you can't help your own flesh and blood. Go figure!

Home Sale Woes

Todd recently moved out of his home and is having trouble selling it. He's considering renting it out for a year or two but he wants to make sure it sells in order to avoid capital gains tax.

Todd is risking a big capital gains tax bill. Tax law dictates that one must live in a primary residence 2 out of the last 5 years in order to qualify for the $250,000 exemption. Therefore, assuming Todd has lived in his home for two years, he has 3 years from that date he moved to sell his house.

Let the Bank Pay You

Many people are heading for retirement with little in financial assets or savings. Are they heading for disaster? Maybe. But there is a possible life-saver—their home.

Many of the people who have avoided stocks and bonds have put much of their money into their homes. The result is they have paid off homes. So, if their retirement savings and Social Security aren't enough (and don't expect very much from Social Security) their homes might be the answer to inadequate retirement planning. Let the bank pay you. It's called a reverse mortgage.

I think reverse mortgages can be a lifesaver for those who need the money. A reverse mortgage enables a retiree with equity in a home to use that equity to provide a lump sum of cash, a monthly income, or both.

Depending on the value of your home, you may be able to use a reverse mortgage to pay off your existing mortgage and still provide you with some additional cash. Unlike a traditional mortgage, a reverse mortgage requires no monthly payments.

The interest that is charged is added to the balance each month, so that the loan balance grows with time. As long as the interest rate is less than the appreciation on your home, your equity will continue to grow. In the event it doesn't, you're guaranteed to remain in the home until the day you die.

Keep in mind that the value of what you will leave to your heirs will be less if you use a reverse mortgage. Your heirs will inherit a home that has a mortgage balance that will need to be paid before they can receive the equity in the home.

In addition, the startup fees on reverse mortgages are much more expensive than those on traditional mortgages (although the interest rates are typically lower).

Living Trust or Community Property? You Decide

The title on Vanessa and Bob's house was originally held as community property. But when it was conveyed to a revocable living trust, it did not include the words "as community property" on the new deed.

Vanessa and Bob assumed that it was not necessary to include the words "as community property" on the new deed because they live in California, which is a community property state.

Without the words "as community property" on the new deed, they are worried that they are going to cause themselves problems. If either the husband or wife dies, they are fearful that both "halves" of their property/house will not receive a stepped-up basis and be treated as community property.

Vanessa and Bob cannot title their house in both a living trust and a community property. To ensure a full step-up in basis on the first death, they should be sure their trust declares their property to be community property. As long as that declaration is in there, both "halves" will receive a full stepped-up cost basis on the death of the first spouse.

Adjustable Rate Mortgages

The so-called "option adjustable-rate mortgages" carry an initial rate as low as 1%. One key and unusual feature is that borrowers get up to four payment choices each month—a minimum payment, which is set at the start of each year; an interest-only payment; or the standard payment on a 15- or 30-year mortgage. Rates typically adjust monthly after the teaser period ends.

But the risks can be considerable and aren't always well understood. For one thing, the low introductory rate can last for as little as 1 to 3 months, after which the rate typically jumps above 4% or more. Plus, rates on these loans adjust frequently; meaning borrowers could see their costs rise as short-term interest rates increase.

Lenders say that option ARMs appeal to borrowers who earn bonuses or commissions or are otherwise looking for flexibility.

For lenders, the low teaser rates are a way to attract customers at a time when business has slowed. Mortgage volume is expected to decline this year, according to the Mortgage Bankers Association. The need to keep loan pipelines full has helped fuel the growth of interest-only mortgages and other creative lending products.

The rise of loans with low teaser rates comes at a time when traditional fixed-rate mortgage rates still remain a bargain. Rates on 30-year fixed-rate loans currently average 5.75%, whereas rates on 15-year fixed-rate mortgages average 5.32%.

"Pay practically nothing on your mortgage for 6 months!" The adjustable-rate loan, which carries a rate a hair above 0% for the first 6 months, came from the 0% popular with autos companies.

But there is no free lunch! Borrowers pay 2.25 points up front, or $4,500 on a $200,000 loan. That works out to an effective interest rate of roughly 4.5%.

Some borrowers who opt for option ARMs could be in for a rude awakening. If interest rates rise, borrowers who elect to make the minimum monthly payment can suffer "negative amortization," meaning their loan balance swells. That's because, as rates rise, the minimum payment isn't enough to cover even the interest that is due. They could also be hit with sharply higher monthly payments several years down the road.

Loans with negative amortization were common in the late 1980s. But they fell from favor because many borrowers didn't understand the risks of a rising loan balance. When real estate prices fell, some borrowers wound up owing more than their home was worth.

Lenders say they have tightened their lending standards and now do a better job of explaining the loans' risks. They have also added new features, such as limits on how big the outstanding balance can get.

Pitfalls? Consider someone who took out a $400,000 mortgage with an introductory rate of 1% in January 2005. The introductory rate is used to calculate the minimum payment on the loan—in this case, $1,287. But after the first month, the actual rate on the loan is roughly 4.6%. If interest rates edge upward, a borrower who made the minimum payment each month could end up owing nearly $407,000 after the first year.

A new minimum payment is calculated at the end of each year based on current interest rates and other factors. To reduce the potential pain, lenders typically set a 7.5% cap on how much the minimum payment can rise in most years. The cap is typically waived once every—years so that the borrower is put back on track to pay off the loan over the original 30-year period. The minimum-payment option is suspended if the loan balance reaches a preset level—typically between 110% and 125% of the original loan amount.

To see how far payments can jump when the cap is waived, assume that interest rates continue to move up gradually. The minimum payment would increase to $1,383 in the second year and by the fourth year rise to $1,598. The real bite comes at the end of the fifth year when the cap on payment increases is suspended. The minimum payment jumps to $3,109—well over twice the original amount.

Pay Off the House

Tom is 43 years old and his wife Trish is 38 years old. They live with their three young children in Anchorage, Alaska. Their home is worth approximately $300,000 with a mortgage balance of $115,000. They have $100,000 in cash and $300,000 in other investments, primarily stocks.

They're considering two courses of action: paying down their mortgage by $80,000 or investing in government bonds. They have no other debt.

Tom and Trish are better off paying down the mortgage. Why? Because the interest they will receive from the bonds will be less than the interest they'll pay for their mortgage. They should pay down the house if that and the bonds were the only possibilities. Fortunately, Tom and Trish are not limited to just those two options.

They can diversify their fixed-income investments over a variety of different types of bonds. They could also choose to invest in some college savings plans for their children, such as the Coverdell IRA or 529 plans.

Unless one has a strong desire to pay off the house, they should think twice before taking their cash and paying down their mortgage. For example, a typical middle-age couple like Tom and Trish still have many years before retirement. So it would probably be easier for them to make mortgage payments each month than to amass an additional $100,000 in cash investments.

Property Swap Yes, But Talk It Over First

Next year Tom plans to sell his long-term rental property at a big gain. But, unfortunately, there is a price for success. Tom will face a large capital gains tax. Therefore, as a tax-saving strategy, he's considering making an exchange. After he sells the rental property, he will buy another property of equal value.

Generally, Tom is using a smart strategy. Under Internal Revenue Code Section 1031, he is entitled to exchange one investment property for another as long as the property is of "like kind" and there is no material change to one's debt and equity.

The property must be exchanged through an intermediary, but, if done properly, there will be no current tax consequences and Tom's cost basis will simply carry forward to his new home. When the property is eventually sold, he will then be responsible for capital gains taxes.

After Tom exchanges his rental property for his new property, if he decides to convert the rental property into his primary residence, he can do so without any tax ramifications. Once he has lived in that home for 2 years, he can sell that home and avoid up to $250,000 of capital gains. On the other hand, Tom may be responsible for recapturing any accelerated appreciation that he claimed.

The 1031 exchanges can be terrific, but there is a caveat: These transfers can be botched—and have been botched—by people who don't understand the technicalities of the transaction. So, Tom must be sure to consult with a firm that specializes in these exchanges and talk with a qualified CPA before starting this process.

Protecting Your Real Estate Gains

For many people, the old homestead represents the biggest asset they will ever have.

The gains from the home often will go to pay for retirement or some other goal. So it is important to them that the home attains the biggest gains with the lowest possible costs. The latter usually means capital gains taxes.

Judy, who is 58 years old, wants to sell her home. The property was purchased for $8,000 in 1970, with $15,000 in additions later. After her divorce, she financed the home for $84,000 to purchase rental property. A real estate agent has told her that she could sell the home for $165,000.

But she is worried about how much of her gains would be eaten up by capital taxes. There is some good news for her. If this property is her primary residence and she has lived in it 2 out of the last 5 years—which she has—there will be no capital gains tax when she sells it.

Judy can also avoid taxes on capital gains of up to $250,000 on the sale of her primary residence. But let's use an example of someone who is not selling a primary residence. That person could be hit with a large capital gain tax.

To determine how much your property will be taxed (assuming it is not your primary residence), you simply take your net sales price (after fees and commissions) and deduct the costs you have expended on the property.

Let's say that you net $165,000 for your home, and then your reportable gain will be $142,000 ($165,000 less $8,000 and less $15,000).

If you sell the home for cash, you will be required to report the $142,000 in the year in which the property is sold. If you take an installment sale, you have the ability to spread the taxation over several years. But you may or may not be reducing your tax liability, depending on your tax bracket. If you are currently in the 28% or higher bracket, and figure you will be for some time, an installment sale will do you little good. But if you're in the 15% bracket, spreading the taxation over years may be a great strategy.

It could mean paying 10%, as opposed to 20% capital gains tax.

Putting $100,000 in Two Homes Poses Risks

Karl recently sold a residential investment property that will provide him with roughly $140,000 of equity with no capital gains tax due (the home was his primary residence). After paying off some car loans, he will have $100,000 to reinvest.

Karl will continue to invest in real estate, but he wonders which is the better of two options: putting $100,000 in residential real estate with 20% down on two $250,000 homes or investing in a single $300,000 piece of commercial real estate with 34% down?

Karl would be wise to put off any investment decision for a short period and think something through: Can he afford to keep the investment in both good times and bad? Owning real estate can provide income from rents, but it also carries with it costs such as upkeep, taxes, insurance, and mortgage payments.

If Karl plans on using 100% of his cash to fund his purchases, he will have some concerns. Most financial experts agree that having cash reserves covering 3 to 6 months of your expenses is essential before you consider setting up a portfolio of real estate or stock investments.

In Karl's case, he should have some reserves set aside for vacancies, repairs, and mortgage payments. Without those reserves, he could find himself in a cash crunch. Then he could fall behind on his mortgage payments. He then risks losing all the equity in his real estate.

His decision to invest in residential rentals versus commercial property should have something to do with his ability to manage the property. Most real estate investors begin by owning residential units before they venture to commercial property.

If Karl can find a viable commercial unit for $300,000 and has the ability to manage it properly, it might work out fine for him. However, it's advisable for Karl to start with one residential rental and put higher than 20% down. If things work out, and Karl is able to generate a positive cash flow, he can always purchase an additional rental down the road.

Real Estate for the Small Investor

Shirley is very interested in real estate and wants to know how to get started. But she doesn't figure to raise the capital to build any housing complexes or shopping centers.

An option for Shirley is to consider real estate investment trusts (REITs). REITs are becoming very popular investment vehicles for both income and growth investors. A REIT is essentially a special type of corporation that owns and operates real estate. As a shareholder in a REIT, you have equity ownership in a corporation and the rights to the profits of that corporation.

It is estimated that the total value of real estate in the United States is in the trillions of dollars, and it is growing fast. The big owners of real estate in the past have been pension funds and insurance companies, but today we are seeing a shift from direct ownership to ownership through REIT securities.

Five years ago, only about 15% of real estate assets were held in the form of a REIT, whereas today that number is rising quickly. One major benefit of a REIT is the liquidity—most REITs are traded daily on stock exchanges.

Although it may be prudent to have a portion of Shirley's portfolio in REITs, it wouldn't be advisable to hold them in lieu of bonds.

Real Estate Investor Goes off a Cliff

You've heard the old saying that it's not what you don't know that hurts you. It's what you think you know that's not true that hurts you.

Here's an illustration of the latter. Andrea, who watches and listens to many money shows, often becomes enthusiastic about some of the schemes presented on these shows.

Her understanding is that if you live in a home before turning the property into a rental, you must live in the home for 2 years to avoid capital gains tax. So far, so good. However, now she believes that has changed. One only needs to live in it for only 1 day.

Andrea is either misled or simply misinformed. Her information is not accurate. There has been a change in the holding period for rental homes that are converted into primary residences. But the change applies to homes acquired through a 1031 exchange. The new rule affects homes that were acquired as a result of a 1031 exchange after October 22, 2004. These homes must be held for at least 5 years before a person can claim the $250,000 capital gains exclusion for a primary residence. See IRS Publication 523 for the full details.

Renting Your Home—A Difficult Issue

Deciding when to sell or rent your home depends on numerous personal, economic, and tax issues.

A big tax issue is the capital gains exclusion, which is only available for someone who has lived in the home for 2 of the past 5 years. Let's say you move out of a home in January 2004, a home in which you lived for at least 2 years. You now decide to rent it. Fine, the clock is running. You have until January 2007 to sell it in order to obtain the capital gains exemption.

Homeowner John is puzzled. He could probably net $75,000 tax-free (including costs) by selling before January 2007. He understands the benefit of selling it now and investing the $75,000 elsewhere. Nevertheless, John is not sure of the benefits of keeping the rental for the long term. He owes $150,000 on it at 6.5%. At his current payment rate (+$100/month toward principal), the loan will be paid off in 23 years.

John is considering several possibilities. If he sells the property for a bigger price in 10 years from now, that might give him a pretax gain of $245,000. John wants to take part of this gain, roll it into another property, and invest the rest elsewhere. He's also looking at keeping the property until it's paid off (let's say 23 years), then selling it for a pretax/postexpenses cost of $400,000. And there's one other factor. John is fed up with the average tenant. He doesn't want to be a landlord the rest of his life.

Indeed, ownership can be a pain. Owning a rental is not a passive investment. It can take some time and expenses to maintain. However, if John has the time and is a patient long-term investor, the rewards can be worthwhile.

The reason John owns a rental home right now is because it was his primary residence at one time. What he should ask himself is this: Is the rental home I own an ideal rental? In other words, if John were to go out and purchase a rental today, would it be the one he currently owns? Odds are it is not.

John has an opportunity to avoid capital gains tax on his home because it was his primary residence. As long as the home is sold by January 2007, he can exclude capital gains. If John keeps the home beyond that point, he will not be able to use the $250,000 exclusion. He will, however, have the opportunity to defer the gain in the future if he exchanges the rental with another one using a 1031 exchange.

John might consider selling the rental home before January 2007 and using the money to purchase a different rental. By doing so, he will completely avoid the capital gains taxes. He will be able to purchase a home that is ideal for renting.

Owning rentals can have some great tax benefits. Many individuals are able to claim losses on their income tax return even when they have positive cash flow from their investment. In addition, capital gains taxes can be deferred for decades by using tax-free exchanges.

Trying to crunch the numbers to see when is the ideal holding time doesn't really work. The outcome is based on the assumptions one uses. If one assumes real estate will continue to grow at a rapid clip, keeping the rental looks fantastic. But if John assumes real estate may flatten out or actually decline over the next decade, the returns don't look so hot.

Retiring Mortgages

June and her husband Skip own their home as well as three rental properties, all of which have mortgages. They would like to have the properties paid off by the time they retire. They have been paying extra each month. Because they have four mortgages, they wonder if one should receive priority.

The key is that there should always be a plan when working toward paying off debt, whether it's real estate loans or credit cards. Typically, the best bet would be to make the scheduled payments on all of the loans and apply additional funds to the loan with the highest interest rate.

By using this strategy, they'll be lowering their overall finance charges. That's because most real estate loans charge higher interest rates on non-owner-occupied residences. So it follows that rental homes probably have the highest interest rates.

One exception to the "highest rate" strategy is if you are paying private mortgage insurance (PMI) on a personal residence. PMI is often assessed if you do not have at least 20% equity in your home. If you are paying PMI, you should apply any extra funds to the home mortgage until the equity is at least 20%, and then you can eliminate PMI.

Reverse Mortgages Sometimes Save the Day

It's happening all over America—the aging of our nation.

Bill's parents are both in their late 80s. For a while now, Bill has been helping them manage their finances. But now Bill's father will be requiring full-time nursing care, and have only about $30,000 in savings.

They have been living off their Social Security and the father's pension, but that won't cover the cost of nursing care. Still, their home is paid for and is worth about $200,000. Bill is thinking about taking out a home mortgage for about $60,000 to cover the costs of the father's nursing home.

Looking to the equity in the home may be a wise idea. Still, Bill may run into difficulty finding a lending institution willing to give the parents a traditional mortgage. There's another alternative.

Bill's parents are good candidates for a reverse mortgage. With this type of mortgage, the parents would receive a monthly income for a specified period of time, perhaps 15 to 20 years. At the end of the term, there would be little or no equity left in the home. The advantage of a reverse mortgage is that it allows the parents to use the equity they have accumulated without having to sell their home or worry about making monthly mortgage payments.

Indeed, the problems of Bill's parents should lead all of us to think about old age. If you wish to avoid facing this same problem, say in 30 years or so from now, you may want to look at purchasing long-term care insurance for yourself. The cost of long-term care can be staggering and can be a burden to other family members.

Should You Buy More House Than You Need?

Many Americans buy more and bigger cars than they need. And many also purchase bigger homes than they need and saddle themselves with huge mortgage payments for many years. One way they can obtain these bigger homes is through the use of interest-only mortgages.

This can be a very dangerous way to buy a house. The concept is built on several assumptions, which must pan out for the loan to work out. One of the assumptions of these interest-only loans is that loan rates will generally stay low. But will they? No one can say with certainty.

These loans can work fine if all the stars line up just so, but what will you do if things don't go as planned? What if rates are higher in 5 years, and you can't afford a higher mortgage payment? Worse still, what if property values have softened as a result of higher rates and your home is worth less in 5 years?

With rates so low, it seems that the smart money would choose a long-term, fixed-rate mortgage. Regardless of what happens to interest rates and property values, you'll know what you must pay for your house with a fixed rate loan. When you have a variable rate loan, whether interest-only or traditional, a rise in interest rates could be a disaster. You could lose your home.

The Bonfire of the Stocks

Let's say you've done well in the stock market and now have a large amount in good stocks and funds. And, as part of the home equity loan craze of the last few years, a fad fueled by unusually low interest rates, you have some debt on your home.

In general, don't sell the stocks and funds to pay off the loans unless you're unhappy with the investments and were going to sell them anyway. Here are a few reasons why.

First, remember, good stocks and funds work most effectively over the long run, over several cycles of the market. Stocks in the short term can be dangerous. For example, if you started investing at the top of the market 5 years ago, then you've likely had bad returns. If you've been in good stocks or funds for 10 or 20 years, you've had some great years and should have had good returns.

Second, home equity loans offer you tax advantaged lending. Much, or maybe all of the interest, is tax deductible. And the interest rate is relatively low because it is a secured loan, unlike a credit card loan. A home equity loan can be a good deal. That's provided you don't take on more debt than you need, don't use the proceeds for frivolous purchases, and pay down the loan over the years just as you did the mortgage. It is a kind of piggy bank. With each payment you gain back more equity in the house.

Third, never consider the opposite—taking a home equity loan to put more money in the stock market. The *Wall Street Journal* in 2000 postulated that the smart money was in refinancing homes to invest in the stock market. In other words, put all your money, or most of your money, into what was then a hot stock market. Of course, anyone who followed that advice has a small stock portfolio and a large mortgage balance to pay off. Don't do this because diversified investing is the best approach for most people. Never put all your money in just one thing, no matter how well it is performing.

There is nothing wrong with using a mortgage to help purchase a house, but for the vast majority of Americans, the mortgage should be paid off by the time one hits retirement. In regard to home equity lines of credits or loans, they can be effective as a source for cheap money, but unless they are paid back, they increase the amount of debt owed on a home.

It's not advisable to use home equity loans to make an investment, but selling investments to pay off a debt is not necessarily the best move. It really depends on where the money from the loan went. If it was used to buy cars and big-screen TVs, it should probably be paid off out of wages. Otherwise, the consequences of spending the money won't be noticed.

One concern with paying off the home equity loans from savings or investments is that it may be too easy to run up a balance in the future. Once the home equity loan has a zero balance, it may be tempting to use some of the credit to purchase additional consumer products. If you're confident that you won't run up the balance again, then paying off the line of credit may, in a limited number of cases, be a wise move.

If you sell some investments to pay off your home equity line there could be another problem: capital gains taxes. It would be a shame to see you liquidate some good investments only to find yourself with a big tax bill in April.

Will Buying a House Beat College Dorm Fees?

Higher education inflation keeps outpacing general inflation. And one of the reasons why this is so is because of the high housing costs.

Donald has two children who are ready to attend a university about 40 miles away. He thinks that buying a house for his kids—both of whom are going to attend the same university—would make more sense than paying for housing at the university. He says this could turn into an investment. He says his two kids may or may not have other roommates to offset the payment. He would be putting down $35,000 on a home cost of $300,000. Donald is well heeled, in his late 40s, and married.

Whether Donald's children live in a rental home that he owns or pay rent to another landlord really makes no difference—there is still a cost involved. Why?

When they're living in a home rent-free, there is an opportunity cost. Donald could be receiving rent if it were rented to someone else.

Before Donald does anything, he should sit down and crunch the numbers. Assume a moderate to no growth rate on the home over the next 5 years. Calculate the total cost paid on the home, including interest, taxes, insurance, and maintenance. Next, compare that expense to what it would cost in rent if Donald rented an apartment to his children.

As for income taxes, if Donald claims the home as a second residence, he'll be able to deduct his interest expense, but no other expenses. If he claims it as a rental, he'll need to calculate a marketplace rent. That's even if his children are not paying rent.

Donald won't be able to deduct all of his expenses if he is not charging his children rent. Unless Donald is betting on a major run-up in real estate prices over the next 5 years, he'll probably find it's much cheaper to pay rent for a shared apartment than to purchase a home for his children.

Chapter 7
Protect Your Wealth

Most people don't do much tax planning. By lowering your tax bill, your savings can go to build wealth.

Robert had just started taking Social Security. He drew some money out of a retirement account that same year, money he didn't really need to pull out, but did for whatever reason. It caused a higher percentage of his Social Security to become taxable. Robert thought he was in the 15% tax bracket, but when he added in the increased taxation of his Social Security, his federal tax rate was actually about 26%. The dollar he pulled out of his IRA, which he thought was going to cost $.15, in fact cost $.26.

Had he done just the bare minimum of tax planning, Robert could have deferred the distribution, or chosen to defer taking Social Security until the following year, and then take a larger distribution. But he didn't do the tax planning.

Tax preparers are the busiest during tax time. They're bombarded. That's not the time for tax planning. It's too late. You really ought to do tax planning throughout the year, particularly in November and December. But most people don't do that.

Our tax structure is a progressive tax system. Some income is not taxable at all; some is taxed at 10%; some at 15%; some at 25%. These rates change on a constant basis when the Feds tinker with them. But the fact is there are big steps at each point. If you can control some of your income, it might be as much as a 10% or 15% savings in income taxes. For instance, you're going to save $2,000 in taxes if you defer an extra $5,000 into your 401(k) this year.

Capital Gains … Again

Carl had a simple question about something that seems to confuse many people—the extent of capital gains exclusion on the sale of a house. That's a tax that was changed several years ago. Carl wanted to know how the capital gains exclusion on the sale of a house worked. He specifically wanted to know how it worked for a primary residence. He was confused and wanted to know if he had to have lived in the house for 5 years to qualify for the exclusion.

The tax treatment on the sale of a primary residence was changed in May 1997. Still, there are many people who are unaware of how the rules work.

When a person sells his or her primary residence, that person can exclude up to $250,000 of gains from capital gains taxes. A married couple can exclude up to $500,000. The only requirement is that the person must have lived in the home as his or her primary residence for 2 of the past 5 years. There is no requirement regarding how long the home was owned.

Gains above the $250,000/$500,000 exclusion are subject to capital gains taxes. The additional gain cannot be rolled over to another home to avoid taxation. In fact, there is no requirement that a person purchase another primary residence. The gain can be spent in any way the person chooses.

Are Your Assets Protected?

Many people have set up revocable living trusts to ensure that, upon death, the ubiquitous taxman doesn't wreak havoc with an estate. For example, sometimes a husband and wife have a revocable trust but list assets in three different banks, each listing the name of the trust.

This may seem a superfluous precaution, but it isn't. It is very important to change ownership on all of your assets to your revocable trust if you want your assets to pass without any glitch upon your death. Simply listing your accounts in your trust binder won't make it easy on your heirs. Too often people spend time and money to establish a trust, but never bother to change the title on their home, savings, and investments.

Suppose your bank accounts are listed under your and your wife's name. You took the time to list the bank and account number in your trust binder. However, you never bothered to inform the bank. Both of you pass away. The trustee of your trust will see the accounts listed in the trust binder. However, now the bank won't simply turn over the assets to the trustee. The bank has no legal proof that the account should be listed in the trust. That's because the bank would need to wait until the courts determined whether the assets should be included in the trust. That could take much time. It could cost someone a good deal of money. Remember, lawyers' meters are running double time whenever they have to go to the courthouse.

Any asset you own (other than retirement accounts) that you want to pass easily upon your death should be listed in your revocable trust. The only times you would want to exclude certain items from your trust is if those assets are titled jointly with another party, held in a different trust, or you wanted that asset to go through probate.

Check to See If Life Insurance Would Offset Estate Taxes

Life has been good to Dave's mom, Grace. At age 84, Grace has assets worth $2 million to $3 million in apartment rental property, land, and stock investments. Grace is considering establishing a trust and giving equal shares of ownership worth $11,000 of a house, rental apartment, and piece of property. An insurance agent has advised Dave's mom to purchase a life insurance policy to protect those assets.

Life insurance can be a great tool to pay for estate taxes if (1) something or someone other than Grace owns the policy and (2) if his mother can qualify for the insurance at a decent rate. The reason life insurance can be useful is because the death benefit can escape taxes.

If Dave's mother were to die without any serious estate planning in place, her heirs would be hit with an estate tax bill upwards of $1 million. Typically, estate taxes are due within 9 months of death, so unless the mother had substantial liquid assets, her heirs could be forced to liquidate some of the real estate, perhaps at fire-sale prices.

There are a number of things Grace should consider doing. These include gifting some or all of her $1.5 million lifetime exemption now, establishing a family-limited partnership, creating one or more irrevocable trusts, and creating a living trust. Grace may choose to do some or all of these techniques, depending on a number of factors.

Dave would be wise to consult with at least two estate-planning attorneys who specialize in estates this size before any life insurance is purchased. See what ideas they have and which techniques they would employ. Ask them about the risks of each technique they recommend and whether the IRS is okay with those techniques. And find out how difficult it would be to unwind these trusts and partnerships after Grace dies.

Once you've looked at all of the options, you may decide it makes great sense to buy life insurance. Or you may find you can accomplish the objectives in a less expensive manner.

Life Insurance—Not on Your Life!

Life insurance is a horrible investment for most people. But life insurance is necessary, and that's why term insurance is an excellent choice for the average American. It's cheap and you can carry the insurance for just the years in which you need insurance, typically when you have kids at home and other people dependent on your income. As people move closer to retirement, their insurance needs decrease because they don't have dependent children. And they now have financial assets saved up to replace that income. That's why term insurance makes sense.

Life insurance is important for a couple of reasons. One is to pay off any debts that you have and second is to replace an income. Let's say you're young and you've got a spouse and 2.2 children and $140,000 on your home and $32,000 on your car. You want to add up what all your liabilities are so that should you die those can be taken care of, and then figure out how much income you've got coming in.

As a rule of thumb, you might need about 10 times your annual income in the form of life insurance. For instance, if someone has $200,000 of debt and is making $50,000 a year, he or she needs $500,000 to replace their income and another $200,000 to pay off their debt, $700,000.

Your life insurance strategy typically changes as you get older. For example, Dave is 39 years old and has bought a $2 million life insurance policy with 20-year fixed, guaranteed, level payments for $1,200 a year. He has two children, 9 and 7 years old. They will probably need support from Dave for the next 15 or so years. After that, they should be somewhat self-supporting and not need Dave's financial support. They'll be adults by that point and will have to learn to fend for themselves. So Dave's insurance needs over the next 15 years are going to be greater than they will be 15 years down the road.

Universal life or whole life is typically a very expensive way to buy insurance. There are times when it is appropriate, but 95% of the time you are much better off just buying some cheap term insurance over the Internet. Whole life and universal life carry huge commissions to the sales rep; sometimes the sales rep will make 50% of your first-year deposits in commission. So if you're putting in $100 a month, he or she is getting $50 a month in commission. Until you're at a point where you're in great financial shape, don't bother with any whole life or universal life.

Only once you've maxed out your 401(k), maxed out your IRAs, and you're out of debt, then it might be the time to look toward universal life. Until that time, use cheap term insurance.

How to Manage the Risk of Buying Corporate Bonds

Kim is a smart investor who intended to diversify. Kim had 90% of her brokerage IRA in stocks and knew it was time to find another asset class. Otherwise she would end up with the same problem as many of her friends who suffered horrific losses in the bear market of 2000 to 2002.

She was looking at an investment in corporate notes. In the corporate notes program, Kim explained, she could buy new issue corporate notes in increments of $1,000 each, and there was no commission.

Kim researched various issues, deciding to limit her bonds to corporations with "A" and higher Standard & Poor's ratings. Kim purchased six bonds meeting these criteria, each in a $1,000 increment. The bonds are due in 2010, 2011, and 2012 and are paying an annual average of 4.5%. Kim realized that these are not stellar returns. However, she wanted some portfolio diversification, and $6,000 is less than 3% of her total brokerage IRA.

Kim's bond component is appropriate for most investors, whether they are purchased individually or as part of a professionally managed portfolio. One reason is that—although stock returns usually beat bond returns most years—there are years in which bonds are a much better investment. When are those years? No one can know for sure, which is why most portfolios should have stocks and bonds, although in most cases more of the former than the latter is a better approach. However, the best approach, over the long term, is to have some of both asset classes.

If you're sold on having some bonds, or what the pros called fixed income, in your portfolio, here are some factors to consider.

You take two types of risks when you own bonds. The first risk is default risk. This occurs when the bond issuer can no longer meet its obligations. There have been many large corporations that have not been able to make good on their bond payments. Examples of this are WorldCom and Enron. Bond-rating agencies, such as Standard & Poor's, can help by evaluating a company. Nevertheless, a good rating today does not guarantee that a company will be good tomorrow.

The second type of risk is interest rate risk. Your bond values will rise or fall inversely with interest rates. If next month's interest rates are much higher than today's, your $6,000 investment in bonds would have a market value of much less than $6,000.

You'll receive your full investment upon maturity, but most investors look at their portfolios at least monthly, sometimes daily. Investors don't like to see the value of any of their holdings fall, regardless of what guarantees there may be in 5 to 10 years.

With regard to commissions, it is true that one does not pay any commissions when purchasing a bond. But that doesn't mean it doesn't cost you anything. The brokerage firm earns what is called a "spread." That is the difference between what it paid for the bond and what it sells the bond for. Typically, the smaller the bond purchase, the greater the spread. Essentially, if you invest $100,000 in a bond you could receive a higher yield than if you invest only $1,000.

Despite the risks of bonds—and every kind of investing has some risks—Kim is to be congratulated on her intelligent approach.

Tax Laws Key to Many Investing Decisions

Variable universal life insurance (VUL) policies tend to work best for those who are already making the maximum contributions to their 401(k) and Roth IRAs. Their use depends on one's individual tax circumstances and long-term financial goals.

This came up recently when Tina and George, who are both in their mid-30s, were advised by their financial planner to contribute $500 monthly to Tina's VUL policy of $250,000, then max their contributions to their 401(k), and then set up Roth IRAs.

The intended use for the money in the VUL is to pay for their daughter's college education (in lieu of a 529 plan, which they might do down the road). Tina and George weren't sure about the value of their planner's advice.

As a general rule, investors should contribute to a Roth IRA and their employer's retirement plan, such as a 401(k), prior to paying extra money to a life insurance policy. Why? Because of the tax laws in place.

Deposits made to a Roth IRA are not tax deductible, but all qualifying withdrawals are totally income-tax free. As long as you're over 59½, you can pull the entire account balance out without ever triggering a tax bill. Under the age of 59½, you can withdraw all of your deposits without getting hit with income taxes.

Money deposited into a 401(k) or 403(b) will lower your current tax bill. Sure, the money will be taxed during retirement. Still, many young families can lower their tax bill substantially by using a 401(k). The money saved in taxes can either be saved or used for other purposes.

Premiums paid to a life insurance policy do not receive a tax deduction, and withdrawals may or may not be income-tax free. Current tax law enables a policy owner to withdraw all deposits before withdrawing gains (similar to a Roth IRA).

But once withdrawals exceed deposits, the withdrawals become taxable as ordinary income. The way to avoid the taxes is to take a loan against the policy rather than a withdrawal, but the policy must be kept until death, otherwise taxation will occur.

There is nothing wrong with universal life, variable life, variable universal life, and so forth. However, many families would be better served with low-cost term insurance and Roth IRAs.

529 College Savings Plan: Worth the Uncertainty

Bob has a young child. Bob wants to know what is the best way to put away money for the huge college bill that will be coming his way in about a decade.

For many parents and grandparents, the 529 college savings plan is the best deal. However, this wonderful deal has one disadvantage—it may not be around in a few years for Bob.

First, let's review how the 529 plan works. Money deposited into the plan does not receive a tax deduction. On the other hand, the account grows tax deferred. Provided the money is used for secondary education expenses, the proceeds are free from taxes.

Prior to 2001, earnings from 529 plans were taxed at the student's tax rate. Thankfully, the major tax package of President Bush's first term, the Economic Growth and Tax Relief Reconciliation Act of 2001 (EGTRRA), changed that. The tax treatment of withdrawals of the 529 was changed.

EGTRRA allowed all withdrawals used for qualified education expenses to escape the clutches of that avaricious Uncle Whiskers.

EGTRRA also dealt with a number of tax issues, including the reduction of income and capital gains taxes and the reduction of estate taxes. It also increased IRA and retirement contribution limits and expanded child credits.

Nevertheless, the entire tax act, including the 529 plan changes, is scheduled to expire on December 31, 2010. That is, unless the members of Congress—the Potomac Poloniuses—pass new legislation to make some or all of EGTRRA permanent.

The Bobs of this world who are using 529s must be warned: It is impossible to know what our income tax system will look like 5 years from now. Possibly, withdrawals from 529 plans will again be taxable at the student's rate.

Still, it's likely that Congress will pass legislation to keep students from paying taxes on college tuition money.

A 401(k) Traffic Jam

It is usual these days for people to switch jobs often. And that means an average worker could end up with several different 401(k) plans and assets scattered across several places.

You have a couple of options. If you are still working and your current employer offers a 401(k), you can transfer your other 401(k)s into your current employer's plan. Simply contact your current 401(k) provider and state what you want to do. The employer should walk you through the process.

If you are not employed, or if you don't much care for your current 401(k), you can transfer your 401(k) plans into a self-directed IRA. You can establish a self-directed IRA at any brokerage or financial planning firm. Because your desire is to manage it yourself, you may want to look at some of the online discount brokerage firms. Once the funds are in an IRA, you can allocate your money in a variety of investments—including stocks, bonds, managed accounts, and so forth.

A Deadly and Confusing Tax

Death is no escape from taxes. After you die, the tax authorities come after your children and others you want to help. But, like many parents who want to pass assets on to their children today or after death, there are things you can do to ensure your demise isn't so taxing. First, retain a tax advisor—preferably a lawyer who specializes in estate taxes—to build your estate plan or help you decide how you might want to help your children.

If you don't have a potential 7-figure estate, you probably don't have a significant estate tax problem. Unless your estate is worth more than $1 million, you can liquidate everything you own and give it to your children free from gift taxes. You will not have to pay any gift taxes, and neither will your children. Each individual can give up to $1 million during his or her lifetime before any gift taxes are assessed. In addition, a person can give $11,000 per year to any number of individuals without triggering a gift tax. It's only when gifts exceed these amounts that there are tax problems.

If you sell your home, you can exclude from taxes up to $250,000 worth of capital gains as long as you've lived in the house for 2 of the preceding

5 years. Once the home is sold, you can divvy up the funds among your children. They will pay no taxes on the gifts. The only taxes they would need to worry about are interest and dividends they will earn from the money received.

However, many people today do have to think about estate taxes. Tens of millions of Americans who have earned only modest incomes through-out most of their lives have saved and invested systematically and have accumulated more than they ever thought possible. Inflation and the fat markets of the 1990s helped to bid up the value of their assets. They have been so busy working—building up a business or making regular invest-ments—that many of them have a net worth today of $1 million or better. Of course, a million isn't worth what it used to be.

If you are in this category, today might be the best time to start gifting to reduce estate taxes. The amount you can pass on while you are living is limited to $1 million. Any gifts you make above that amount will be hit with a gift tax, which starts at 37% and can run as high as 48%. This $1 million exemption is in addition to the $11,000 per year you can give to any number of persons.

The amount you can pass on at death is currently $1.5 million. It is sched-uled to remain that amount through 2005. For the years 2006 to 2008, the amount rises to $2 million. In 2009, the exemption rises to $3.5 million. If you die in 2010, there is no estate tax, and you can transfer an unlimited amount at death.

But in 2011 and beyond, the limits drop back to $1 million. But I stress, these estate tax numbers are all projections. Another reason why you need a tax advisor is because Congress is fickle. Who knows what they will do with estate tax schedules? because the tax rates and exemptions often fluc-tuate, the advisor can, potentially, save you much money. A good advisor can more than earn his or her fee.

Taxes are wounds that we can't escape. Do you want a flesh wound or some-thing more serious?

A Home Is a Tax Bill

Do you want to get stuck with a big capital gains bill because, although your father was trying to help you, Uncle Whiskers was trying to help him-self to a generous slice of your property?

Well, it can happen. Indeed, it is on the horizon. Recently, Mr. Braun (86 years old) added his two sons as owners of his house. He wanted to help them. But will he be giving them a tax headache some day? He could be.

If the father's home is transferred to the sons by means of joint tenancy, they could be stuck with a capital gains tax. When the father listed the sons on the title of his home, Mr. Braun technically gave both sons a portion of his house.

The portion that will transfer to the sons upon the father's death will receive a stepped-up cost basis, but the portion that was given to the sons will have a cost basis tied to what he paid for the home.

Mr. Braun can remove the sons' names from the title and can create a will that states that the brothers should receive the home. But this won't avoid probate, which could run several thousand dollars. To avoid this cost, Mr. Braun should establish a revocable living trust.

What the sons should do is ask the father if he would have his attorney set up a living trust. If Mr. Braun were reluctant to do so, the sons should offer to pay the costs. The price of establishing a trust today is much less than paying either capital gains tax or probate upon the father's death.

Selling a Property

Tina receives Social Security payments because she is disabled. She pays no income taxes. She sold her home a few years ago and cleared $90,000. She lived in the home for 5 years and, like so many others fearful of Uncle Whiskers, she is now worried about running up a tax bill.

Tina can feel reassured. Taxation on the sale of a personal residence has nothing to do with one's income, working status, age, sex, race, political persuasion, and so forth. Furthermore, it has nothing to do with what one does with the money one receives from the sale of a home.

Tina can spend the money, save it, reinvest it, burn it, bury it, or smoke it. The determining factor for taxation is based on how long she lived in the home.

All gains on the sale of a personal residence are taxable unless one has made that home one's primary residence for at least 2 of the preceding 5 years. If so, one can exclude up to $250,000 of gain if single or $500,000 if married.

Because Tina had lived in the home for more than 2 years, she will owe no taxes on the gain.

A Tax Avoidance Strategy Run Amuck

Taxes are the biggest expense for many people. And certainly there are good reasons to utilize many tax avoidance strategies. However, it's possible to go too far.

Charles retired 3 years ago at age 56. He began a constant dollar withdrawal from his savings/investment account—which had recently performed very well—to supplement a pension. The withdrawal was designed to deplete the account by age 65, assuming a 10% rate of return. Social Security would provide a large part of the supplemental income when the account was gone, Charles figured.

The investments have increased in value and now Charles is looking ahead to taxes on Social Security income. He is thinking of increasing withdrawals at age 59½ to deplete the account by age 65, or possibly staying the course and paying the higher tax rate on 85% of his Social Security income.

The idea of depleting all of his investments before age 65 simply to avoid taxes on Social Security income is a ludicrous plan. Most people would rather have a large financial base and pay some additional taxes, as opposed to no financial base while paying little in taxes. What is Charles' goal here? To be broke? Or to enjoy a long and prosperous retirement?

Just because the financial markets have given us phenomenal returns over any short period does not ensure good returns tomorrow. In other words, the gain Charles just experienced may be needed to keep his income going until age 65.

Furthermore, who's to say Congress won't change the tax law with regard to Social Security income? Charles should plan an income stream that will keep his investments intact forever, not just for a few years.

An Unhappy Investor

Investors sometimes don't fit a stereotype. Take Phil, a 60-year-old man who has a good retirement plan. He should be happy with low return and safe investments, right?

Phil, who is retired from a school district and has a 403(b) with an insurance company, is "fed up." Phil is unhappy with the 6% interest he is currently earning. He would like to have the money transferred to another 403(b) that he has, one that is paying much better and has been for quite a while.

Phil, who won't need this money for several years, says his only concern is the tax consequence of the transfer.

There is good news for Phil. He can transfer a 403(b) plan to another 403(b) without any tax consequences. That's provided he elects for a "direct transfer." A direct transfer is simply when the 403(b) transfers the funds directly to a new plan. As long as Phil does not receive the funds, the transfer will take place free of any income taxes or tax withholding.

If Phil, or Phil's agent, made a mistake and did not elect a direct transfer, but instead had the funds payable to Phil, the 403(b) would withhold 20% federal income taxes.

Although Phil is entitled to transfer his 403(b) to another plan without any tax consequences, his current insurance company may impose an early withdrawal penalty. Phil should be sure to look into any withdrawal penalties before he initiates the transfer.

Annuity Hi-jinks

Annuities, in the right circumstances, can be a helpful retirement vehicle. On the other hand, some annuities come with outrageous setup costs and unreasonable penalties for terminating the contract.

A general rule of thumb is to try to find annuity contracts with low setup and maintenance fees. In general, the less you pay, the more you can earn. As with so many other things, one must examine annuities on a case-by-case basis.

Here's a case of an annuity to avoid. An elderly couple is offered a 20-year annuity—5 years guaranteed at 6%. The couple can withdraw 10% per year, but cannot get the total they will invest ($25,000) without a penalty for 11 years. The husband is in bad health and has a greater chance of dying before the wife.

This is a bad deal. First, there is no reason to invest in a deferred annuity that ties your money up for 11 years, regardless of your age. The company is offering a 6% guarantee for the first 5 years, but what happens after that? Odds are, the rate you'll receive will be half of the rate credited for the first 5 years.

In addition to the long-term time commitment on the annuity, it's questionable why the agent offering the contract didn't list the husband as the annuitant and his wife as the beneficiary. That way, if the husband predeceases his wife, she could receive all of the couple's money without any surrender penalties. Perhaps the annuity salesman was concerned about losing his commissions if the husband died in the near term.

Unless the couple has no intentions of ever spending the $25,000, the agent's motives in selling such a long-term contract should be questioned. Typically, the commissions paid to an annuity salesman are larger for annuities with long-term surrender schedules.

Bum Advice

Claire is 58 years old and will be retiring this summer. She likes her 401(k) plan and expects to leave her money in the plan, taking withdrawals as needed. Someone working for the plan informed Susan that this would invite a penalty, something that shocked Susan into seeking advice.

Claire should be skeptical about any financial advice received from a 401(k) service rep on the other end of an 800 number. More often than not, these people are not adequately trained in all aspects of tax law. And they can sometimes give out erroneous information, as in Claire's case.

The tax code clearly states that if an employee leaves the service of an employer after reaching age 55, the individual can pull money from the employer's pension plans, including 401(k)s, without any penalties or restrictions. (See Internal Revenue Code Section 72 or a qualified tax advisor for specific details.) Claire is okay to move forward with her original plans.

A Probate Avoidance Strategy

Probate is not beer and skittles or a walk in the park on a Sunday afternoon. It can be very unpleasant. It can be expensive. It can be time consuming. It is the process by which a court straightens out an estate, determining who gets what. But you can spare your relatives some pain by setting up an IRA in such a way that probate can be avoided.

When an individual owning an IRA dies, his or her IRA can both be cashed out and distributed to the beneficiaries, or a "beneficiary IRA" can be created. A beneficiary IRA is listed in the deceased's name, but the beneficiary is listed as the new and rightful owner. The beneficiary will pay only income taxes when money is withdrawn from the IRA.

IRAs that have beneficiaries designated are not subject to probate, but they are certainly subject to estate taxes. In fact, for larger estates, the estate tax due can add up to half of the account balance. Unless the estate has other cash to pay the taxman, the IRA may have to be cashed in to pay the estate taxes, which would trigger income taxes.

If you hold a beneficiary IRA, see if there were any estate taxes paid from the deceased's estate. If there were, you could receive a tax credit to help offset your income taxes when you withdraw money from the IRA.

A Tax Simplification Complicates Things

Can the taxing authorities in Congress, the presidency, and the IRS ever get it right? Year after year they pass more and more changes in the tax code. And yet we're all still as confused as Albert Einstein, who said he couldn't understand the tax code. The Tax Reform Act of 1986 was supposed to simplify tax issues. That's not exactly how it has worked out.

Today, there are still a number of issues over how one can withdraw money from an IRA penalty-free to pay for a child's education expenses.

If one does this, how does one figure out one's taxes? Let's say a wife and her husband have each had an IRA since the early 1980s. They were able to fund deductible IRAs for only a couple of years.

The questions—which were supposed to be cleared up by the big tax reform of 1986—just keep coming. At what rate should a withdrawal be taxed? Some think the withdrawal would be treated as ordinary income. Others think it would be taxed only at the rate for long-term capital gains, at least that portion of the withdrawal that was earned with after-tax dollars. Most people, after a determined effort to find an answer to this madness, are reaching for the aspirin bottle.

The problem is many people have had IRAs that were funded with both before-tax and after-tax dollars. Prior to 1986, there were no income limits for IRA contributions. Therefore, all deposits were tax deductible. The tax act of that year put limits on higher wage earners. As a result, many people lost the ability to deduct IRA contributions.

To avoid paying taxes twice on your IRA money, you need to keep track of your after-tax contributions. You should have been filing IRS Form 8606 each year with your income taxes to let the IRS knows how much of your IRAs are made up of after-tax contributions.

If you have not been filing this form, you should start doing it with your taxes next year. Without it, the IRS will assume all of your IRAs are before-tax and your withdrawals will be fully taxable.

All interest and gains in an IRA will be taxed as ordinary income upon withdrawal. You do not receive favorable capital gains treatment within IRAs. However, because you have some cost basis in your IRAs from the after-tax contributions, not all of your withdrawals will be taxable.

To determine how much of a withdrawal is taxable, simply calculate what percentage after-tax deposits make up of your IRA balances. For example, if you have $20,000 of after-tax contributions and your IRAs total $200,000, then 10% of your IRA account has already been taxed. Ninety percent of any withdrawal you make will be taxable as ordinary income and will be taxed based on your income tax bracket.

Double Trouble

Jerry, who is retired and collects Social Security and a pension, unexpectedly had to pull $10,000 out of his annuity. Now he has double tax trouble.

Jerry has two different taxes about which he needs to be concerned. First, there is the income tax due on the $10,000 he withdrew from the annuity. Second, there is the income tax that could be due on his Social Security. Let's start with the Social Security.

Some retirees pay no income taxes on their Social Security benefits, whereas some can pay as much as 30% in federal income taxes. It all depends on how much other income a person has.

To determine what portion of Social Security is taxable, the Internal Revenue Service looks at "provisional income." Your provisional income is determined by adding all of your taxable income plus any tax-exempt interest you may have received plus one-half of your Social Security benefits. When this number exceeds a certain threshold, your benefits start becoming taxable. That threshold is $32,000 if you're married and file a joint return or $25,000 if you're single.

Once your provisional income exceeds the threshold limit, a portion of your benefits becomes taxable. From $32,000 to $44,000, up to 50% of your benefits become taxable. Provisional income above $44,000 results in up to 85% of your benefits being taxable. For singles, the numbers are $25,000 and $34,000, respectively.

As you can see, additional income, such as Jerry's withdrawal from an annuity, can create additional taxes on Social Security benefits. With regard to the tax treatment of Jerry's $10,000 withdrawal, any withdrawal from an annuity is treated as gain first and return of deposit second. If Jerry's gain in the annuity is $10,000 or more, his withdrawal is taxable as ordinary income.

On the other hand, if Jerry's gain is less than $10,000, only the gain is taxable as ordinary income. The remainder is treated as a return of premium, which is tax-free.

Forget Whole Life Insurance as a Retirement Vehicle

There are several excellent retirement saving vehicles discussed in these pages. Whole life insurance is not one of them.

Joe received some strange advice from a "financial planner." The so-called planner, who is actually an insurance salesman, told Joe that he should reduce his 401(k) and Roth IRA contributions and put the difference in a whole life insurance policy.

The planner/salesman told Joe that the long-term tax benefits are better in whole life than in the retirement accounts. This sounded odd to Joe, so he hasn't acted on the advice.

Joe is wisely thinking twice about this sales pitch disguised as great financial advice.

Countless people have accumulated large amounts of money in their 401(k)s and IRAs and are comfortably retired because of the money they stashed away in these plans.

Only a few lucky people have successfully used life insurance as a primary means to accumulate wealth. Who are these lucky people? They all happen to be life insurance salespeople.

Nevertheless, if someone has a need for life insurance, then by all means that person should buy life insurance before doing anything else. If Joe does this, he should find a low-cost term insurance policy. He should also max out his retirement accounts before buying a whole life policy, if he ever does decide to buy one.

Most people don't need life insurance throughout their lifetime—they need it only while they are working and supporting a family. There are times when whole life insurance makes sense, but 9 times out of 10, people would be better off using cheap term insurance and investing in tax-favored retirement plans. Whole life policies do offer some unique tax benefits, but 401(k)s and Roth IRAs should be used first.

Most people are better off buying term insurance and investing the difference.

How to Beat the Gift Tax

You've worked many years and paid huge amounts of taxes during your working life. Now you're set. You have more than enough in financial resources to take care of you and your spouse for the rest of your lives. There's just one thing: How can you help your kids without running up another big tax bill?

That was the problem that confronted Sara and Joel. They were planning to give gifts of $10,000 or more (possibly as much as $20,000) to each of their two adult children and wanted to know how to minimize the gift tax.

There will be no tax consequences if they keep their gifts within limits. Each person can give to another person up to $11,000 per year without triggering any gift taxes. That means Sara can give $11,000 to each of their children, and Joel can give $11,000 to each of their children.

If their gifts exceed $11,000 per year, per recipient, then they will trigger a gift tax. Each person can give up to $1 million during his or her lifetime, in addition to the $11,000 per year. By the way, it makes sense to talk these things over with your tax advisor because tax rules are always changing.

Once a person's gifts exceed $1 million, gifts become taxable to the donor, but not to the recipient. Gift tax rates run as high as 47%. Try your best to avoid this. Everyone—rich, poor, and in-between—already pays plenty in taxes.

Baby Boomers Bankrupted?

First, it was that house. Then it was providing for the kids. After that, it was that car that you just had to have. Sound familiar? It is the story of tens of millions of baby boomers who always talk about saving tomorrow. This generation could be called the *tomorrow generation*.

Many of us are always buying something. We rationalize that whatever it is, it is critically important at that moment. So we put off savings—especially retirement savings. Well, now many of the "I'll do it tomorrow" boomers are running out of tomorrows. They're in their 50s and want to retire soon. But they have little in savings.

Larry and Suzanne are both successful professionals. They have made good money throughout their lives. They have a nice home, three vehicles—one is an RV—and have just finished putting their two kids through college.

But, unfortunately for Larry and Suzanne, they have little in savings. Now, about 20 years late, they are ready to do something about it. Their only debts now are a home mortgage with $18,000 and a $20,000 RV loan. Although they agree that it's time to get going, they are disagreeing over how to do it. Suzanne wants to pay off the house first, then the RV loan. She then would put what's left over into the IRAs. Larry says max the IRAs first. After that, he wants to pay off the house and RV loans.

Larry and Suzanne are examples of this "worry about it tomorrow" lifestyle that is seemingly everywhere in our culture. Larry and Suzanne should save for retirement, regardless of how much debt they have. If you always wait until all your debts are paid before you save, you'll never save enough for retirement.

Retirement savings need to be a higher priority than an RV or other expenditures. Put aside a minimum of 10% of your income toward retirement savings. If you don't, you may find that you won't have a choice but to work well into your 70s.

Look Closely at Investment Taxes

It happens just about every year. Sometimes it's big. Sometimes it's small. But it happens just about every year. Congress tweaks the tax code. Sometimes—as in the 1980s under President Reagan—it is more than a tweaking; it is major surgery. But whether it is big or small, tax changes could have huge implications for your investments.

Any time there is a tax change given to us by Capitol Hill, it's smart to look at your savings and investment strategies to see whether any adjustments are necessary.

For example, Bob says that even though his employer doesn't match any of his contributions to his 401(k), he has been putting money in his retirement plan. That's because it is made with pretax dollars and the tax on the contribution and earnings will be deferred. However, recently the tax rate on dividends and capital gains was lowered to 15%. Now the 401(k) distribution will be still taxed as ordinary income.

Bob's current marginal tax rate is 25%. So if he invests money outside of a retirement account instead of 401(k), any capital gain and dividend will be taxed at a lower rate now rather than at a higher rate as ordinary income when Bob retires. Now, in certain circumstances, it appears that tax-deferred investing isn't as good a deal as when capital gains tax rates were much higher.

One of the primary benefits of the 401(k) is the tax deductibility of the deposits. Every dollar that is saved is a dollar that is reduced from your taxable income, thereby lowering your tax bill. Because of this tax savings, many people are able to save more per paycheck than they could otherwise.

Consider the following example. Suppose you are putting $1,000 per year into your 401(k). If you chose to take that money and invest it somewhere else, the $1,000 would be taxed. It would be added onto your W-2 at the end of the year. At a 25% marginal tax rate, you would have to pay $250 in taxes and would be left with only $750 to save.

As a 401(k) investor saving $1,000 a year, you would have an account balance of $14,486 after 10 years, assuming an 8% growth rate. The 401(k) account would be taxable and after a 25% tax reduction, the after-tax balance would be $10,865.

The non-401(k) investor has only $750 per year to save, so after 10 years, that investor's account balance is $10,865, the exact amount you have remaining. However, the non-401(k) investor still has capital gains and dividend taxes to worry about. Assuming a 15% tax on capital gains, the tax bill would be $505, leaving the investor with $10,360.

As you can see from the previous example, it's typically a good idea to use an employer's 401(k), regardless of whether there is a match. The one time it does not make sense is if an investor is in a lower tax bracket today but believes he or she will be in a higher tax bracket in the future. For the time being, Bob has continued making contributions to his 401(k), although he now watches Congress almost as closely as he watches his investments.

Looking for a Tax Haven? Stay Where You Are

Municipal bonds belong in many portfolios, especially those of conservative investors. Others who can potentially benefit from municipals are those who just want to lower the risk level of a portfolio or those who find themselves surrendering much of their investment gains each April 15th.

The key element in why these fixed-income investments work is that they can be free of almost all taxes. You can sidestep federal taxes. And, if you are living in the state and city in which the municipal bonds were issued, then you avoid both state and city taxes on your investment. In fact, you miss all investment taxes. So the return you get is actually a good deal better than what the bond is paying. Rates of return on municipal bonds often have been around 4% or 5%. However, the returns are actually a little better than that. That can mean municipal bonds are a good deal for someone in a high tax bracket who often pays a lot in investment taxes. You will pay state taxes on a municipal bond if you reside outside of the state.

Municipal bonds also have their downside. As with all bond investments, they generally pay less than stocks, unless the stock market is declining. (That's one reason to have some bonds even in an aggressive portfolio because although stocks usually beat bonds, there will be years in which bond returns beat stocks.)

Municipal bonds are generally considered a fairly safe investment. That's because the state or city issuing them has pledged that these obligations must receive top priority for repayment. Still, it's good to check on the credit worthiness of any bond you might buy. You want to be sure that a bond issuer have an investment grade that is at least BBB or BAA. These are some of the ratings given by the two main bond-rating agencies, Standard & Poor's and Moodys.

Prepare for Next Year's Taxes This Year

Tax planning should be a year-round concern. That's because whether we like it or not, we all have a perpetual partner with our family's finances— the tax collector.

Most Americans choose to ignore that partner until April 15, but the best time to make tax plans is prior to January 1.

Unlike other types of partners, we cannot negotiate with the tax collector. The only thing we can do is plan ahead to ensure that we pay no more than our fair share.

Late in the year is actually a good time to start tax planning. The techniques you employ during this calendar year can have a dramatic impact on your tax bite for next April. Here are a few things that you can do to lower your income tax bill.

Pay your state and local income taxes early. For whatever reason, the IRS lets you include any state and local income taxes paid in your itemized deductions. If you pay $1,000 in state and local income taxes throughout the year, you can deduct that $1,000 against your income for determining your federal income taxes. That savings can range from $150 to $350 per $1,000 paid. It all depends on the tax bracket. One gets the deduction only on what one actually paid during the year, not on what one owes.

Harvest tax losses. If you have been an investor in the stock market during the past few years, some holdings are possibly worth less than what you paid for them. By selling the holding this year, you can lock in those losses for your income tax return. One can use an unlimited amount of losses to offset capital gains, but one can deduct only a maximum of $3,000 worth of losses where there are no gains. Many investors will sell a stock near the end of the year simply for a tax deduction. You cannot repurchase the same security within 30 days, but you can purchase a similar security. For example, someone might sell Home Depot and purchase Lowe's. The stocks won't track with each other exactly, but will probably move in a similar direction. After 30 days the Lowe's stock can be sold and the Home Depot stock can be repurchased. Harvesting tax losses in this way can save thousands in income taxes.

Give to charities. Fortunately, our government thinks it is a good idea for Americans to give to charities. If you itemize on income taxes, you can deduct whatever you give to charities against your income for determining your income taxes. Depending on your combined federal and state income tax bracket, you could save up to $450 in taxes for every $1,000 given away. Planning on making large gifts to charity? Consider giving appreciated property or securities rather than cash. Typically, you can deduct the current market value of a security or other asset. And that's regardless of how much gain you've had in the asset. For example, suppose you paid $100 for a stock that is now worth $1,000. You can give the stock away and take a $1,000 deduction. You will not owe any capital gains taxes, even though you had a tremendous gain. Giving money to charities is not only good for your taxes but also good for you. Giving money to the needy can help you keep a proper perspective about your own money and life.

Don't forget deductions for business owners. If you own and operate a business, whether it is a large corporation or a small, home-based business, year-end planning is critical. Equipment, supplies, and so forth that are purchased before the New Year can frequently be deducted. The tax law allows small businesses to deduct up to $100,000 worth of business equipment that would otherwise need to be depreciated. That means a home-based business can purchase a new computer, furniture, and other equipment and deduct the full amount against this year's income.

Roth IRA conversion is another potential tax-saving opportunity. Converting money to a Roth IRA will not reduce income taxes on next year's return; it will increase them. So why do it? Because it could reduce your long-term aggregate tax bill. If you are in a low tax bracket this year, but figure you'll be in a higher tax bracket in the future, it might be a good idea to convert a portion of your IRAs to a Roth IRA. You'll pay taxes on the conversion, but paying taxes this year could dramatically reduce your taxes in the future.

There are other techniques that can be employed to reduce your income taxes. But don't wait until April to do your income tax planning. The best planning is done now, while you still have a chance to reduce your tax bill.

States Serious About Residency Requirements

Who doesn't want to escape from high tax states? That's why tens of millions of Americans move from them to lower tax states. Jan and David want to move from California to avoid the high state taxes, which are eating into David's annuity payments.

With plans of retiring, and because David would like to spend a year sailing, they are thinking of establishing residency in the less taxing state of Florida (maybe for a year). But they intend to keep their house in California.

Jan and David aren't the first ones to think up this tax-avoidance strategy. Establishing residency in another state to avoid California income tax can be a little tricky. If one doesn't actually leave the state but merely sets up a P.O. Box or other mail drop in another state, one may find oneself in a mess with the California Franchise Tax Board.

What makes you a resident of a state? A resident of a state is where you have your primary residence. There are few clear-cut guidelines that will ensure treatment as a primary residence.

Consider doing the following: Change your address for everything to your new address; register to vote; register your vehicles; set up a checking account; get a driver's license; and join a church, synagogue, or civic group. Once you physically move, you can establish residency from that day forward.

Florida has some of the lowest taxes anywhere, which is one reason why it is one of the fastest growing states. But Florida isn't quite Utopia. Although it has no income or sales tax, it does have property taxes, so Jan and David shouldn't think they'll be able to avoid all taxes. Furthermore, there are certain types of income that may be subject to California income tax. So Jan and David should consult a tax professional before they make a major move and maybe even go over it with their attorney.

Superfluous Life Insurance

You buy garden-variety life insurance to protect your family or spouse or anyone who would be hurt should you die and your earning power be removed from the household. If the primary breadwinner dies and he or she has no life insurance, then the family may face serious financial problems. The standard of living of the survivors declines. Besides the grief accompanying the death, there is the added misery of family members trying to maintain a decent standard of living.

Adequate life insurance would prevent that. However, there may come a time when the protection offered by life insurance would no longer be necessary. That time comes for many when there is no longer an income stream that is dependent on a living person. Life insurance is designed to replace an income in the event of one's death. When someone is young and working, life insurance can guarantee the future earnings of one's life. During retirement, life insurance can replace a pension that may cease upon death. When a person is not working and has no pension, there is little income that may be lost. In that case, there is no need for life insurance to replace an income.

Your house is paid off. The kids are no longer kids, but adults who have good jobs and take care of themselves. You and your spouse have accumulated considerable financial assets and property so that neither will have to worry. In this case, life insurance is probably superfluous unless there is some special need such as having money available to pay some expensive bill in the future. Otherwise, you should think seriously about canceling the life insurance, especially because as you age the life insurance rates are likely to rise.

Although many retirees don't need life insurance, there are some who do. Life insurance can be used quite effectively for estate planning for those with estates subject to estate taxes.

Tax Avoidance Strategies for Your Children

The government, in its relentless pursuit of money to fund its various crackpot schemes, finds endless ways to take more and more of your hard-earned property. That's even after you've met your Maker and spent a lifetime keeping Uncle Whiskers fat and happy.

Currently, millions of elderly Americans have considerable financial assets—much of them in qualified accounts such as IRAs—but are unsure how they can pass these assets to children without creating family, legal, or tax problems. For example, tax law bars direct rollovers from a parent's IRA to a child's IRA.

Passing assets or property to the next generation can be a dicey proposition. When Joe Don Robbie, the former owner of the Miami Dolphins died, his beneficiaries had to sell the team to pay the estate taxes. Most small American businesses don't make it from one generation to the next. Taxes are a big reason.

There is a way to give your children your IRA. And it can be done without starting a family argument and in a way that might help them defer and reduce taxes. Put your IRA or IRAs in a living trust. Name your children as the beneficiaries. This can be a very smart strategy that will give your grateful offspring another reason to smile when they think of their dear departed mom and pop.

And when you can no longer avoid that pressing appointment with St. Peter, the IRAs will be split as many ways as you have children.

This can also avoid arguing among siblings as the proceeds are split equally. One child may take all of his or her windfall and buy a house. Another may use it to pay off intolerably high credit card bills. A third child can use these IRAs as a tax dodge that could last forever because the IRA can, in the right circumstances, go as long as "The Simpsons."

The tax authorities will require a minimum withdrawal from the IRA each year based on life expectancy. But, if an IRA has good investments, it could go for decades, providing a steady stream of income for one or more of your children in a tax-advantaged environment.

It's almost as good as life after death.

The Advantage of Fixed Annuities

Fixed annuities have their disadvantages. The same as with some annuities, they can be expensive to set up and maintain. In the case of the fixed annuity, the rate doesn't change. So you could start out with an adequate income stream. However, if you income needs change, you could be stuck with a problem—not enough income.

Provided the income stream you have is sufficient, your principal is safe with a fixed annuity. There is no need to worry about an investment decision. The issuing insurance company guarantees fixed annuities, and the investment is protected.

There are some positive features of fixed annuities, and some negative ones. The benefits of fixed annuities, which are easy to understand, are guaranteed returns, tax-deferred growth, and avoidance of probate. You really can't get hurt buying a fixed annuity as long as the issuing insurance company is in good shape.

The disadvantages are that most annuities are long-term investments, with surrender charges that last several years. If you need to withdraw your funds early, you could get hit with charges as high as 7%. Furthermore, interest earned on fixed annuities is only tax deferred, not tax-free. Income tax on the interest will be due either when you withdraw the money or when your heirs do.

What most fixed-annuity investors don't understand is that if they buy an annuity contract when interest rates are low, the interest rate on the annuity could remain low, even if market interest rates rise. Many insurance companies match their investments with annuity deposits. That means the insurance company locks in long-term investments to match their obligations on the annuities. What an insurance company might offer a new annuity purchaser in the future, when interest rates may be higher, could be substantially different from what it pays to existing annuity holders.

There are times when fixed annuities are an appropriate investment, but they are not for everyone. Too often, banks push them as an alternative to lower yielding, short-term bank deposit accounts.

The Answer for Estate Taxes

Karen wants to know if her 79-year-old mother is receiving good estate-planning advice. Her mother's financial advisor is recommending she purchase a life insurance trust to pay for estate taxes. Karen is having difficulty understanding why her elderly mother would need life insurance.

Life insurance can be a great source of cash to pay estate taxes, particularly for those estates that are tied up in nonliquid assets, such as real estate. If Karen's mother's taxable estate exceeds a certain amount (the amount is often changing), her estate could be subject to estate taxes. And if estate taxes are triggered, the taxes will be due within 9 months of her death.

Life insurance proceeds are income-tax free, but if Karen's mother is the owner of her policy (as in most situations), the proceeds will be included in her taxable estate. If her estate is large, up to 55% of the life insurance proceeds could be lost to estate taxes.

By having someone other than Karen's mother own the policy (such as Karen or a trust), the proceeds will not be includable in the estate and will not be subject to estate taxes.

If the mother's estate is large, using life insurance that is owned by an Irrevocable Life Insurance Trust (ILIT) to pay estate taxes might be a prudent planning technique. But if her estate is not large, life insurance may not be necessary and an ILIT may not be cost effective.

The Downside of the Annuity

Buying an annuity contract is a logical move for many who are planning for retirement. It can provide a steady income stream. Annuities are backed by some of the strongest financial institutions in America (insurance companies, unlike banks, were not failing during the Great Depression). Still, annuities also have disadvantages, especially if your retirement plan changes and you have to terminate the contract.

It's easy to get into an annuity. It's getting out of one without losing your shirt that can be the tricky part. To get your cash out of the annuity, you need to request a full surrender from the insurance company. Unless you've owned the annuity for years, you'll probably get slapped with early-withdrawal penalties. Furthermore, any gain you have in the annuity will be taxed as ordinary income, not as capital gains. In addition, the gain will be subject to a 10% federal penalty because you are not age 59½.

There is no way you can avoid the taxes on your earnings. You can defer the taxes by leaving the money in the annuity; nevertheless, one day the earnings will be taxed. (You can learn more about the specific details by reading IRS Publications 575 and 939.)

Be sure you fully understand how annuities work before you purchase one. If you buy one (or, as in most cases, are sold one) and decide you don't like it, it can be expensive to unwind.

The Relative Importance of Tax Deductions

The United States was started by a bunch of hotheads who hated taxes. They railed and bayed about taxation without representation, then dumped taxed tea in Boston Harbor.

More than 2 centuries later, despite all the hype about taxes as the price of civilization, the American tradition of detesting taxes continues. But it sometimes takes counterproductive forms. Take the home mortgage deduction. Many Americans believe it is a great idea to buy big houses. Their reasoning is the bigger the mortgage interest deduction, the better off they will be. This is a mistake. The tax deductibility of anything can help—but only on the margins.

Tax breaks shouldn't be the primary reason why one buys property or makes an investment. Rarely should anyone do something just for the tax implications of the action.

Indeed, making massive mortgage interest payments just to get a tax deduction is a waste of money. No red-blooded American wants to pay more taxes than is necessary. But given the choice of paying $1 to the government or $3 to The Very Large Bank, you may be better off giving the dollar to Uncle Whiskers.

There is not a one-to-one relationship between mortgage interest payments and income taxes. When you pay your $600 interest payment to the bank, you don't get to reduce your income taxes by that amount. You get to reduce your income by that amount. When you include the interest payments as an itemized deduction on your taxes, the interest charges reduce your taxable income, which will in turn reduce your taxes.

If having a small mortgage is good for your taxes, then having a large mortgage must be even better. Why not refinance for a $100,000 loan? Or a $200,000 loan? Think of the tax savings you could receive! Yeah, and think of the debt you will run up. And even if a deduction is grand, there is one looming danger—it can always be abolished or reduced. The home mortgage deduction, which I doubt will ever be discontinued, has been reduced over the years.

Twenty-five years ago, billions of dollars went into limited partnerships that lost tons of money. That's because in the 1970s and 1980s these dicey partnerships offered huge tax breaks. Then something terrible happened—the government decided to withdraw almost all of the tax breaks under the tax reform act of the Reagan era. Many people and businesses were ruined.

The Taxing Implications of Selling Property

Bob is a small capitalist living in San Francisco. He bought a pair of apartments or, as he puts it, a "set of flats" (a single structure that includes two units). Both units are rented. Bob finds tax law (as do most Americans) confusing. He believes that, as an owner, he can claim tax relief if he occupies the dwelling for 2 out of 5 years, that is, if the structure is sold within the 5 years.

But here comes the confusing part. He wants to live in one unit for 2 years while renting the other, then move into the second unit for 2 years (again renting the other), and then sell the flats within the following year. He hopes that this strategy will allow him to write off the building, and the gains that come from selling it, as a primary residence, qualifying him for capital gains exclusion.

Well, maybe. The Taxpayer Relief Act of 1997 allows individuals to exclude from income capital gains of up to $250,000 on the sale of a primary residence. For a property to qualify as a personal residence, one must have lived in the home 2 out of the last 5 years.

But the problem Bob may encounter is not the 2- out of 5-year rule, but another stipulation that states he can only take advantage of this exclusion once every 2 years. However, if Bob sells both flats at the same time, he will only qualify for the exclusion on one of the flats, not on both. One way to avoid the tax is to sell the flats separately, with the sales occurring at least 2 years apart.

Use Tax Breaks Carefully

What's your biggest bill? Well, if you live in an average state in the Northeast or in California, it could be taxes. So, you should take maximum advantage of tax breaks whenever you can. Don't spend money or sell property just to take advantage of a tax break, but use the latter whenever you can and in a way that maximizes the tax reduction.

For example, there is the $250,000 capital gains exclusion one gets for selling a primary residence. It's double that if you are married.

If you have more than one home (and the taxing authorities of the IRS say you have only one primary residence), be sure to live in the one that will give you the biggest tax break if you are going to sell a home. Some lucky people split their time between two homes.

You can have only one primary residence (hence the term primary). The one the IRS will consider as your primary residence is the one you treat as your primary home.

There is no one thing that determines whether a home is your primary residence, but there are many factors that come under consideration: Your primary residence will most likely be the home where your mail is delivered, you are registered to vote, your friends send notes and cards, you register your cars, the IRS sends your tax documents, you receive W-2s and 1099s.

If you plan to sell one of your homes, you can avoid up to $250,000 of gains ($500,000 if you are married) if you have lived in that home as your primary residence at least 2 of the past 5 years. If the home you want to sell was not your primary residence, you'll have to convert it to your primary residence and wait for at least 2 years to sell it to avoid the taxes. Remember; sell the home that yields the biggest potential gains and the biggest potential tax savings.

Weigh Your Needs with Life Insurance

Jennifer is 61 years old and married. She is thinking about canceling her $100,000 life insurance, which will stop at age 70. The insurance company will require a new physical evaluation and premiums will be whatever is in effect for her age at that time.

Jennifer thinks that maybe she should change the policy to one that does not have the above stipulations, or cancel and set aside the premiums into a savings account (to cover cremation) and rely on her IRA to sustain her husband upon her death.

If an insurance policy should be necessary upon Jennifer's death, then the best type of insurance is the type that will actually be in force when she dies. If there's a strong possibility that her existing policy may not be in force upon her death, then the current policy may be a waste of money.

If Jennifer has plenty of other assets and her husband could survive financially without her, there is little need for $100,000 of life insurance. If her only goal is to provide for cremation costs, she should be able to cover those costs with much less than $100,000 (unless Jennifer wants her ashes flown to the moon).

It wouldn't take Jennifer much time to save enough money to cover her cremation costs. Once she has enough funds set aside to meet her family's goals, she may want to drop her life insurance altogether.

Where's Your Retirement Account?

God knows we already pay beaucoup taxes. And, given the pricey wars we wage and the obligations of our welfare state, higher taxes—either directly through taxes or through inflation—are likely on the way. So, because you plan on saving for retirement anyway, why not take advantage of every tax break you can get?

The government offers tax breaks for every member of the family who is saving for retirement and has earned income, and you should use every one of them. Yet many people don't. There are millions of people who have access to a 401(k) plan at work, with a generous employer ready to match your contributions to a certain point, and yet they don't think they can afford to contribute.

Actually, it's the reverse. Most people can't afford not to contribute to a plan. A financial planner, who advises businesses how to set up these plans, believes that it is critical to convince employees to contribute to the 401(k). "For many of them," he said, "this will be their only chance to accumulate significant retirement assets."

There are situations in which the husband takes maximum advantage of retirement savings break at work and with his own IRA plan, but his wife saves nothing—and vice-versa.

Here is a case where the maximum advantage—both in savings and in tax benefits—will come from the husband and wife working together. Each must do his or her part; otherwise, the couple won't have enough savings when they want to retire.

A good starting point for retirement savings is 10% of your combined income. The bottom line is that both must save for retirement, and the company's 401(k) usually is the best solution.

There may not be much money left over each month, but even families with relatively small incomes are sometimes able to save greater than 10% of their income. Conversely, there are families that make huge incomes and have nothing in retirement savings. The key is establishing a goal and sticking with it.

If you have a spouse who doesn't get this, there's a simple technique to get his or her attention. Tell your husband or wife that either he or she starts putting money into his 401(k), or he or she can keep working until age 80.

Where Will You Be When You're in Your 80s?

Cathy likes to plan ahead. She and her husband are both in their early 60s and in good health. But Cathy is thinking about the potential perils of getting older. "Old age," said Charles De Gaulle, the famous French leader, "is a shipwreck."

To avoid any shipwrecks, Cathy was thinking about purchasing a long-term care insurance policy. But the premiums for Cathy and her husband would be very high.

Cathy should begin with a question: What would be the costs of not having long-term care insurance? In the event that either she or her husband should ever have to go into a skilled nursing facility or require home health care, the costs would be staggering, easily exceeding $40,000 to $50,000 per year. Long-term care (LTC) insurance can be purchased to pay some or all of those costs, should the need ever arise. The decision to purchase LTC insurance should be based on several factors. For starters, could Cathy afford the care if she or her spouse ever needed it? If the answer is yes, she may not need the insurance. It is a question that tens of millions of Americans, many of whom are living longer than they imagined they would, must also answer.

If the answer is no, then you should seriously consider purchasing the insurance. Are you married or single? If you're married, you certainly wouldn't want LTC to drain your savings, leaving your spouse with nothing to live on. But if you're single, you may not care if the costs of LTC eat up your savings.

LTC insurance should be considered in every retirement plan, but it is not for everyone. Figure out what your financial life would look like if $150,000 or more were spent on LTC. If that dollar amount would wipe you out, purchasing the insurance would be a prudent move.

Who Gets the Life Insurance and the IRAs?

If you're married, the decision of who is the primary beneficiary for your life insurance and IRA is obvious—your spouse. But the contingent beneficiary can be a trying decision. Maybe you want to list your children. Maybe you want to set up a trust that would take care of your children.

Your decision to list your trust as a beneficiary is dependent on whether you want the trust to direct what happens to your IRAs and life insurance after you die.

When families have young children at home, listing a trust as the beneficiary is prudent. That's because a trust can provide guidance as to how and when the dollars can be used. A trust can ensure that the children won't receive all of their inheritance on their 18th birthday, an event that could be unfortunate.

Once the children are grown and capable of making financial decisions, it is typically advisable to simply list the children as beneficiaries. Otherwise, the children may have to deal with a trust that can be both time-consuming and costly to maintain and administer.

Because every situation is unique, it's a good idea to consult an attorney before making this choice. Even if your children are grown, there may be a reason why you would want to list a trust as a beneficiary.

Chapter 8
Grow an Investment Portfolio

Making wise investments is obviously important, but not the most important thing to know.

Unless you're extremely lucky you're not going to get rich by picking the right investments. You're going to build net worth through all the other painful choices that most people need to make, such as living on less of your income than you could otherwise, staying out of debt, and delayed gratification. You must separate your wants from your needs. That's how you build net worth and that's how you get financial independence. Not by picking the right investments. You're not going to pick the right investments if you're taking big risks trying to hit a home run. That's when you can blow up your portfolio.

A Fool and His Money

Wall Street is always coming up with new schemes to separate you from your money. Market timing—the idea that someone can consistently pick market lows and highs, getting clients in or out at precisely the right moment—is such an old scheme that it's almost new. But whenever and wherever the charlatans offer this crackpot idea, you must disdain it just as you would a politician who promises to cut your taxes while expanding government's spending.

The case for market timing is that it can work. And indeed it can—over short periods. However, the reason market timing can't work over the long term is that you have to be right all of the time. No one is right all the time.

Market timing cannot reduce risk. On the contrary, market timing will increase risk. Moving in and out of investments is wonderful if you make the right decisions, but what happens if you make the wrong decisions? Risk is reduced through diversification.

In 1998, the bear market erased the myth of market timing. Most market-timing managers didn't get out before the market dipped. Also in 1998 there was a hedge fund named Long-Term Capital Management run by two winners of the Nobel Prize in Economic Sciences who thought they could time the bond market. With all of their brilliance, they managed to lose over $3 billion and caused a global currency crisis. If guys with Nobel Prizes can't figure it out, how can a local investment advisor?

Most pension plans, foundations, endowments, and the like use an investment strategy that stresses diversification among a broad array of investments. There may be minor adjustments to their allocations from time to time, but they do not manage money by moving in and out of different investments. It is expensive to move in and out of investments. You're charged commissions and other transaction costs whenever you jump in or out of markets.

Diversified portfolios may not get you rich, but they'll keep you from becoming poor.

Annuity Woes

The best financial products can blow up if someone buys them without thinking about the long-term tax implications. For example, an annuity as a tax deferral vehicle can work, but without careful planning it can just as easily become a headache. The latter is what happened to Doug and Lee.

This husband and wife have been retired for several years and have been living on their pensions and Social Security. About 10 years ago, they deposited $75,000 into an annuity. It is now worth some $160,000. Now they would like to supplement their income by taking some money out of the annuity, but they don't want to increase their taxable income.

Tax-deferred annuities usually work great for reducing current income taxes. However, without careful planning, they can hit you with big tax bills in later years. All of the interest that has been accumulated in their policy will one day be subject to income tax. The key is to keep that tax to a minimum.

Doug and Lee can receive income from an annuity one of two ways: The first method would be to set up a systematic withdrawal of a fixed dollar amount. When money is withdrawn from an annuity, all of their interest comes out before any principal. So, until they've withdrawn all of the interest, 100% of the withdrawals will be subject to income taxes.

The second method would be to annuitize the policy. That means Doug and Lee give up control of the principal in return for a fixed dollar amount for a specified period, such as a fixed number of years. Their monthly income from the annuity will be only partially taxable—a portion of the income treated as a return of principal.

Both methods have their pros and cons, and it's up to Doug and Lee—along with their tax advisor—to decide which method is best for them. The longer they defer their income in the annuity, the larger the taxable income may be down the road.

Backdoor Roth IRA

When does income qualify as earned income even though you weren't actually working at a job? That, in essence, is what Gary was recently able to do. He was able to claim earned income for a job that he no longer had. Therefore, he was able to able to open a Roth IRA.

Gary retired from a major airline several years ago. He had only worked for a short time under a contract that provided him with stock options based on company profitability. Four years ago he exercised some of those options. In doing so, he determined that this money came to him as ordinary income, subject to federal and state income taxes as well as FICA payroll taxes.

But Gary wasn't sure if this deferred income qualified him to open a Roth IRA for last year. That's because he never actually turned a wheel for his former employer in the last tax year. Part of Gary's compensation package from the airline was in the form of stock options. And, because our taxing authorities view the financial gain derived from the options as the same as wage compensation, they tax it with FICA payroll taxes and issue a W-2.

Here was the good news for Gary. Any income he received that was reported on Form W-2 was considered wage income. Therefore, this entitles Gary to contribute to a Roth or traditional IRA.

One doesn't necessarily need to work to have wage income. Any time someone receives a W-2, he or she has wages. In addition, some types of alimony may even qualify as wage income. This means that even if you don't work but receive alimony, you may be entitled to make an IRA contribution.

Bewildered in Belmont

James Leer lives in Belmont, a suburban community. Like millions of other Americans, he is relatively new to stock investing.

James is trying to determine how to use a stock's P/E ratio. He's researched several stocks with P/E ratios ranging from 7 to 43. He doesn't know how to make any sense of these numbers.

A stock's P/E ratio is one of many yardsticks that can be used to evaluate if a stock is currently a bargain or overpriced. The P/E ratio is calculated by dividing a stock's price by its earnings. For example, a company that is currently trading at $20 per share and earned $1 per share last year would have a P/E ratio of 20.

Companies that have high P/E ratios are priced high relative to their earnings and generally are considered more speculative.

A shortcoming of the P/E ratio is that it looks at what a company earned yesterday, not what it will earn tomorrow. When you purchase a stock, you should be much more concerned about what the company will earn in the future.

For example, you may be willing to pay a premium for a stock that is expected to grow its earnings over the next few years, but would probably want to pay a discount for a stock whose earnings are expected to decline.

In the long run, the overall performance of a stock will be tied directly to the company's earnings. You'll want to own stocks that have not only current strong earnings but also good growth on those earnings.

Compounding

Imagine a pond in your garden with a floating lily pad that doubles in size every day. If it takes 80 days for the lily to entirely cover the pond, on which day is half the pond still uncovered, open to the sun and the outside? Answer: the 79th day.

Compounding is the process of earning a rate of return on your invested money, and then reinvesting those earnings to realize an aggregate rate of return. This can be done with dividends, interest, or new contributions. For example, a $100 investment earning compound interest at 10% a year would total $110 at the end of the first year, and $121 at the end of the second year, and so on. The actual formula is: compound sum = (principal) (1 + interest rate), to the Nth power—where N equals the number of years.

The essence of the formula is that, on a regular basis, a return is earned not only on the original amount but also on all previously accumulated earnings. You earn a return on your return. The typical compounding table below shows you how a single investment of $10,000 will grow at various rates of return. Five percent is what you might get from a bond; 10% is about the average historical return of the stock market, and 16% would have been possible over the last 20 years.

GROWING AT:			
Year	5%	10%	15%
1	$10,000	$10,000	$10,000
5	$12,800	$16,100	$20,100
10	$16,300	$25,900	$40,500
15	$20,800	$41,800	$81,400
25	$33,900	$108,300	$329,200

A simple way to figure how long it takes your money to double is the Rule of 72. Divide the number 72 by the interest rate, or rate of return, you anticipate earning. The result is the number of years it takes your money to double. For example, if you are earning 10%, your money will double in 7.2 years. If you are earning 12%, it takes only 6 years for your money to double.

Diversification Is an Essential of Good Investing

Your stocks or other investments go up; you get excited and pour more money into them. Your good investments run into some temporary problems; you jump ship and sell. This is the exact opposite of what good investors should do.

Carmen contributed the maximum to her employer's 401(k) plan and has amassed quite a large balance. But the majority of Carmen's money is invested in her company's stock, which has almost doubled in the past 4 years.

Carmen should diversify her 401(k), but she hesitates to do this because the stock has done so well. The stock has performed well over the past 15 years, but that stock has not been the star performer Carmen believes.

Carmen's 401(k) plan, if it is like most, probably has some type of diversified stock portfolio as an option. Had she been invested in that option, she would have actually achieved higher returns than her company stock returned.

Furthermore, Carmen would have been diversified into several hundred companies (as opposed to just one). Carmen's employer provides her income, medical and dental, and retirement. Is it really wise for her to tie most of her savings to her employer as well? Carmen is thinking it over.

Don't Go Wrong!

You want to find people who solve your financial problems. And to the extent that advisors understand how to solve problems, the more effective they are. Often, advisors listen to clients and then tell them what they want to hear, instead of trying to understand their clients' needs and then educating clients as to what is in their best financial interest.

A good example is the typical stockbroker who pushes products designed to fit most every financial situation. This type of stockbroker typically has a credenza lined with prospectuses and financial sales literature. When a new prospect walks in the door and wants an investment that can provide growth and income, this broker picks a growth and income mutual fund off the shelf. But when the prospect rejects it saying, "No, I think I want a tax advantage," the broker regroups and reaches back to the shelf to select a variable annuity product. If the investor now says he or she wants tax-free income, the broker obliges by pulling municipal bond sales literature off the shelf. The broker is really just a product pusher. If, instead, the broker would take the time to understand his or her prospect's specific needs, and then take a firm stand on what type of investment would (in his opinion) best fit those needs, he or she would have a much higher level of success.

Don't Trust Averages

For 11 years, Dr. and Mrs. Greene had been in the Merrill Lynch Select Professional program. "It's supposed to be their highest level of retail program," Dr. Greene began.

The year was 1991, toward the end of the bull market and the Greenes were upset because they hadn't made any money—at least not the amount they have been promised. The broker had told them they were making about 11% a year. However, Mrs. Greene, who was pretty sharp in math, said, "My figures showed we were way under 11%, so we had an actuary figure the rate of return on every year simply by taking all the cash inflows, beginning balance, cash influence by date, cash outflows by date, and calculated the rate of return. The calculated returns were just over 6% compound for the 11 years."

"How could this be?" the doctor asked. The broker had showed them the average rate of return.

Here's an illustration: Suppose Dr. and Mrs. Greene gave the broker $1,000, and 1 year later it was worth only $500. But the year after that, it was worth $1,000 again. After 2 full years, how much money have they made? Nothing, right? They're right back where they started. But the broker can legally claim that their average annual return was 25%!

Averages can be deceiving. Here's the math: In Year 1, the mutual fund return was −50%; it dropped from $1,000 to $500. But in the second year the fund doubled—now it was worth $1,000, or +100%. When you subtract the −50 from the +100, that equals 50. When that figure is divided by the 2 years, the annual average rate of return is 25%!

The solution: Look at your compounded rate of return, not at your average rate of return with a broker who understands math.

Fabulous Returns, No Risk and Maximum Liquidity

People are funny—and not in a comic sense—funny as in strange, odd, and bizarre.

The police officer walking the streets on a cold winter morning sees a CPA in her warm office and thinks how lucky she is. The accountant sees the cop and thinks how much more exciting it would be if she were outside, instead of stuck in an office with ledgers as her only companions. A man has a lovely wife. He sees a movie star with a super model and wonders what went wrong with his life. An investor who started with nothing, who once lived from paycheck to paycheck, now has a net worth of $1 million. He constantly thinks of all the people who have more. The man suffers from the same affliction as the cop, the accountant, and the moviegoer—envy.

The anomalies of life are limitless. And they are no different from the anomalies of investments. People always seem to want what the other person has. People want the impossible. They want maximum returns but no risk. They want immediate investment gratification, even though it's well known that the best returns usually come from patient, long-term investing.

Judith was blessed with a $10,000 windfall. Now she wants to invest her money and "gain the most money in the short term, but still be able to access the money immediately in case of an emergency."

This is reminiscent of the 1990s when people were perpetually complaining because they were getting "only" a 20% annual return. Their comments prove the usefulness of history (Henry Ford was wrong. History is not "bunk." It proves an understanding of how we got to where we are and is the *sine qua non* [essential element] of clear thinking about the future). These historical folk were ignoring the painful fact that the long-term returns of the stock market had been about 8%. Judith wanted her $10,000 to become $20,000 within a year.

The fact is that in investing, there are risks and rewards. The greater the risk, the greater the potential for rewards—and for disasters. The key to investing is to know thyself and to find the golden mean.

Do you have many years to achieve your goal of $1 million? Then you can be a bit risky. If you are in your 20s and if you have the temperament of an aggressive investor, you can put money in small cap stocks and developing market equities. But you should do this realizing that there is more than a chance of investment disaster. Still, you will have many years to make it up if you stumble.

If you are a middle-aged and moderate investor, you could invest in a few small cap stocks, but also use more conservative, large-cap stocks and also some bonds. Why bonds? There are some bad years in the stock market in which bonds beat stocks. There are even some disastrous years in the stock market when cash—money markets, certificates of deposit—will beat the stock market.

If you are old (ahem!) and have accumulated enough to take care of yourself for the rest of your life, then you can be conservative, keeping most of your money in bonds and cash, leaving a small bit in some stocks because inflation can erode the buying power of even large portfolios.

In short, one size doesn't fit all in investing. It depends on many factors—what kind of person you are, what you trying to accomplish, and how many years you have to do it. Sometimes you need an uncompromised, independent financial advisor to help you get these answers. The tortoise usually beats the hare. Time, steady investing, and unspectacular investments are probably the best course for the average investor. For example, you invest $300 a month for 30 years and earn only 7%. After 30 years, you have $368,126 before taxes. By the way, if you can keep going for another 10 years, you will have $792,037! Not too shabby.

Judith got over her "funniness" and split her money between two low-cost bond and large-cap stock funds. She says she plans to invest for the next 10 years and hopes to get a long-term return of 8% a year.

How Risky Is That Investment?

Whenever someone says he or she can obtain an outsized return for you, it is either because it is a shady investment or because he or she is offering you something risky. The greater the risk, the greater the potential for gain—or loss. Your job as a savvy investor is to match your investment with the proper amount of risk.

What is the proper amount of risk? That depends on you. What kind of person are you, and what is your investment time frame? Generally, the longer out you can go, the more risk you can take. The shorter the timeframe, the more conservative you should be.

Ensuring that your risk profile matches your investments is one of the most important things you can do. Advisors will establish the risk profile of their clients by reviewing myriad personal factors such as age, investment goals, temperament of the investor, and so forth.

Why is the risk profile possibly the most critical factor for successful investing? An investment train wreck can illustrate the point. Back in the late 1990s, millions of investors were cleaning up on tech stocks, sometimes making 100% or better a year. Unfortunately, many of them had no idea of the risk factors in investing in these dicey investments. They had much or all of their investments in tech stocks. They believed in the drivel that was going around then that bull markets were permanent. By the way, moonshine of this order was also consumed en masse just before the stock market crash of 1929.

In the bear market of 2000 to 2002, many of these no-risk wonders took incredible losses, losses they could have avoided had they diversified and had they understood that every investment—even a federally guaranteed savings account—has risks.

For instance, from time to time I'll see ads for investment notes yielding uncommonly high rates. Some rates are up to 12% for a 12-month period. How can companies pay so much? Anytime a company is offering an above-market rate of return, you have to ask why.

If the average Joe can go to a bank and get a low-interest loan, why is a company offering 12%? Does it have bad credit? Why not simply go to a bank and get a lower interest loan? Why does it have to pay such a high rate? Why not pay an investor a much lower rate?

Obviously, there must be some risk involved. To determine the amount of risk, you must figure out what it is you would be buying and what the guarantees are. Once you've done some research, you may decide the risk is worth taking and invest in the notes. But it's doubtful.

However, risk is an individual measure. And, to complicate matters, the individual risk measurement can change throughout life as we accumulate or lose wealth. There are risks in excessive aggressiveness. When you buy those investment notes you may be buying equity in a company that could file for bankruptcy. On the other hand, there are also risks to excessive conservatism.

Some readers might wonder why there is a risk in putting money in a savings account. After all, you'll never lose your principal. The problem is the probability of loss of buying power. Savings accounts pay low interest, maybe about 1%. Inflation, since the Great Depression, even in good periods, always seems to run at least 1% or 2% a year. Throw in penalties on thrift called taxes and, through the magic of our rulers on the Potomac, the buying power of your savings accounts—your ability to buy goods and services—has declined. That's even though the savings account balance amount has gone up. You may feel richer, but you're not.

This just scratches the surface of this complex thing called risk. Risk is a complicated matter; yet, in one sense, it can be summed up in a simple concept. It's risky to invest all your money in one thing. Diversification can reduce risk.

How a Young Person Should Invest a Small Distribution

Ms. White is 30 years old; she is still employed and has many working years ahead of her. She is also covered by a pension where she works. Her main objective is long-term growth. Ms. White can afford to be more aggressive in her investment selection.

Smaller companies tend to be the fastest growing companies in the economy; however, their prices tend to fluctuate more than larger companies. Although a common stock portfolio will fluctuate, Ms. White will have many years before she needs her money and she can withstand the ups and downs of the market. Diversification among many different securities and professional management reduces the risk that she would take if she invested in only a limited number of securities.

If It Looks Like a Dog ...

If it sounds too good to be true, it probably is. George was approached by a financial planner who wanted him to buy a "can't-miss" investment. Whenever someone invokes that "can't-miss" moonshine, be very careful. The first thing you must do is check that you still have your wallet and silverware.

The planner told George that, with his wondrous equity index annuity product, he could have a stock market return if it goes up or a guaranteed 3% if the market goes down.

George should run, not walk, away from that planner. There may be a few good equity index annuities in the marketplace. However, most appear to be garbage.

There are drawbacks to index annuities. First of all, the salesperson representing these products does not need to be licensed to sell securities or have any investment training. (The guy trying to sell this bow-wow to George is about as much a planner as he is the starting second baseman for the New York Yankees.)

The only license a person needs to sell these products is an insurance license. Too often the salesperson has little understanding of the intricacies of the product or how it would fit in with an investor's portfolio. His or her main motivation is the sale, which is how they get paid.

And, by the way, the fees and commissions on some of these products are outrageous. There are no upfront costs, but George's money would be tied up for years, if not for decades. Typically, the longer your money is locked up, the larger the commission paid to the salesperson.

Commissions can run as high as 15%! Guess who pays the commission? Ultimately, people like George.

An equity index annuity is a contract issued by an insurance company. Returns are based on the stock market while guaranteeing the principal. Unfortunately, the investor does not receive the stock market return.

The upside is limited to only a portion of the market's return. Indeed, many contracts have a maximum gain in any 1 year, a point that the salespeople usually don't emphasize. Unsurprisingly, many owners of index annuities have been very disappointed with their results.

If the person who has been trying to sell George an index annuity is a financial planner, George should find out if he or she is a *certified* financial planner. Most likely not.

George should also ask what other types of investments might be available from this planner. George will probably discover that the "financial planner" is not a planner at all, but an insurance agent in disguise.

More Capital Gains Strategies

Jerry rents out a property in which he has considerable equity. He has been holding on to it to avoid capital gains taxes. He knows if he sells it he will be handed a big tax bill. His best bet may be to opt for a 1031 exchange.

A 1031 exchange allows a person to exchange one investment property for another while avoiding capital gains taxes. A tenants-in-common (TIC) exchange is where a person sells his or her property, joins with other investors, and acquires a fractional interest in a larger property, such as an apartment complex or office building. If done properly, the exchange will avoid capital gains taxes.

A TIC exchange can work for Jerry. He could get rid of his rental home and have an interest in a piece of commercial property. But there is also a disadvantage.

He'll give up control of the property. Rather than owning a rental where he can call all the shots, he'll be an investor with several others. Decisions will be made jointly. And of course, his return will be based on lease income and the real estate market.

Before making any investment decision, Jerry should ask himself if he would want to buy that investment if there were no tax breaks. Never purchase an investment solely for tax reasons.

Market Volatility Should Not Change Long-Term Outlook

It happens in every crash and in every bear market, and even in any 1- or 2-day period when the market dramatically drops.

Some investors become shaky. They lose their nerve. They are suddenly ready to ditch a perfectly good investment plan and sell all their stocks. They're like the nervous Nellie baseball fan whose team has just lost the first two games of the 162-game season and is now ready to give up.

Dennis was planning to retire in a few months when he turns 55, which is not very old these days. He has about $300,000 saved for retirement and was going to take 8% per year from his account ($24,000). Now that the market is doing so badly, he's concerned that he won't be able to earn much on his retirement money.

There's no question that the financial markets are volatile right now, and volatility will probably be a factor. (By the way, have you noticed that no one ever complains about upside volatility?) However, the current market environment should have little bearing on whether Dennis can afford to retire.

If Dennis' retirement dollars were invested similarly to most U.S. pension plans, they would be allocated about 60% stocks and 40% bonds, cash, and real estate. Since 1946, a portfolio with that allocation returned an average about 10% per year (according to Ibbotson Associates).

But here's the catch that those investors with high blood pressure should understand. The market did not return 10% in every year. In fact, there were many years when that portfolio lost money. But over the long term, accounting for both good and bad years, it averaged about 10%.

Just because the market was heading down in any short period doesn't mean it will never go up again. Instead of focusing on the current financial markets, try focusing on the long-term markets. After all, if you're planning on retiring at age 55, then you'll be retired for a long time.

Not All Qualified Retirement Plans Are the Same

Not only is it difficult to save for retirement, but also it can be bewildering. Qualified retirement plans such as 401(k) s and 457s—to name just two of the many options—differ. And there are also differences within each type. Some employers match contributions to a 401(k) plan. Others don't. Also, the types of investments offered can vary from plan to plan. And, to complicate matters, because most people today will have many jobs in a typical career, it is likely that the average worker will accumulate assets in several kinds of qualified plans.

Willie has assets in both a 401(k) and a 457 plan. He has his retirement assets almost evenly split between fixed income and equities in the two plans, with a small amount in stable value funds. He is in his 50s and still contributes to the 401(k), but no longer works in the place where his 457 assets are.

Willie has two decisions to make with these accounts: Does he leave the money in the 401(k) and 457 plans or move them elsewhere, or does he just want to change his investments?

The money in his 401(k) is tied up until age 59½, barring a few exceptions. On the other hand, the money in his 457 plan is free from penalties once he quits his job. One does not have to be age 59½ to pull money from a 457. Once Willie is separated from his employer, he is able to withdraw money from the plan without any penalties, regardless of age.

Willie may not want or need to take a withdrawal at this point. But given the flexibility of withdrawals, he should keep the 457 plan in place until he reaches age 59½. He should not roll these funds to a 401(k) or IRA unless he is absolutely certain he will not need the money prior to age 59½.

In regard to the 401(k), Willie can keep the money in the plan, transfer it to his next employer's 401(k), or roll it into an IRA. It doesn't have any impact on his taxes. If Willie is comfortable with the investment selections he has, he might want to keep his money where it is.

Willie's current investment mix is about 45% stock and 45% fixed income, and the rest is in stable value funds. This is a moderate allocation for someone his age. Although he may be quitting his job next year, he is not planning on spending all of his money right away.

If he is planning properly, he should expect that this money would last the rest of his life. Willie does not need to reduce his exposure to stocks, provided he can stomach the ups and downs of the market. Willie is in good shape and will probably be around for 30 or more years. So he probably will see some good times and some bad times before he pulls any money from his account. If history is any guide, his investments in stocks will outperform the stable value funds, given enough time.

Odd Lots Not Wanted

Odd lots are not strange pieces of real estate in an out-of-the-way part of town. They are stock trades of 100 shares or less. The problem with selling just a few shares is that the cost of the transaction could take a large chunk of the proceeds.

To sell small amounts of stock, one must hire a broker to find a buyer for the shares and to facilitate the transaction. Odd lots are not wanted in most big brokerages, which usually have little or no interest in the average individual investor who is just starting out. (Of course, this myopic thinking ignores something—many large investors begin as small investors, small investors who will remain loyal to a firm or a financial professional who helped them when they didn't have huge assets.)

So what does an average investor do who has a small amount of stock to trade?

You do what most people do today—night and day, sometimes 24 hours a day. You go on line. Your best bet is to find an online broker and shop by the lowest price. This is not always the most cost-effective route for a large portfolio, but for a few shares, you'll want the cheapest commission possible. Simply Google online stockbrokers and you'll find myriad options.

Play Defense

If you're a baseball fan, you've probably heard that pitching is the most important element of the game. The premise is a sound one. It's not only how many runs you score but also how many runs you prevent that will determine whether your team will go to the World Series.

A similar philosophy can and must be applied to investing. It's not only how much you make on an investment; it's how much you pay to get the return. Investment expenses are critical. You can have an excellent fund that generates a healthy return. However, if the fund has a big expense ratio and you're paying a sales charge every time you buy shares, or if your fund generates a big tax bill, then your investment isn't nearly as good as you think.

The expense ratio is what the fund charges you, the investor. The average stock fund has an expense of around 1.3%. But let's say you shop around and you find a good fund company that charges 0.2% for its stock fund. Let's also assume that you have a more tax-efficient fund, and that you don't buy funds that charge you a commission for buying a fund. These sales charges mount up. So let's say that you are as finicky about buying a mutual fund as you are about buying fruits and vegetables. And let's say you can save 2% a year in fund expenses. That may not seem to be a large number. But over long periods, we are talking about gains that mean the difference between investment success and so-so performance.

Don't believe it? Look at Fred Mertz. He's a first-team all-star tightwad, who will not buy expensive, tax-inefficient funds. He invests $500 a month in his fund over 20 years and earns 9% a year.

Then there's Diamond Dan, a fund investor who doesn't care that his fund company lives high on the hog and who seems content to send the maximum amount to Uncle Whiskers in investment taxes because his fund is run in a tax-inefficient manner. He also puts $500 a month in a fund over 20 years. He earns 7%.

You know Finicky Fred Mertz is going to come out on top, but can you guess by how much? Diamond Dan has $261,000 at the end of 20 years. However, Finicky Fred has $75,000 more. He has about $336,000. By the way, these numbers don't figure in the effect of taxes, which will give Freddy a bigger advantage.

And if you go out in 30 years instead of in 20, then the disparity widens. Freddy has $922,000, and Diamond Dan has $613,000. That's $309,000 or some 50% more, just because Freddy is a smart shopper. Do you think almost a third of a million dollars could make a difference in your life?

If you throw away runs in a baseball game—if you give the other side easy runs—you usually lose. It's no different in investing. If you cheat yourself of a higher return because you pay too much for an investment, you could be throwing away some $300,000 over 30 years.

Defense pays—in investments and in baseball.

REIT Woes

It's a classic case of investor cold feet. Anne wanted to invest in real estate. So she put 10% of her portfolio in real estate investment trusts (REITs). But her real estate investment has declined by about 10% over the past 8 months, and now she wants to sell.

Having 10% of a portfolio in real estate is not out of line, assuming the remainder of Anne's portfolio is well diversified. REITs are companies that own and operate real estate and, historically, real estate tends to move in different directions than the stock market in general, so REITs can help balance out a portfolio.

REITs have performed very well over certain periods, with the exception of 1998. Like all other stock investments, REITs should be considered long-term investments, and a slight downturn in prices shouldn't cause any alarm for the long-term investor. Anne should think twice before selling.

How to Manage the Risk of Buying Corporate Bonds

Kim is a smart investor who intended to diversify. She had 90% of her brokerage IRA in stocks and knew it was time to find another asset class. Otherwise she would end up with the same problem as many of her friends who suffered horrific losses in the bear market of 2000 to 2002.

Kim was looking at an investment in corporate notes. In the corporate notes program she could buy new issue corporate notes in increments of $1,000 each, and there was no commission.

Kim researched various issues, deciding to limit her bonds to corporations with "A" and higher Standard & Poor's ratings. Kim purchased six bonds meeting her criteria, each in a $1,000 increment. The bonds are due in 2010, 2011, and 2012 and are paying an annual average of 4.5%. Kim realized that these are not stellar returns. However, she wanted some portfolio diversification, and $6,000 is less than 3% of her total brokerage IRA.

Kim's bond component is appropriate for most investors, whether the bonds are purchased individually or as part of a professionally managed portfolio. One reason is that—although stock returns usually beat bond returns most years—there are years in which bonds are a much better investment. When are those years? No one can know for sure, which is why most portfolios should have stocks and bonds, although in most cases more of the former than the latter is a better approach. However, the best approach, over the long term, is to have some of both asset classes.

If you're sold on having some bonds (or what the pros call fixed income) in your portfolio, here are some factors to consider.

There are two types of risks when you own bonds. The first risk is default risk. This occurs when the bond issuer can no longer meet its obligations. There have been many large corporations that have not been able to make good on their bond payments. Examples of this are WorldCom and Enron. Bond-rating agencies, such as Standard & Poor's, can help by evaluating a company. Nevertheless, a good rating today does not guarantee that a company will be good tomorrow.

The second type of risk is interest rate risk. Your bond values will rise or fall inversely with interest rates. If next month's interest rates are much higher than today's, your $6,000 investment in bonds would have a market value much less than $6,000.

You'll receive your full investment upon maturity, but most investors look at their portfolios at least monthly—sometimes daily. This is not a good idea. Investors don't like to see the value of any of their holdings fall, regardless of what guarantees there may be in 5 to 10 years.

In regard to commissions, it is true that one does not pay any commissions when purchasing a bond. But that doesn't mean it doesn't cost you anything. The brokerage firm earns what is called a "spread." That is the difference between what it paid for the bond and what it sells the bond for. Typically, the smaller the bond purchase, the greater the spread. Essentially, if you invest $100,000 in a bond you could receive a higher yield than if you invest only $1,000.

Despite the risks of bonds—and every kind of investing has some risks—Kim's approach is an intelligent one.

Should Mama Have All Her Money in CDs?

Kara, who is active in investing, is upset with her 78-year-old mother. You see Mama lived through the Stock Market Crash of 1929 and the resulting Great Depression. That was a time when stocks crashed and a generation gave up on equities. So Kara's mother has her entire retirement assets in low-interest certificates of deposit, which Kara, who loves stocks, thinks is foolish.

Kara should take it easy on her mother. Sure, Kara's intentions are good, but it may not be appropriate to convince her mother to purchase stocks if she never has before. Over the past 20 years, stocks have lost value on the average of about 4 months per year, so they do carry some risk.

If Kara's mother has zero tolerance for risk, those down months may cause more anxiety than they're worth. Perhaps a better alternative is to start by shifting a portion of her money to bonds. If Kara's mother can be comfortable with the little volatility those carry, maybe she can warm up to the idea of having an investment that fluctuates in value. Perhaps then she can allocate a portion to stocks. But if Kara pushes her too fast, her mother will be calling her the first time she sees a loss in her account. Like Pearl Harbor, or September 11, 2001, some people have never forgotten the terrible years of the stock market crash of 1929.

The Fixed Annuity Dilemma

You see the ads everywhere for one of the oldest retirement saving vehicles around. And your brain goes into overdrive.

Should you buy a fixed annuity? That was the question before Charles, who is 76 years old. As with all financial products, it depends. This is not the convenient double-talk of some congressional candidate on the make. Finding the correct answer depends on a person's circumstances and outlook. And remember, the reason why there is not one easy answer is that each person is different. And, to further complicate the answer, a person's circumstances and outlook can change—sometimes several times—as he or she goes through life.

But let's get back to Charles. He has $40,000 in a bank certificate of deposit (CD) that has matured. He is wondering if a fixed annuity would be a good option. He is looking for the highest yield on a guaranteed investment. The bank is offering an annuity that would pay him 7% guaranteed for the first year.

Annuities have some features that can be attractive to retirees such as Charles. They offer a guaranteed interest rate, tax-deferred growth, and an option to convert the annuity to a guaranteed monthly income. However, there are some drawbacks.

Most annuities have a surrender penalty if you pull your money out during the first 7 years of the contract. Additionally, many annuities offered today have artificially high "teaser" rates during the first year, like the 7% Charles was quoted, but pay below-market rates in the following years. Furthermore, all of the earnings are tax deferred, not tax exempt. So one day Charles or his estate will be responsible for the income tax.

Buying an annuity may be the right option for Charles, but it is important that he understand how they work before he dumps a chunk of money into one. Otherwise, Charles may make an investment he will later regret.

The Inevitable Bumpy Ride of Markets

It's inevitable. Wars, lower than expected earnings reports, trade and fiscal deficits that seem endless, even which team wins the Super Bowl. Any of these things can and do roil markets. They have and they will continue to do so as long as we have markets. It is the nature of the beast. And, if one wants the long-term gains of the market, one must be prepared to ride them out through some bad times.

There's no question that volatility is now a permanent part of the financial markets. And it can certainly spook those who are, say, only 5 or 10 years from retirement. We've experienced phenomenal growth in the stock market in the 1990s. However, the current market environment—which over the last few years has been nothing like the roaring 1990s—should have little bearing on whether or not you can afford to retire. That's if you have a plan to weather good markets and bad.

Indeed, if your retirement dollars are invested similarly to most U.S. pension plans, they will be allocated about 60% stocks and 40% bonds, cash, and real estate. Since 1946, a portfolio with that allocation returned an average of slightly over 10% per year, according to Ibbotson Associates.

But here is the key. It was a rocky ride to get that number. It did not return 10% every year. In fact, there were many years when that portfolio lost money. But over the long term, accounting for both good and bad years, it averaged 10%.

Just because the market has been heading down lately doesn't mean it will never go up again. Instead of focusing on the current financial markets, try focusing on the long-term markets. After all, if you're planning on retiring at age 55, you'll be retired for a long time. And, if you're an average investor, you should continue to have some money in stocks even after you retire.

The Joys of Dividend Reinvestment Plans (DRIPs)

Rick is investing in DRIPs to build long-term wealth.

What are DRIPs? DRIPs are a convenient method of investing in stocks. The dividends paid by the stocks are simply used to purchase more shares in that stock, typically with little or no cost. However, what bothers Rick (and tens of millions of other investors) is that when he purchases new shares through DRIPs, he is running up a tax bill.

That's because any and all dividends earned by Rick's stocks will be fully taxable to him. That's regardless of whether the dividends are reinvested or not. (The same thing happens with mutual funds.) Rick will receive a 1099 for each DRIP and have to pay ordinary income taxes on the dollars that were reinvested.

One way of reducing your taxable income is to purchase stocks that pay little or no dividends. There are many great companies that do not pay any dividends and from a tax-planning standpoint, stocks of these companies can be a great option to avoid taxable dividends.

What's the Utility of These Stocks?

Clark inherited a couple of utility stocks from his mother when she died 5 years ago. She had held them for as long as he could remember, so he decided to hold them as well. However, they've cut their dividends and haven't grown much in the past few years.

Utility stocks were once known as widow and orphan stocks. The utilities were basically guaranteed a profit through their monopoly power in government-regulated industries. Therefore, the stocks paid hefty dividends with little price fluctuations. Today, however, all that has changed.

With the massive deregulation that has been occurring in the utilities industry, utility companies are facing tough competition from all fronts. Maintaining profits has become difficult. That's because the companies' prices have been squeezed. As a result, dividends have been cut and stock prices have been volatile.

What was once the ideal investment for Clark's mother may not be ideal for her son. Now is probably a good time for Clark to evaluate whether these stocks are appropriate for him.

Where Should I Invest, Smart Guy?

So often people read investment books looking for the "One Big Answer." They have a large amount of money and they want a financial writer to tell them where they can find the next Microsoft so they can get in on the ground floor and become a millionaire by the evening of the day they buy their shares.

If the authors of investment books knew of a superb investment such as that they wouldn't be sharing it with anyone; but rest assured they don't. Successful investing takes time, self-discipline, and persistence. Even Warren Buffett's fortune wasn't created overnight. He was once middle class, worrying about paying for his house in Omaha.

You should stay away from any big investment idea that promises to make you rich overnight. Many people have gone broke looking for that.

So let's say you have a windfall to invest. What should you do? Take your time. Many brokers and financial planners will want to rush you into making an investment decision. Benjamin Graham, the fabled guru of value investing, was the author of *The Intelligent Investor,* a book well worth your time. He was Warren Buffett's teacher, and he had three rules: Don't lose money. Don't lose money. And, finally, don't lose money.

So you should be in no hurry to get your dollars invested. And by the way, in selecting an advisor, anyone who wants to rush you into a portfolio—in other words, he or she immediately has places he or she wants to put your money in the first hour in which you talk—is someone who you should avoid. A good investment advisor—like a good tax advisor—needs to know as much about you as possible before making any recommendations.

Before you make any investments, you need to determine what you want your dollars to do for you. Do you want to use some of the money to buy a new home? A new car? Do you want to pay down your house? Pay off bills? Will some go to help pay college costs for a child? Or will most of your money go for your retirement?

The best advice is for you to visit a financial planner—a certified financial planner is recommended—to help you develop an investment strategy based on your goals. If you are about to receive a large amount of money that can make a big difference in your life, you don't want to make any major investment mistakes.

Which Way to the Stock Market?

You might as well try to guess who is going to win the next Super Bowl. You may be right, but you just can't be sure.

Marian is some 2 years away from retirement, and the stock market is starting to make her nervous. The stock market makes all investors nervous, but that's one of those things that anyone who invests must understand.

Most of Marian's 401(k) is invested in stocks. She's read that money in stocks should be invested for the long term, such as 5 years or more. So now she wants to move all her retirement money out of stocks and into bonds and cash.

It is impossible to predict accurately where the market is headed. No one has a crystal ball. Instead of trying to guess, look at the stock market as a long-term investment.

Just because Marian will be retiring in the next 2 years does not mean her investment time horizon is only 2 years. If she's like most retirees, she'll want income from her portfolio. But she'll also want her account to last her until her dying day. That is probably 20 to 30 years from now.

If Marian views 20 to 30 years as her time horizon, rather than the 2 years until her retirement date, she'll see that there is nothing wrong with having long-term investments in her portfolio. However, she may want to consider moving some money out of stocks if she plans on making withdrawals upon retirement. Marian should always keep a few years worth of withdrawals in a stable, fixed-income-type account to prevent her from having to sell stocks in a down market.

Chapter 9
Plan Your Retirement

You've reached a place of reflection in your life, where there's nobody telling you what you have to do next. You no longer have to jump out of bed to fight your way to work on crowded freeways. You can shelve those uncomfortable suits. The chapters in this book will present you with a guideline for building a new future and life, a life designed by you.

You may discover that managing your own life is very exciting. But the absence of discipline or a guiding hand can wreak havoc. You'll have to learn to function without someone else calling the shots or establishing the framework; you will have to come to terms, perhaps for the first time, with excess time and space.

Millions of baby boomers have a date with destiny, specifically their last day of work. The challenge of dealing with the largest generation in human history, the generation that has the longest projected life expectancy, is about to erupt.

If you are 65 years old, you have a 93% probability of reaching age 81 and a 63% probability of reaching age 90. Toss out all those old insurance actuarial books. They are wrong!

A recent study points out that many boomers expect to retire from their current jobs and launch into an entirely new endeavor. Only 17% hope to never work for pay again. Boomers reject a life of either full-time work or full-time leisure. When probed about their ideal work arrangement in retirement, the most common choice among boomers would be to repeatedly cycle between periods of work and leisure (42%), followed by part-time work (16%), start their own business (13%), and full–time work (6%). It's not about the money. Although 37% of boomers indicate that continued earnings is a very important part of the reason they plan to keep working, 67% listed mental stimulation and challenge as their motivation.

From "me" to "we." Boomers are now 10 times more likely to "put others first" (43%) than "put themselves first" (4%). They are 3 times more worried about a major illness (48%), their ability to pay for health care (53%), or winding up in a nursing home (48%) than about dying (17%).

Boomer women are better educated, more independent, are simultaneously juggling more work and family responsibilities, and are more financially engaged than any generation in history. In fact, they are more than six times more likely to share responsibility for savings and investments compared to their mothers' generation (33% now, 5% then). They also view the dual liberations of empty nesting and retirement as providing new opportunities for career development, community involvement, and continued personal growth.

You're on Your Own

The government wants out of the retirement business. What does this mean to you? You are going to have to do it yourself. This comes at a time when most Americans are not disciplined savers. They'll spend what comes into the checkbook.

Only 19% of retirees roll over their 401(k)s intact. This means that 81% of rollover participants have to pay penalties, cut into them, and spent their principal. Most people are not planning a future.

Only a small percentage of this generation is secure for their later years; the masses have still not been brought into the game. It has little to do with income. Most people's lifestyles will adjust to whatever their income is. Some people who make $30,000 a year have a lot of financial independence. Others who make $300,000 a year are up to their eyeballs in debt.

The main value in your 401(k)s and IRAs is not the tax deferral. Although that is important, the best thing about them is that your money is yanked out of your check before you have a chance to spend it. Whether or not you have the discipline, it's not there for you to spend.

Second, and also very important, is the tax deferral. It cuts down on the amount of income tax you must pay today. And that reduction of income taxes can enable you to set aside even more than you would otherwise. For instance, if you set aside $500 a month in your 401(k), your paycheck might only be reduced by $300 or $400 a month. If your goal is to set $500 aside, you might actually find that you can put up to $800 a month in your 401(k) and your paycheck will only be reduced by $500 a month. So it enables you to set aside more dollars in your retirement account.

The money is going to be taxed one day, but you might be able to control some of the taxation. You can decide what year you're going to have it come out of your income taxes. You can let it grow deferred. And when you die, your kids can take over those accounts if they're IRAs and continue with the tax deferral for years and years.

Another one of the beautiful things about retirement accounts is that you can make changes without any tax consequences.

In the late 1990s, people had many stocks that went way up. They didn't want to sell because they didn't want to pay the taxes when the stock was up. When the stock market crashed, they ended up crashing along with the market. With money in a retirement account, you can sell stock, mutual funds, CDs—it doesn't matter. There are no tax consequences until you withdraw the money. It's very flexible for people who want to make changes in their investment allocation.

Don't Nibble Away Your Retirement Funds

Stan, who is 38 years old with many years to go before retirement, needed money. He wonders if he can withdraw money from a 401/457 plan without penalty while still being employed.

One reason some people never accumulate significant retirement funds and end up working much longer than they want to is because they can't keep their hands off of their retirement nest eggs.

Why would you want to spend your retirement savings while you are still working? What will you live off during retirement? Money that is deposited into retirement accounts should be left untouched until retirement. This is not fun money. It's true that all kinds of needs and emergencies arise, but if paying for them is tough while you're working, think what they'll be like once you've retired.

For whatever reason, age 59½ is the magical age that allows you to withdraw money from your retirement account. If you pull money before that age, you'll be slapped with 10% federal and 2.5% state penalties. You can avoid the early withdrawal penalties if you (1) die, (2) become totally disabled, or (3) receive money that is part of a series of substantially equal periodic payments.

Stan should forget about touching his 401(k) and leave the money alone until he quits working and fully retires. He should stop, take a deep breath, and seriously consider the consequences of this action.

How About Having It All?

That's the issue that faced Jack in retirement planning. He was considering putting money in both a Roth IRA and a 401(k) plan that had just begun to be offered at his job. The Roth IRA and the 401(k) are two distinct retirement plans, and Jack's participation in one would have no impact on the other. He can contribute to both plans.

The maximum you can contribute to the Roth IRA is scheduled to rise each year, so you must check with your tax advisor. But, as long as you have some earned income, you can contribute. You cannot contribute if you are retired and have no wage or self-employment income.

If you are married, your spouse can also contribute to a Roth IRA. If, like Jack, your employer offers you a 401(k), you can contribute the maximum allowable to that plan, usually a percentage of your earned income. Your contribution to a 401(k) has no bearing on how much you deposit in your IRAs.

If you contribute money to a regular IRA or a SEP-IRA, you will not be allowed to contribute to the Roth IRA. For most individuals, the Roth IRA may be the best bet. But the 401(k) also is a good retirement savings vehicle. Jack is lucky to have the chance to take one from retirement column A and retirement B. Eat hearty.

Investing in Retirement

Many people make the mistake of not accounting for inflation. They begin retirement with a sufficient nest egg to maintain their lifestyle. But they put all their money in cash or bonds and nothing in stocks. Inflation outstrips the rate of return on their investments as they go through retirement. Soon, they no longer have a comfortable retirement. They are pinching nickels and dimes, which is no way to live in their golden years. That is why it is important to have an intelligent investment plan, even after you have made your money.

Sara and Sam are about to retire. They have about $300,000 in Sara's 401(k) and $300,000 in outside investments. Their goal is to split their investments so that they have about 50% in stocks and 50% in bonds, a smart allocation for people who have just retired and might live another 20, 30, or even 40more years. Their plan is to live off a pension and Social Security and a small portion of the interest their investments earn. They are contemplating whether they should own stocks within or outside the 401(k).

The conventional wisdom is that you hold long-term investments (stocks) inside retirement accounts, such as your 401(k), and shorter term investments (bonds) outside retirement accounts. The theory is that because stocks should perform better over the long term, they should be held in a long-term account.

However, tax changes a few years ago may have replaced the old school of thought. Today, withdrawals from retirement accounts and income from bonds are taxed as ordinary income. Tax rates for ordinary income can start at 15% and sometimes go as high of 39.6%.

If Sam and Sara hold stocks in a 401(k), any appreciation in those stocks will be taxed as ordinary income upon withdrawal. But, if they hold stocks outside a 401(k), any appreciation from a sale of stock will be treated as capital gains, with long-term rates ranging from 10% to 20%.

Because current tax laws favor capital gains, Sam and Sara probably want to consider owning the majority of their stocks outside retirement accounts and their bonds in their 401(k) or IRA.

Tacano Returns

Costs matter in investing. That's because excessive fee or management charges can drive down returns, turning a decent investment into a turkey. That's what Brett realized a few years ago.

In March 2000 (at the peak of the market), Brett opened a traditional IRA and funded it with $2,000. The following year his employer began a profit sharing plan and 401(k), so Brett was no longer able to contribute to the traditional IRA. He has, however, contributed to a Roth IRA each year since then along with contributing to the 401(k).

The traditional IRA took a beating the first year or two and was valued at about $850 by 2003. But just to add insult to financial injury, Brett was charged a $35 yearly maintenance fee by his investment firm just for having the account as well as a $35 yearly fee for the Roth IRA account.

Brett is now disgusted with yearly maintenance fees that eat into his returns, which since 2003 have been better, but not great.

Maintenance fees can really eat away at smaller accounts. A $35 fee isn't a big deal on a $100,000 account, but on an $850 account, it is over 4% of the account's value. In other words, you would need to earn 4% just to break even.

Brett's account is probably what is known as a brokerage IRA. This gives one the ability to invest in stocks, bonds, and so forth. With the small account size, Brett really doesn't need that much flexibility. He could transfer the account to a bank or other investment company and avoid the $35 fee.

To do so, Brett can simply contact a bank or other financial institution, establish an IRA with that firm and complete some transfer paperwork. His account will be moved electronically. Here's the part Brett likes. There will be no taxes due on the transfer, and will not have any paperwork to file with the IRS.

Age-Weighted Retirement Plans

At times, life is unfair. There are some problems you can do something about, and there are others you can't.

Take Fran. She works for a small company that set up a retirement plan in 1988. The plan favored older employees by allocating more of the company's contributions to the older employees' retirement accounts and less to the younger employees. Previously, the only older employees were the company owners. However, the company recently hired some older employees, so they changed the retirement plan to reduce costs to the company.

The problem for Fran is that the old plan hurt people like her. Under the old plan, she was slated to receive $2,700 per month at age 55. But, under the new plan, she will receive only $1,000 per month.

The company's original retirement plan was an "age-weighted" plan. This is a plan designed to fund the owner's retirement plans first and foremost. The owners' may never have intended keeping the plan in place until Fran and others reached age 55. Unfortunately, there is little Fran can do about the change in retirement plans.

Over the past decade, employers have been scrapping traditional pension plans and replacing them with less costly 401(k)-type plans.

What this means to Fran is that she can no longer rely on her employer to fund her retirement. She must take care of it herself. Advice to the millions of Frans is to save your own money and plan as though your retirement plan at work will be your only source for retirement income. That way your retirement fund won't be dependent on anyone but yourself.

How to Foul Up Your Rollover IRA

There it is. You get a statement every 3 months or so, and the balance has been on the rise. It is a lot of money. Maybe the most money you've ever had. But there's one limitation. It's in your rollover IRA and if you break into it before age 59½, generally, you will pay a huge tax bill.

But that new house is something you've always wanted.

Tom recently plans to use part of the money from his IRA, combining it with the proceeds from the house he is going to sell. This will allow him to purchase that super deluxe house he always wanted. Also, by doing this, Tom says he'll be able to make a much bigger down payment. Therefore, his monthly mortgage payments will be much smaller.

Tom should discuss this with an advisor before going ahead. Withdrawing money from an IRA to use as a down payment on a home is tricky business. It may seem as though it could help reduce monthly payments, but the taxes due on the withdrawal could be enormous—wiping out a significant part of an account it took years to build up.

Distributions from IRAs and other retirement plans are taxed as ordinary income. Unlike the favorable tax rates dividends and capital gains receive, IRA withdrawals receive no special tax treatment. The tax rates for retirement withdrawals range from 10% to 35%, depending on your other income. Indeed, April could turn out to be the cruelest month in your new house. You could withdraw $50,000 today, only to find yourself with a tax bill of $15,000 next April.

The best way to withdraw money from your IRA and other qualified retirement plans is gradually. Do it over a period of years rather than pull a chunk out now. You might consider starting to draw a monthly income from your IRA that can be applied to your monthly mortgage payment.

Tom's goal is to reduce mortgage payments by $300 per month. On a 30-year mortgage, this would require about $50,000. Because of the taxes triggered by a withdrawal of that size, Tom could be forced to pull $70,000 to net $50,000. Tom would be sending $20,000 to the tax folks.

Rather than paying unnecessary taxes, I told Tom that he could simply set up a monthly withdrawal from your IRA so that he could receive $300 per month. That way his IRA would remain intact. He wouldn't be giving a huge chunk of his IRA to the government.

IRA and 401(k)s Are Different

Qualified retirement plans are generally the key to the average middle-class person effectively saving for retirement. But, as with many good things, they can also be potential headaches.

That's because most people will accumulate more than one kind of qualified plan during their working lives. And although all qualified plans provide tax breaks for those saving for retirement, they can have very different rules.

Phil recently turned 55 years of age. He hopes that the withdrawal rules for 401(k) plans are the same as IRAs. Bad news. The 401(k)s and IRA rules are different for those retirees between the ages of 55 and 59½.

Individuals who retire at age 55 or beyond can withdraw money from their employer's retirement plans without restrictions or early withdrawal penalties. The only taxes due are ordinary income taxes. This early withdrawal exception applies only to those who reach at least 55 in the year in which they retire. Those who retire under that age do not have full, penalty-free access to their 401(k)s.

IRAs do not receive the same special treatment. One must be age 59½ or older to have unrestricted access to his or her retirement plan.

If Phil moves his 401(k) to an IRA, his money will fall under the IRA rules. He'll lose his ability to withdraw funds as needed and avoid penalties. Phil can still take withdrawals using a series of equal payments, but his withdrawals would be both limited and restricted.

Unless Phil's 401(k) choices are abysmal, it may be to his benefit to leave his 401(k) intact until age 59½. That way he can have access to his funds as needed.

401(K) Assets Are Yours. Do You Know What You're Doing?

Bob is worried. He works for an airline that is losing large amounts of money. He fears that his pension could be in trouble. Bob's problem could happen in a number of ailing industries.

There is a potential pension fund crisis in our nation, a crisis as profound and threatening as the banking crisis of the late 1980s and early 1990s. That's when thousands of banks went belly up and the federal government had to bail out the depositors. The same dangerous situation now threatens thousands of underfunded pension funds.

But it could be worse.

The government corporation designed to make good on the promises of these pension funds is also underfunded. Here is an example of the difference between traditional pension funds—defined benefit plans—and 401(k) plans, which fall into the category of defined contribution plans. If you have the former, then you want to be sure that your employer is in good shape and is fully funding the pension plan. However, if you are part of a 401(k) plan—as is Bob's brother Steve, who doesn't work in the airline industry—then you don't have this problem.

That's because your 401(k) is not an asset of the employer. The company cannot use your funds for its own purposes. And the money in the plan is not subject to any of your employer's creditors.

The 401(k) is set up in a special trust account, often with a big mutual fund company such as Fidelity or Vanguard. It is apart from the company's other accounts. The fund company gives the employees of the participating company a special phone number, but it is administered in the same manner as other mutual fund 401(k)s.

If the company goes bankrupt, the 401(k) is protected. We've all heard the stories from Enron employees, but many Enron employees had their 401(k)s invested in Enron stock. Those who did not own Enron stock saw no losses as a result of the bankruptcy.

The risk you have in your 401(k) is the investments you hold inside your 401(k). As long as you don't own company stock in your 401(k), you won't suffer a loss if your employer goes bust. However, although 401(k) (or defined benefit) plans have many advantages, there is at least one big disadvantage.

It requires the employee to pick the investments. It forces the smart employee to learn something about investing; about the advantages of modern portfolio theory and diversification.

Many 401(k) plan participants are not smart about investing. They put too much money in company stock, which is a dangerous move, as former Enron employees will tell you. Sometimes, they put all their contributions in money market accounts. That's also a dangerous move. Over the long term you will probably lose buying power as inflation and taxes outperform your rate of return. People end up with not enough to save retire comfortably.

Some 401(k) participants put either too much money in stocks or not enough. Again, the assets in a 401(k) are yours. But you have to know a little something about how to invest them properly.

401(k)-to-IRA Shift Offers Choices

Tim is an unusual worker. He contributes to his company 401(k) plan, but he also studies the plan and is aware of its expenses. He was recently upset. "I'm getting socked with high 401(k) fees—over $400 each year—and want to know if I can roll over my 401(k) into an IRA, which should reduce my fees," he explained.

Tim has some choices. Until the early 1990s, the only time one was permitted to transfer a 401(k) into an IRA was at retirement. Furthermore, to qualify for the rollover, an employee had to roll over at least 50% of his or her account balance. However, the rules became much more flexible after 1992.

Currently, tax law allows for unlimited transfer from 401(k)s to IRAs. Tim doesn't have to quit or retire from his employer and he can transfer as little or as much as he'd like. That's provided the funds are transferred directly to an IRA.

Unfortunately, many employers do not permit distributions from their 401(k)s while employees are still working for them. If this is the case with your employer, you may want to see if the company can amend its plan. There are many circumstances where transferring money from a 401(k) to an IRA may be of benefit. Besides greater investment flexibility in a self-directed IRA, you can access your money penalty free for educational expenses, the purchase of a first home, and utilizing the now-popular Roth conversion. None of these transfers are permitted from 401(k)s.

457 Strategies

Mary is retiring in 2 years. She has approximately $40,000 in a 457 plan that is invested in a stock account. She worries that, because retirement is just 2 years away at age 55, she should be moving her money into a conservative option. She is thinking of a money market or savings account.

Retirement at age 55 isn't the end of the road. In fact, Mary, who is in great health, could live another 30 or 40 years.

The question is: Are you really planning on spending all of your 457 plan the day you retire? Many investors equate the length of time until a retirement date as the time horizon for their retirement funds. But the reality is your retirement dollars will typically be there for many years after you retire. So stocks—because they perform better than bonds over the long term—should continue to be some part of the portfolio.

This advice can apply to almost any people in their 50s who are in good health. If you are not planning to pull all your money out the day you retire, you probably shouldn't worry so much about what the 457 plan will be worth 2 years from now. You should focus more on what the plan can do for you for the rest of your life.

A 401(k) All-Points Bulletin

A 401(k) is a defined benefit plan. You decide how much to put in the plan and your employer will often match your contributions to a certain point. Generally, you are in control of the assets. You determine how much of your contributions will go into the various investment options, which are set up by your employer.

This contrasts with defined benefit plans in which the employer tells the employee how much to put in a plan and controls the assets.

However, there are times when an alarm bell should sound for someone who is part of a 401(k) plan. Let's say the employees have recently found out that the funds have not been sent to the plan administrator on a regular basis. Let's say they suspect that the employer is pocketing this money or using it for other things. This, if true, is a serious offense, an offense that could land an employer in prison for many years. The employer has both a legal and a moral obligation to see that the funds are deposited into the 401(k) account in a reasonable period of time.

All 401(k) plans are governed by strict ERISA guidelines that place a fiduciary responsibility on the employer. The employer must see to it that employee funds are deposited in a timely manner. Failing to do so could put the employer in a position where both civil and criminal penalties are imposed.

The best plan of action for employees at this point is to contact the United States Department of Labor and file an official complaint. The DOL will then contact the employer and investigate the situation. If funds have been diverted, the 401(k) participants will be among the first to be repaid in the event of bankruptcy or liquidation.

A Regular or Extra Crispy IRA?

Millions of Americans seeking to avoid scandalous tax bills on their retirement savings have a choice. Do they want a regular IRA or a Roth IRA, a proposition that sometimes comes down to whether it makes more sense to pay Uncle Whiskers now or later.

With a regular IRA, normally you start to pay taxes when you begin to pull money out of it at age 59½. If you want to convert your regular IRA to a Roth, you pay taxes when you convert. But then the account can build up without any further taxation. The latter can be a tremendous selling point for a Roth. However, each person is in a different tax situation.

One needs to proceed carefully because there are numerous ways that one can trigger taxes and penalties. Rules on withdrawals and conversion rules are longer than *War and Peace*. And, unlike Tolstoy's seminal novel, the rules governing IRAs, and all qualified plans, will get bigger and bigger.

The Roth, the regular IRA, and the 401(k) plan you may contribute to at work are all part of what are called qualified plans. Through qualified plans the government will give you special tax breaks as a way of encouraging retirement savings. But the rules for contributing to and pulling money out of these plans are arcane and subject to endless revision. Just when you have figured out all the answers, the government changes the questions.

For instance, say you plan to retire at age 55, which is 3 years from now. You only have $100,000 in your 401(k), but you have a $2.5 million IRA. You think: Why don't I just roll the money over to the 401(k)?

Sorry. Cannot do, the government says. Money can be withdrawn penalty free from an employer's retirement plan if you retire on or after the year you reach the age of 55. This age-55 rule applies to all qualified retirement plans an employer may have. Unfortunately, IRA money specifically is excluded from the age-55 exception. Tax law currently allows a person to transfer a traditional IRA into a 401(k), but getting at the money prior to age 59½ could create a problem.

A simple solution to your problem is to start a monthly income from your IRA. As long as the income is designed to last the rest of your life, you can escape the early withdrawal penalty. Keep in mind that once you start the income, you cannot modify it until the latter 5 years or age 59½.

Here is just one of myriad distribution issues for people with qualified accounts. It's just as bad for people at the other end of spectrum. We're speaking of those who are just starting out to save for retirement or those who have been saving but still have 10 or 15 years to go before they plan on accessing their money.

One needs to discuss "to Roth" or "not to Roth" with a tax advisor. The latter probably should be a CPA and someone who has done your taxes for many years and knows your lifestyle, income, and financial needs. One reason to convert to a Roth now is to avoid higher taxes down the road. If you have the slightest inclination that income taxes may rise in the future, paying taxes at the current low rate can give you a nice tax-free check down the road.

Let's say that converting an amount from your IRA to a Roth each year keeps you in the 15% tax bracket. That could be a very smart move. Too often people defer retirement withdrawals into the future, only to be taxed at higher rates. Converting to a Roth assures that you won't be taxed at a higher rate because qualified withdrawals from a Roth IRA are free from income tax.

Nevertheless, there are potential downsides to this tax strategy. There are two areas you need to be aware of. First, any money that you convert to a Roth IRA will trigger a tax bill. You'll need to take some of your savings to pay the income taxes.

And for people who are retired, a Roth conversion could cause your Social Security benefits to become taxable. Depending on the size of your pension, your benefits may be tax-free. But converting to a Roth will add income to your tax return, which could in turn trigger the taxation of your benefits.

By the way, if one is hard up and needs money, a person could take the principal contributions one has made to a Roth IRA—the amount you put in without the buildup of capital gains, dividends, and so forth—without a penalty before age 59½. But even this loophole can hurt you if you don't know what you're doing or if you find out later on that you can't put the money in the account.

The problem with using the Roth to fund purchases is that once the money is pulled out, it's difficult to get it back in. The only way to get money back into a Roth IRA is by making annual contributions, which are limited by wage or self-employment income, or by converting money from a traditional IRA.

In countless situations people have taken cash from their Roth to purchase cars, pay for vacations, and so forth. There are times when the Roth is the right place to get the dough, but all alternatives need to be looked at prior to a withdrawal. Given the fabulous tax benefits of the Roth, other avenues should be explored before a Roth is touched.

Before you tap a Roth, think about it carefully. And before you convert anything to a Roth, run a quick tax projection that not only looks at your income taxes but also focuses on the taxation of your Social Security check. If a future Roth conversion causes your benefits to become taxable, it could negate most of the income tax reduction aspects. Also, Roths have their drawbacks for certain people. For example, say you try to move money from your current 401(k) plan into a rollover IRA with the idea of moving it into a Roth IRA. You never touch the assets because you hope you can avoid any penalty and assets.

Wrong. That used to be a loophole that permitted people to move assets penalty free to Roth IRAs. That doesn't exist. For those under age 59½ who convert money from a traditional IRA to a Roth IRA, the converted portion of the Roth must remain in the Roth until age 59½. Withdrawals of the converted dollars prior to that age will be slapped with a 10% early withdrawal penalty.

If that loophole was not closed, anyone could avoid early withdrawal penalties from retirement accounts by converting money to a Roth IRA prior to withdrawing it.

The Roth IRA can be a tempting place to go to when in need of cash. All contributions can be pulled out free of taxes and, if you're over 59½, any growth and interest can be tax-free as well.

Given the fabulous tax benefits of the Roth, one should think about buying the extra crispy version of the IRA. But, once one has opted for a Roth, one should think very carefully before using the account before age 59½.

A Retirement Saving Caveat

Many people are not saving enough for retirement. And, given the persistence of inflation, a kind of invisible tax that eats away at your standard of living, and the certainty of higher taxes, most people aren't considering that their needs will be great in 20 years or more—especially if they're expecting to achieve financial independence.

But there are actually circumstances in which contributing more may not be the right strategy. Let's take Nancy, who is 52 years old. She works for the state, earns $100,000 a year, and wants to retire in 3 years. She's unsure if she should make maximum contributions to her 401(k) or 457 plans or both.

Her employer recently said that she could contribute both $16,000 to her 401(k) and $16,000 to her 457 plan for a total of $32,000.

It is an unusual situation. Blame the recent tax changes. They made it possible for people to contribute to both a 401(k) and a 457 plan. The limit for these plans, for example, in 2004 was $13,000 each, plus an additional catch-up of $3,000 each for those ages 50 and older. Added together, Nancy could defer up to $32,000 of her pay this year.

Still, it doesn't always make sense to max out your retirement accounts. By contributing the maximum, people sometimes receive a tax deduction at the 15% tax rate only to be taxed at the 25% level once they've retired.

Nancy should contribute only the pay that will be taxed at 25% and not the pay that will be taxed at 15%.

And because she plans on retiring at age 55, it doesn't matter which plan she uses. Both plans are available at age 55. The 457 plan is available at any age once she retires. And the 401(k) is available penalty free at age 55. That's provided Nancy waits until she is at least 55 when she retires. She doesn't have to wait until age 59½.

With regard to risk factors, there is a subtle difference in the two plans. 401(k) plans are held in trust. They are not assets of your employer, whereas 457 plans are technically deferred compensation plans. Therefore, they are plans that can be subject to the employer's creditors.

A SEP-IRA Can Go into Extra Innings

When will you be allowed to go into extra innings on a qualified plan contribution?

Juan had to get an extension on his April 15 tax deadline, but he wanted to know if he could contribute to his SEP-IRA within the extension.

The answer is yes for SEP-IRAs, no for IRAs.

A SEP-IRA, by the way, is a type of retirement account for self-employed individuals. Any deposits can be made up until an income tax return is filed, even if that date is beyond April 15. However, regular IRAs must be funded on or before April 15. Extending your tax return filing date will not help you when it comes to IRAs.

A Stretch-IRA

There is another way to pass on assets to your children, a way that will free them of some of the stress and strain of estate taxes. It's called the "stretch-IRA."

The term stretch-IRA refers to a strategy used with an IRA. The stretch-IRA is what can happen to an IRA after your death.

When an IRA has people listed as beneficiaries, as opposed to a trust or estate, the individuals have an opportunity to stretch the IRA disbursement for the rest or their lives. Children cannot roll the IRA into their own IRAs, but they can leave it intact and take distributions based on their life expectancy.

The benefit of stretching the withdrawals for several years or decades is maintaining the tax-deferred growth. If the IRA were fully distributed at death, the money would be fully taxable and would lose the ability to grow tax deferred.

For your children to have the greatest flexibility, you'll want to make sure your IRA custodian can do two things at your death: (1) Split the IRA so that each child can control his or her own money. (2) Allow a beneficiary IRA to continue for the remainder of the beneficiary's life. Although tax law permits stretch-IRAs, not all IRA providers are accommodating. Check with your investment firm to be sure your children can take advantage of the stretch rules.

Consulting Business Retirement Contributions

Teresa's husband, Buddy, is 64 years old and owns a consulting business with no employees. Teresa and Buddy have set up a SEP-IRA. Teresa and Buddy also want to contribute $13,000 to a "K" plan. Before retirement, Buddy contributed $4,000 through his company. Now they're looking to contribute the $9,000 difference.

I told Buddy and Teresa that retirement contributions must be aggregated with other retirement plans. For example, if the maximum income limit is 20% of pay, that percentage applies to any combination of retirement plans. One cannot contribute 20% of pay to one plan, 15% of pay to another, and so on.

The 401(k) plan designed for the self-employed must be established prior to the end of the business fiscal year (typically the calendar year) to receive a tax deduction for that year.

If your goal is to receive a tax deduction for the current year, then the solo-K should have been set up by December 31.

A Year and a Half Is a Long Time

Some people just can't wait in our hurry-up world. Even people who have been putting money in their 401(k) plans for 20 years or more, and are 18 months away from the magical age 59½ mark, the point at which one can withdraw money from a plan without tax penalty, sometimes can't wait a year or so more.

Normally, you have to wait until age 59½ for penalty-free withdrawals from an IRA, but there are exceptions. Say you are age 55 or older when you stop working for your employer. You can withdraw money from your 401(k) without penalty. You are not required to be age 59½. However, if you transfer your 401(k) balance to an IRA, the age-55 rule no longer applies and you must either wait until you are age 59½ or start a series of withdrawals that cannot be changed for 5 years.

Nevertheless, it's advisable to leave enough money in your 401(k) to last until you reach age 59½ and transfer the remainder into an IRA. If your 401(k) provider doesn't permit partial withdrawals, simply withdraw what you need to last until age 59½ and roll the rest into an IRA. Either way, that would accomplish the objective of receiving penalty-free money without tying you to a 5-year payment stream.

A Youngster's Retirement Questions

There are limitless examples of retirement distribution puzzles. That's because, in our grand republic, there are a limitless number of lawyers who write a limitless number of rules affecting these retirement systems and, therefore, there are a limitless number of ways these rules can affect us— even people who have no intention of retiring for 20 or 30 years.

Young people who are changing jobs and trying to figure out what to do with their retirement assets must face some of the potential retirement distribution problems.

Jeff is a 30-year-old plant manager. Does he have to worry about how he is going to get retirement benefits from his pension? Well, yes. He is a member of a safety retirement system and has already accumulated 10 years of service. He is eligible to retire at age 50. He is planning to leave his employer in order to stay home with his family.

So now he has the option of deferring 10 years of service and then drawing his retirement pay at age 50 at $24,000 per year.

Should he defer his retirement, or should he take a lump-sum distribution of approximately $25,000 and roll it into an IRA, allowing that money to grow?

Our thrifty young person has made the maximum contributions to his deferred compensation plan and a Roth IRA. He will not need the retirement income to survive. He considers it "fun money."

Here, again, the answers are not always clear-cut. There are times when taking a lump sum is better and times when opting for a monthly pension is better. It depends on how large the lump sum is relative to the pension.

To determine whether the lump sum is a good deal, a few calculations are necessary. To run the numbers, one will need to use either a financial calculator or one of the many calculators available on the Internet.

The first step is to determine the future value of one's pension income. We'll project a growth rate of 8%. A $24,000 annual pension for a 50-year-old will pay 33.1 years on average, according to an IRS life-expectancy table. The calculation: How much money would he need to set aside to pay $24,000 for 33.1 years? The lump sum needed for a 50-year-old to pay $24,000 per year at 8% is $274,000.

The second step is to calculate how much cash a 30-year-old would need today in order to grow to $274,000 by the time he reaches age 50. If we again use an 8% growth rate, that number would be about $58,000.

If the lump sum were greater than $58,000, and if this youngster was confident that he could do better than 8%, he should take the lump sum. But if the lump sum were only $25,000, he would need to earn in excess of 11% on his money before the lump sum would be worth more than his future pension. The historic long-term return of the stock market has been about 9% a year, but many individual investors don't achieve this. That's because many of them tend to jump in and out of the market.

More than 80% of those whose employers offer traditional pensions have the option of a lump sum. Don't take the cash just because it is offered to you. Have the numbers run to see what type of return you would need to equal the pension before you make any final decisions. Again, even though you are young, it is probably a good idea to retain an advisor, at least on a part-time basis.

Life Begins at Age 50

Do you want to get out of the rat race? Do you want to tell your boss where to get off? Well, someday you can. In fact, let's look at a couple who are young and on the road to accomplishing financial independence at a relatively young age.

Sean is 31 years old. His wife, Kate, is 28 years old. They both have 457 plans, to which they have each contributed the maximum since beginning their employment (combined $135,000 balance).

They both belong to a safety retirement system, which will provide them with a pension of 3% for every year of service (beginning at age 50). They both have contributed the maximum to Roth IRAs since their inception (combined balance of $31,000). They have a 1-year-old daughter for whom they have established a 529 college savings plan with savings of $250 month (balance of $3,800).

Sean and Kate are well on the road to financial independence. For starters, they have a government pension that will be coming to them that is unbelievably rich. They can retire at age 50 with a pension that will almost replace their salary.

If they work 25 years, by the time they reach age 50, they will receive 75% of their salary for the rest of their lives. No job in the private sector can come close to that.

Second, they are fantastic savers. Not many people at their ages have the level of retirement savings they do. Even if they never saved another dime toward retirement, their retirement plans will be worth more than $700,000 by the time they reach age 50, assuming an 8% growth rate.

If they continue plunking away $20,000 per year, they'll be worth over $1.5 million. They are more than on track for retirement. They're on track for a house on the Gold Coast.

At the rate they are saving for their daughter, her 529 plan should be worth about $120,000 by the time she heads off to school.

Given how college costs keep increasing, this may not be enough to pay for all of her college expenses. However, they may not want to add too much to the 529 plan in the event she doesn't go to college.

Avoid Nondeductible IRAs

Our nation needs more savings. The greater the pool of savings, the lower the costs of capital, which is a fancy term for interest rates. The lower the interest rate, the more people can buy and businesses can borrow to expand.

So everyone who can should save, especially those who realize that their retirement will cost huge amounts of capital. IRAs are an excellent way to save. That's provided they are deductible. Unfortunately, there is a problem with IRAs. As your income increases, the deductibility of the IRA decreases until it reaches a point in which there is no deductibility.

Claude and Lily, who have built up a successful business, recently arrived at this point. Now they're unsure if they should stash more in their IRA. That's because, at their tax rate, there is no tax benefit.

Nondeductible IRAs are undesirable for a number of reasons. You receive no tax deduction on your contributions, although the money grows tax-deferred. But the growth is taxable as ordinary income when it is withdrawn.

Another big problem with nondeductible IRAs is that the only way to get at all of your after-tax deposits is by cashing in all of your IRAs. When you pull money out of a nondeductible IRA, all of your IRAs must be taken into account when determining your tax bite.

Let's say you have contributed $10,000 to a nondeductible IRA over the years, and the IRA is now worth $20,000. In addition to this IRA, you also have a rollover IRA worth $180,000. That brings your total IRA balances to $200,000.

You decide to withdraw your $10,000 from your nondeductible IRA balance. The tax-free portion of your withdrawal will be calculated based on the percentage your after-tax contributions constitute of your entire IRA balances. In this example, the contributions amount to 5% of the total IRA balances. Therefore, $9,500 of the $10,000 withdrawal will be taxable.

Another problem with nondeductible IRAs is that all of the growth is taxed as ordinary income rather than as capital gains.

Claude and Lily should scrap the nondeductible IRA contributions. In their case, there is an alternative. Buy a tax-efficient investment outside of an IRA. It could net more after-tax income than holding the investment inside an IRA.

What Do You Do With the Retirement Assets?

Seven years ago Valerie left a company and was told she would have to transfer her 401(k) out of the account. It's only $20,000 and Valerie is 50 years old. Along with other accounts, Valerie is planning on retiring at age 60.

Valerie rolled it over to her bank's IRA even though she thought that was the worst place to roll the 401(k) money. Actually, it is the opposite. An IRA is typically the best type of account to transfer money from a previous employer's retirement plan. An IRA can offer many benefits. Rolling money to an IRA avoids current income taxation. The account grows tax deferred, and tax law allows for a variety of investment options for IRAs. Furthermore, money that is sitting in an IRA can be rolled back into a current employer's 401(k) should the need arise.

There are two situations in which leaving money in a 401(k) may be the wrong choice. First, if a person is being sued or filing for bankruptcy. Then, a 401(k) offers greater protection than an IRA.

Second, if people are between the ages of 55 and 59½ when they leave their employer and require income from a retirement account, the 401(k) works better. Money can be withdrawn from a 401(k) without penalties or restrictions for that individual. By transferring money to an IRA, those individuals would have to wait until age 59½ for the same flexibility.

Can't Keep Your Eyes Off Your 401(k)

Many Americans don't like their jobs. Some people just become fed up with their company or their boss (or both), and they depart. But then there is the question of their 401(k) savings. Many people have accumulated triple-digit balances at a job. Some want to start spending the balances immediately, not wait until age 59½.

Jonathan is a 45-year-old worker who will get a pension at age 50 and has $170,000 in his 401(k). He wants to break into it and pay off his mortgage. It may not be a good idea.

The problem lies with the rules imposed by the Internal Revenue Service. If you cash out your 401(k) and have a check sent to your home, the 401(k) people will withhold 20% of your account balance for federal income taxes. But your tax bill doesn't stop there. The 20% will be only a down payment on the taxes you'll owe.

In Jonathan's case, the $170,000 will be added to his income this year, pushing him into the 33% bracket. Add to that the 10% federal early withdrawal penalty and the applicable state income taxes, and Jonathan could easily lose more than 50% of the account balance. He could have a tax bill next year in excess of $50,000.

Rather than wiping out the 401(k), Jonathan could start a monthly draw and avoid the early withdrawal penalties. Under Internal Revenue Code

72(t), the IRS allows individuals to take a monthly income from retirement plans so long as the income is designed to last one's life expectancy. Based on an account balance of $170,000, Jonathan could receive approximately $850 per month. He would avoid the early withdrawal penalty, and probably would be taxed in his current tax bracket.

It would be for Jonathan to leave his 401(k) untouched until he reached his actual retirement age. Perhaps he can do some other work to bring in enough money to make the mortgage payments. But if he has to start a penalty-free withdrawal, he should learn about all of the rules by talking it over with his financial advisor.

Capital Gains Blues

We've already discussed how people who sell their primary residences within a certain period can use capital gains tax breaks. Using the break effectively, a taxpayer can obtain an exclusion from all gains on a primary residence. However, there are some people who were hurt when the capital gains exclusion was rewritten a few years ago.

Sara has been a sage real estate investor over the years. She's moved several times over her life and has always made money on her homes. Her current residence is worth about $500,000. She would like to sell it and move to another part of town. She's worried about the capital gains taxes.

She's rolled over the capital gains on each house and has heard that she can't do that anymore. Sara wonders if the current capital gains exclusion law has any "grandfather" provisions that could help her.

Unfortunately, Sara is one of the few people hurt by the capital gains tax exclusion changes of a few years ago. The law allows a property owner to exclude from income up to $250,000 worth of gains on the sale of the primary residence. But here is the downside: It does not allow the property owner to roll forward any gain.

So, if like Sara, you have a low cost basis in your home, you will have to pay capital gains taxes on the sale. And that is regardless of the huge price you might pay on your next home.

Paying Off a Mortgage Is Smart if Income Will Drop

Terrence and his wife Terry are in their mid-40s. They earn $100,000 combined, and have no kids and no debt other than a 6% $90,000 mortgage on a $200,000 home.

Terrence and Terry have $400,000 in savings (IRAs, 401(k)s, and savings accounts). Their two cars and the house roof will need replacing in 2 to 5 years.

But both Terrence and Terry will be laid off this year, and they're both considering switching to "feel-good" jobs that will slice their combined income by 50% by the end of the year.

Terrence and Terry have a question: Should they pay off their mortgage now or save the $90,000 in case of real disaster (can't find jobs, sudden health issue, etc). Terrence and Terry are healthy, conservative, and fairly risk-averse.

It's an excellent idea for them to find jobs they enjoy. Too often people spend their entire lives doing jobs they hate only because the pay is good. People are more content enjoying the journey through life than trudging through life with only the goal of financial success.

Although 6% is a great interest rate on a mortgage, Terrence and Terry would need to earn greater than 6% on their investments to come out ahead. That may be doable, but not without taking some risk. If their investments work out, they'll be in great shape in the future. But if they don't work out, Terrence and Terry might have to give up their feel-good jobs to earn enough to pay off the home.

They should plan on paying off their home once they are secure in their new jobs. With a 50% cut in pay, coming up with the mortgage payment each month could be a bit of a burden. If Terrence and Terry have no mortgage payments, they should be able to get by each month with less money.

Check With Your 401(k) Administrator

The record keeping on 401(k) plans can be a headache. Don't assume that your plan administrator has all the correct details. Check your statement and immediately alert the administrator to any errors.

Tina has been in her plan about 5 years, but has recently retired. She has made all contributions to the plan. Her employer made no contributions.

Recently she received a distribution form from the 401(k) manager that states she was only 80% vested. Tina thought that was ridiculous—she couldn't be only 80% vested in money that was totally hers.

By law, a plan participant is always 100% vested on one's contributions. Only funds contributed by an employer can be restricted by a vesting schedule.

It was clear that someone made an error. Tina contacted the plan administrator and he corrected the problem.

By the way, if you have this same problem and the employer doesn't correct it, then you should contact the Department of Labor. An employer who doesn't properly administer a plan can run up big fines and be faced with all sorts of other problems.

Don't Pay More in Payroll Taxes than You Must

Tens of millions of Americans who began working in the 1970s have been paying high payroll taxes, which have been raised many times since then to prevent the system from cracking up.

For many Americans, the payroll tax is their biggest tax bill. Some, who have been paying the maximum payroll amounts for years, have little incentive to keep funding Uncle Whiskers and big government dreams. (The surpluses from the Social Security taxes fund all sorts of government projects.)

Diane has been paying the max in Social Security taxes since 1970. She sold her business and retired last year at age 53. Diane is not planning on working between now and age 62, the earliest she can start collecting Social Security.

For people in Diane's situation—those who paid the most for many years—there is good news. Social Security benefits will be based on their highest 35 years of wages, adjusted for inflation. So Diane's lack of work from now until age 62 won't reduce her benefits, but future wages could increase her benefits.

She still has 9 years to go before she can collect benefits, and there may be some changes to the way benefits are calculated by the time she reaches age 62.

However, if she'd like to see how her lack of wages could impact her benefits under the current system, Diane could visit the Social Security Web site at www.ssa.gov. There is an online calculator where you can estimate your benefits.

Getting Behind the Retirement Eight Ball

The typical American doesn't save enough. Some don't save at all. This typical American waits until Junior is in the third year of high school before thinking about a college fund. He promises himself that he's going to save for that house, then lives most of his life in a crowded apartment because he can never manage the down payment. And, most alarming of all, he puts off saving for retirement until his mid or late 50s.

Sometimes he rationalizes this by saying that he plans on working forever. That, of course, ignores whether one will be able to work forever or whether one will always feel that working 40 or 50 hours a week is a great thing. We change in our lives. Change can be good or bad, but it is also inevitable.

Nevertheless, there are tens of millions of Americans who have $10,000 or less in financial assets. They think of schemes to fund retirement savings such as borrowing against a house, attracted by the potential tax benefits of such strategies. They might as well look for financial advice from Seinfeld's Kramer.

These people are fooling themselves. They refuse to face this difficult fact: Saving is not easy. If you want a comfortable retirement, if you want financial independence by age 45, or 55, or 65, there is no substitute for a sustained program of saving and investing over a protracted period.

Borrowing on your house to contribute to a tax-deferred retirement plan may help you on your income taxes this year, but it isn't going to help you much in the long run. You'd have more money saved for retirement, but you'd also have a larger liability against your home.

To be frank, you need to get serious about saving for retirement. Borrowing money against your home to sock into a retirement account isn't saving.

Saving is taking a portion of your earned income and setting it aside for the future.

Start saving for retirement on a monthly basis by using your 401(k) at work or any other qualified plan. Treat your retirement savings as important as making your mortgage payment. You wouldn't dare miss a mortgage payment, would you? You'd be risking the loss of your home and all the equity that you have. And if you look at saving the way you look at the mortgage payment, you'll not only save on your income taxes this year but also be in a better position for retirement.

Getting the Jump on Retirement Savings

Ten years ago a large pizza cost $9. Today it costs $15. Forty years ago, a ride on the wretched New York City subway cost 15 cents. Today a ride on the equally egregious subway is $2. In the early 1960s, a gallon of gas was about 50 cents. Today, well, it costs a hell of a lot more.

It's called inflation. Governments cause it by printing too much money. They debase their currencies. And it is probably the single reason why it is so difficult to figure out how much one will need 20 or 30 years from now. One rule of thumb is that it is much better to have more than you think you need. So how does one build up a big retirement stash?

Without doubt, the most important element in achieving a goal is the number of years you save and invest. This can be even more important than your investment returns. So get started as soon as you can, especially if you have some automatic savings plan at work; one in which an employer will match your contributions. You can also set up an investment plan with a good fund company. It will take money out of your checking company each month. A good fund company is one with a long record of good—not great—returns and with a record of low expenses.

But time is the greatest key. That's because the more your money compounds, the more the dividends thrown off dividends. You're much better off investing small amounts of money over long periods than huge amounts over short periods.

Let's say you invest $300 a month over 40 years and get 7% a year. You've invested $144,000. Another person invests $500 a month, but does it over 30 years. He's invested $180,000. He also gets 7% a year. He's invested $36,000 more than you, but he did it for 10 years less. Who is better off?

You are. And it's not even close. He only has $613,544 before taxes. However, you have $792,037. You had 10 more years of the compounding effect, and it made a difference of almost $179,000. Start saving as early as you can and continue with it a long as long as you can. Just 10 years extra can make a world of difference.

How You Invest a Roth

A Roth IRA will be a source of untaxed benefits when you start drawing it down in retirement. That is probably its greatest benefit—a nest egg that is beyond the power of our omniscient taxing authorities. But how does one ensure that the account obtains the best gains over long periods?

This was an issue before Doris. She is 51 years old and expects to invest $21,000 or so in some qualified retirement account over the next 15 years. She is starting with just $36 in the account. Doris wants to know the best way to make the account grow.

With 15 years to go before Doris needs to tap the $21,000, time is on her side. Her main goals should be to build a portfolio that can provide long-term growth.

Given the fact that she only has $36 in her Roth IRA, she may want to put the $21,000 into a Roth IRA. The Roth will provide for tax-deferred growth, and as long as she doesn't touch it until age 59½, all of her gains will come to her income tax-free, always a good deal given the long-term tendency of our lawmakers to raise income taxes.

To have the best opportunity for long-term growth, Doris should consider investing the funds in a portfolio highly weighted toward stocks. Why stocks? Since 1925, there has never been a 15-year period in which stocks have not made a profit. Furthermore, there has not been a 15-year period in which stocks have not outperformed bonds, according to Ibbotson Associates.

Depending on Doris' tolerance for risk, she may want to consider a portfolio something like this: 25% bonds, 50% large-cap stocks, 15% mid-cap stocks, and 10% small-cap stocks. The stocks should be highly diversified with companies representing many industries.

A Lump Sum or a Monthly Payment?

Many people have to make this decision. And it can only be intelligently made by crunching numbers and looking at your personal planning goals.

Lisa recently left a job where she had worked for 12 years. Her pension fund with the company added up to $78,000. This was based on her years of service and annual salary.

Lisa elected to leave the assets with the current holder of the plan so that she will have a guaranteed retirement payment of $808 monthly when she reaches age 59½.

But now Lisa is questioning her decision. She is 43 years old and still is about 15 years away from retirement. She had been thinking of rolling her money over into an IRA and trying to make it grow at a faster pace than what she would get from her own retirement plan.

The decision to take a pension lump sum or opt for a monthly payment or roll it over to an IRA should not be taken lightly. Often, it is one of the most important financial decisions one will face.

Lisa's employer needs to earn only about 4.5% on her $78,000 to pay her a pension of $808 per month at age 59½. If she had the cash, she would need to earn 4.5% to generate the same income.

If Lisa thinks that she could have earned more than 4.5% over the next 15 years, then she made a poor choice. And remember, the historic return of the stock market over long periods—10- to 20-year holding periods—is about 9% annually.

So be careful making this decision. Lisa is unsure whether she wants to take greater risks and put her money in the stock market. It's not a matter of whether Lisa is right or not. It is a matter that Lisa didn't thoroughly go over all the possibilities of what to do with this money.

Now, like it or not, right or wrong, there is nothing she can do. Unfortunately, her decision is irrevocable.

Diversification of Investments

Diversifying your investments is the principal method of reducing risk. Diversification is such an important concept that the law requires it for company retirement plans. Trustees of company pension and profit sharing plans must diversify the plan investments to minimize the risk of large losses.

There are two types of diversification: diversification among different companies and among different types of securities.

Investing in a portfolio that contains many securities of different companies will help you to avoid the risks that are present if you invest in only securities of a few companies or companies in only one industry. The economy and the financial markets are ever changing, and spreading your investment among many different companies in different industries can significantly reduce the risk of unpleasant surprises.

The other type of diversification is to spread your investments over different types of securities: bonds, stocks, and short-term investments. Each of these securities has different risks and will fluctuate over time. Selecting different types of investments will help to reduce the risks present with only one type of security.

Relationship of Risk to Rate of Return

Reducing risk is important, but equally important is obtaining rates of return that will enable your money to grow. To improve your rate of return, you will have to take some risk. Every investment has risk of one type or another. It is important for you to understand the risks that you will be willing to assume and the returns that you may get for assuming these risks.

If you wanted an investment that doesn't fluctuate and has no financial or credit risk, you would select certificates of deposit, money market funds, or treasury bills. However, these investments have historically provided the lowest return. Long-term bonds involve financial risk. Common stocks have historically provided the highest rates of return and the best potential of offsetting inflation. On the other hand, they involve higher degrees of market and financial risk.

When financial professionals talk about conservative investments they tend to focus on investments that have lower volatility and financial risks; aggressive investments tend to involve more of these types of risk.

Choosing an Investment Program

There is no one-investment program that is right for all people. Each person has his or her own needs for present or future income and his or her own concern about how much risk to assume. The key to creating an investment program that you will be comfortable with is to understand the roles that different investments can play in providing you with the income and growth that you need, while at the same time keeping risk at a level that you find suitable.

To meet your long-term needs, you have to select from among several types of investments with different risk and return potential. Some of you will opt for more conservative investments, recognizing that you will receive a lower rate of return, whereas others are willing to accept more aggressive investments in seeking a higher rate of return.

Setting Your Personal Objectives

When you set your objectives, it is important that you be realistic; the higher the rate of return that you seek, the greater the risk. Beware of persons who promise you rates of return that seem unbelievable; generally they are unattainable, or the investments entail a risk level that most people would not wish to assume. There are several considerations that you should take into account in selecting your investment program.

When will you need to take your money out? If you plan to start withdrawing money shortly after you receive your lump sum, you would normally want to reduce the volatility of your rollover investments. On the other hand if you will have many years before you need your money, you can accept greater fluctuations in the search of a higher rate of return. Remember that even if you plan to start withdrawals shortly, you will have to live off this money for many years and that you should have some portion of your money working to help offset inflation.

Is your lump sum your only source of retirement income? If your lump sum is the main source of your retirement savings, you will generally want to have a more conservative attitude toward investing. On the other hand, if you are going to receive a pension from your employer, its payments are generally guaranteed for many years into the future. However, the monthly payments normally don't increase, so you should invest your lump sum to provide for the growth of the assets in order to offset inflation.

"Solo K" Retirement Plan Aimed at Small Businesses

Teddy is a small businessman who wants to know how he can most effectively use a retirement plan.

Solo K is a retirement plan designed for small business owners with no full-time employees (hence, the name Solo K). Unlike traditional 401(k) plans, the Solo K is easy to establish and simple to maintain.

Solo K plans are available for both incorporated as well as unincorporated businesses. The maximum that can be contributed is 25% of the business's net income plus the $13,000 annual employee 401(k) limit, up to a maximum of $41,000 per year.

For example, a business owner with $50,000 in profits can sock away $13,000 for his or her annual contribution, and the company can sock away another $12,500, for a total of $25,500.

An individual does not need to be working full time in the business to utilize the Solo K. Even part-time home businesses can receive the Solo K benefits.

To take advantage of the Solo K, a business must establish a Solo K plan prior to December 31, but much of the deposits can be delayed until the time the income tax return is filed. Most brokerage and financial planning firms can help you establish a Solo K.

Are You Still Employed?

If you are still working, you can generally take more risk in your IRA. Over time you will have other money to invest to offset any declines in the securities markets.

The purpose of retirement income is generally to replace a significant portion of the income that you were earning while you were working. Because you are still working, your current income will be increasing. Your IRA also has to grow to provide future income to match the income that you will be earning when you actually retire.

Do You Have Investments Outside Your IRA?

If you have other investments, you should balance the investments in your IRA so that you have an appropriate portfolio, taking into account the investments inside and outside the IRA. Because an IRA is a long-term holding, you will generally use investments that have a longer time horizon in an IRA than investments that you may need before you retire, for example, common stocks that fluctuate more than money market investments and would be better in an IRA than in money market funds. Money market funds would be better used for savings outside an IRA where they would be available to meet emergencies.

How Experienced Are You?

If you have had experience in investing, you generally will understand its risks and rewards and you may be more willing to accept more fluctuations than if the thought of fluctuations will unduly concern you.

As the years go by and your needs change, your investment program should also change. The investment that you make today should be appropriate for you at this point in your life. However, over time your investment program should be modified to meet your future needs. It is therefore important to select investments that can easily be modified to meet your future requirements.

Moving Bonds into a Roth IRA

Joe wants to transfer $6,000 in savings bonds. He is out of luck.

All Roth IRA contributions must be made from cash deposits (check or money order). The only circumstances in which one can deposit investments into a Roth is when converting some assets from a traditional IRA to a Roth IRA or when completing a rollover from one plan to another.

To get his $6,000 into Roth IRAs, Joe would need to cash in his savings bonds and pay the taxes (and potential early penalty). Once the cash is in the Roth, Joe can invest the cash in a variety of investments. Still, he cannot own savings bonds inside an IRA.

Unless Joe plans to make a major change in his investment strategy, he should probably just keep his savings bonds and look for other cash to fund Roth IRAs.

Moving to a Roth

Let's assume you want to start a Roth. Bill, a contractor, wants to know the mechanics of converting his IRAs to Roth IRAs, which means paying a tax bill. What are the mechanics of doing this? Should Bill convert a bond fund first instead of a stock fund? And is there a way of making the transfer and keeping him in the lowest possible tax bracket?

There are a number of factors to consider before converting an IRA to a Roth IRA, and Bill appears to be looking at each of those factors. It is that type of analysis that sound financial plans are built on.

Because Bill believes he will be in a higher tax bracket upon retirement, he's a great candidate for the Roth conversion. He'll be paying taxes today at a lower tax rate to enjoy tax-free benefits when retired.

When deciding which assets to convert first, convert those assets you believe will have the highest growth over the next few years. Because stocks have outperformed many other investments over the long term, converting stocks probably should be the first priority.

With regard to the timing of Bill's conversion, this is an issue that should be discussed with a tax advisor who keeps up-to-date with the doings on

Capitol Hill. That's because Congress is forever tinkering with the tax code. So Bill should come up with a plan with his advisor before going ahead.

Overdoing Retirement Savings

Shelly is a schoolteacher in her late 30s who has taught for 14 years. She is doing something that few Americans are doing these days. She is probably saving more for her retirement than necessary.

She has no kids, one rental property, and will have her current home paid off by the time she is 50 years old. She contributes the yearly maximum to her 403(b) account of $13,000.

She is also contemplating a contribution of an additional $13,000 yearly to a 457 plan. If she begins contributions to a 457 plan, she hopes to resign from the school district (say at age 52) and use her 457 plan at that time and wait for pension until age 60.

Shelly is an aggressive saver who is already looking at the advantages and disadvantages of planning this type of retirement. Indeed, Shelly is well on her way to a comfortable retirement. By the time she retires, she'll not only have a good pension, but also have a boatload of money in her retirement plans, and no mortgage payment.

There is a tricky balance that should be maintained between how much is spent and how much is saved. Most people spend too much today and have too little saved for tomorrow. But there are a few people on the other end as well: They spend so little today that they wind up with more than they need during retirement.

Before Shelly starts kicking in an additional $13,000 into her 457 plan, she may want to run some projections on where she'll be by the time she retires. If she's been putting money for years into her 403(b), she may find her income in retirement far exceeds her current income. If that's the case, she needs to ask herself what she plans to do with the extra money once she retires.

By putting more money into a 457 plan, she may push herself into a lower tax bracket. In that situation, it's not advisable for Shelly to put aside any additional income. Given the way things are going for her, she'll be in a much higher tax bracket when she retires.

Assuming any additional 457 plan contributions will result in a tax savings of 25% or higher, there is no reason she couldn't max out those contributions and use the 457 plan money to fund her retirement income at age 52. There is no age requirement for 457 withdrawals. The only requirement is that one must leave his or her employer, either through retirement or other termination.

If most of Shelly's savings are in her tax-deferred retirement accounts, it might be wise to begin saving in a nonretirement account. She won't receive a current tax deduction, but she will have access to capital during retirement that won't cost her an arm and a leg in taxes.

Pension Portability?

Congress has finally come to its senses on pension portability. Even though there are still some issues about moving assets from one qualified plan to another, it is today now much easier to transfer money from, say, a traditional IRA to a Keogh pension or do the reverse.

Until recently, one could not transfer IRA balances to company retirement plans unless the IRA money was a result of a rollover from a previous retirement plan.

That has all changed. Today, pension plans are portable, and tax law allows you to transfer any IRA balances to any retirement plan, regardless of the originating source.

All retirement plans are subject to early withdrawal penalties prior to age 59½. Keogh plans have generally allowed withdrawals at age 55. However, there are a few exceptions to the penalties. (It's a kind of full-employment plan for lawyers, an idea that originated in Congress, a place dominated by, yes indeed, lawyers!).

In addition to the death and disability exceptions (both of which one should try to avoid), there are two other exceptions that could work for prospective retirees: the age-55 rule and the SEPP rule, also known as the 72(t) rule.

John has both a Keogh and a traditional 401(k) plan and wonders about transferring assets from one place to the other. If John is at least age 55 or older in the year in which he retires, he can pull money from the company's retirement plans (Keogh, 401(k), 403(b), etc.) without any restrictions or penalties.

John can also pull $5,000 from his Keogh one month, $10,000 the following month, nothing the next month, and so on. He has total and complete flexibility. All withdrawals will be exempt from the early withdrawal penalties, but will still be subject to ordinary income taxes. Well, there are a few times when Congress actually gets it right.

Still, money that is left in an IRA follows a different set of rules. The age-55 rule does not apply, regardless of the source of the funds. Money in an IRA can be received penalty free under the Series of Equal Periodic Payments method, but this method is quite restrictive and should be used only as a last resort.

If John transfers his IRA balance to his Keogh prior to retirement, his IRA no longer exists. Therefore, all his money is considered "qualified dollars." He'll be able to withdraw funds during retirement as he pleases.

Retirement Confusion

Chris worked for the New York City Public Library as a printer for some 40 years. He began in the 1930s. That would be his only full-time job in his life. He had only one retirement plan.

That was the norm for people of Chris' generation. But that is no longer the norm. Indeed, most people will work in multiple jobs over the course of their lives. That means they will accumulate assets in multiple places and have money in different kinds of plans. It can be maddening. And, until Congress decides to make plan portability easier, it will be a continuing problem that almost all of us will confront sometime in our work lives— maybe multiple times.

For example, Tyler recently switched jobs. He has a 401(k) from his previous employer, and now he has an opportunity to participate in a 403(b) or 457 plan. Each kind of plan has its advantages and disadvantages, but how many people actually understand this? Very few.

These myriad plans with their endless rules for everything from contributions to how often you can blow your nose show how insane our tax system is. Why in the world should someone have to choose between so many dif-

ferent types of retirement plans, particularly when they all provide basically the same benefits?

As an investor saving for retirement, the options range from a 401(k),
403(b), 457, 401(a), IRA, Roth IRA, SEP-IRA, Simple IRA, Keogh, and so
forth. Once someone sorts through all the retirement plans available, he or
she still has to pick the right kinds of investments to own inside the retirement accounts. Congress should simplify the ever-increasing complexity of
retirement savings.

A 403(b) has an advantage over a 457 plan in that you can borrow from
a 403(b), but you cannot borrow from a 457 plan. However, the 457 plan
could be more advantageous because there is no age requirement for withdrawals once you leave your employer. You can retire at any age and receive
income from a 457, whereas withdrawals from a 403(b) are more restrictive
prior to age 59½.

One distinct drawback of a 457 plan is that it is technically a liability of
your employer. Unlike a 403(b) or 401(k) account, you do not own the assets until they are paid to you. Money in a 457 plan is deferred compensation and is a promise from your employer to pay you upon retirement. In
the unlikely event that your employer goes bankrupt, your 457 plan could
be in jeopardy.

In regard to leaving your 401(k) where it is or rolling it over, it really doesn't
make much difference. Choose the plan that allows you the greatest degree
of investment flexibility. Still, it makes sense to spend some money and
hire a good advisor—preferably a certified financial planner—and discuss
the various options.

Switch in Pension Plans Can Spell Trouble

Jerry worked for FedEx for 14 years before quitting to pursue a teaching
career. Jerry was informed at the time of his leaving that his traditional
pension would yield $680 a month if he chose to collect at 55 years of age,
or about $800 if he chose to collect at age 60. Jerry said that he would like
to collect at age 55 years to supplement his income.

Now Jerry is worried. He fears the possibility that this traditional pension
may be turned over to something called a cash balance pension with a much

lower yield. Jerry wants to know if he can fight this. Neither his taxman nor his financial advisor knows anything about this.

Many companies have been moving away from traditional defined benefit plans and adopting cash balance pension plans. Although cash balance plans may benefit some employees, the main reason companies are switching to cash balance plans is simple: economics. Financial technocrats created cash balance plans as a means for corporations to save money on their pension contributions.

Don't believe it when your employer tells you the company is changing to a cash balance plan because it is concerned with your financial well-being. Your employer is concerned about his financial well-being, not yours.

Traditional pension plans provide a monthly income upon retirement based on an employee's years of service and pay. To qualify for retirement, an employee must have a certain number of years with the company and attain a stated age. Once an employee meets these requirements, he or she is vested for a pension.

Cash balance plans are quite different from traditional pension plans. Employees become vested after only a few years with a company.

Cash balance plans look somewhat like a 401(k) in that there is an account balance that receives contributions and interest. However, unlike a 401(k), the employer both contributes funds to the plan and guarantees the account balance. Contributions are typically based on a combination of pay and years of service.

As a general rule, traditional retirement plans favor long-term employees, whereas cash balance plans favor more transient workers. However, the majority of workers in this country would be better served by a traditional pension plan.

Under pension law, a company may change future retirement benefits but cannot reduce a benefit an employee has already earned through vesting.

If Jerry is currently vested for a monthly benefit at age 55, he is guaranteed to receive the value of that pension. The employer cannot take that away from him. However, the employer can pay Jerry the equivalent present value of that retirement in a lump sum.

Retirement Now or Later?

Retirement planning is probably the most difficult problem of all. How can we know exactly how much we'll need and whether we risk running out of money?

The problem is that we're human beings. We're not omniscient creatures with the exact answers to questions such as: How long until we meet St. Peter? What are we planning for? Thirty years? Forty years?

Indeed, let's take a real-life case. Jim is thinking of retiring at age 51. Unfortunately, he's not sure if he has adequate financial resources. Jim is considering retirement after nearly 35 years on the job. Currently he is single. His pension will be $2,150 per month minus $70 for medical. His Social Security projection shows that he will be entitled to $1,264 at age 62. Jim is not sure whether this will be reduced if he does not work between now and when he reaches age 62.

Jim's pension plan has an option that will pay him half this figure until age 62 and then reduce it by $1,264 when the Social Security kicks in. This would provide him a steady check of $2,782 for life.

Jim may look as though he has an address on easy street, but he has some potential problems. Let's look at his situation. It looks as though his company wants people to retire. The company is creative in designing ways for people like Jim to have a larger retirement check today rather than sticking them on the payroll for another decade.

The two pension options provided by Jim's employer have the same dollar value. That's assuming he lives an average life span. One option pays him a fixed-dollar amount for life, whereas the other offers an increased benefit. But that is reduced when Jim reaches age 62.

There are a number of problems with Jim's plan to retire at age 51 and opting for the higher pension. The number 1 issue is inflation. If inflation grows at just 3% per year, Jim's monthly income of $2,782 would buy only about $2,000 worth of goods when he is age 62. By the time he reaches age 73, his purchasing power would be reduced to just $1,450 per month.

These are serious issues. Indeed, people are living longer than ever before. Living into one's 90s is nothing extraordinary these days.

The estimate that Jim received from Social Security is based on his continued employment until age 62. If he quit working now and no longer contributed to the system, his retirement income would be reduced. In that case, the higher pension will be cut by an amount greater than his Social Security income. That would result in a hit on his monthly cash flow.

If Jim plans on leaving his employer at age 51, he should not to take any option that will result in a reduction of income in the future. If he can afford to retire at such a young age, Jim must be sure of something: that his retirement plan doesn't provide just a steady retirement check. Jim needs a retirement income that increases to offset the ravages of inflation.

Reverse Dollar-Cost-Averaging-Out of Employer's Stock

Julie has been with the same company for 26 years, and plans on retiring when she reaches 30 years of service. Her concern is with her company savings plan. She has always put my money in the company stock, but her employer's stock has been doing horribly. "My 401(k) has fallen from almost $300,000 to $230,000 and I have no idea what to do."

She doesn't want to *sell* the stock while it's down, but doesn't want to risk her retirement either.

The danger is having all her investments in the company she works for.

It's understandable why she doesn't want to sell her employer's stock while it's down, but how does she know where the bottom is? It is conceivable that the stock could fall another 25%. Or it could increase 50% in the next few months. No one really knows.

Rather than worrying about the stock price, Julie could make a plan to diversify the 401(k) plan over a period of time. She could transfer out 25% of her employer's stock this week, 25% 3 months from now, 25% 6 months from now, and 25% 9 months from now; then invest the proceeds into a balanced strategy comprising stocks and bonds spread among many types of asset classes or mutual funds. This is a form of "dollar-cost-averaging-out" of employer's stock. This also takes the guessing out of marketing timing and better prepares Julie for retirement.

Rigid Roth Rules

A Roth IRA offers a unique ability to access IRA assets with minimal taxes. But there's a catch. There are many withdrawal rules that can catch you if you're not very careful. Taxes, penalties, and all sorts of terrible things can catch you.

Here's an example of a potential problem. Simon turned 60 years old in 1998. He converted his $26,000 traditional IRA to a Roth IRA. The account has since grown to $66,000, of which $35,000 is profits and $5,000 is total contributions, $2,500 in 2000 and another $2,500 in 2001.

Simon believes that he can now withdraw $21,000 without tax penalty, taking into consideration the first-in, first-out rule. Still, he's not sure how the $5,000 in contributions will affect future withdrawals of profits, including the existing profits of $35,000.

Anytime you withdraw money from a Roth IRA you must pay attention to the "ordering rules." According to the IRS ordering rules, Roth IRA withdrawals are distributed in the following order: (1) annual contributions, (2) Roth conversions, and (3) earnings.

There is also the 5-year rule that essentially states that you must keep your conversion dollars and earnings on contributions in your Roth for at least 5 years.

You could withdraw almost all of your Roth without any taxes. All of your contribution money can come out tax-free (there is never a tax on return of contributions). Your conversion dollars can be withdrawn tax-free because the 5-year rule was satisfied, and you can withdraw most of your earnings. The only money that cannot be withdrawn tax-free is the earnings on your $5,000 contributions. That amount won't be available until 5 years after your first contribution.

But consider this. Although you could withdraw most of your Roth without any taxes, why would you want to? The main benefit of the Roth is the future tax-free growth of assets. Your Roth IRA should be probably the penultimate place to take money.

Roth Conversion

Two years ago Angie quit her job at a local hospital. She has a cash balance retirement account of around $36,000, which is getting about 5.5% interest. She is 52 years old and plans to continue working to age 65. But she wants to move some or all of it into a Roth. She knows she must have a tax plan to accomplish this.

This year Angie's household income—she is married—will be considerably lower than usual due to a temporary disability. She wants to roll the money into a Roth as soon as possible. Now might be an excellent time to convert a portion of Angie's cash balance account to a Roth IRA. Still, she cannot convert the retirement plan directly to a Roth, but she can roll the plan to an IRA. And, after that, she can convert the IRA to a Roth IRA.

Angie should talk this over with her tax advisor before going ahead. She needs to examine her tax situation carefully before converting to a Roth. If she converts the entire balance, the conversion could push her into a 25% federal tax bracket. However, if she plans carefully, she could convert a portion of it and be taxed at only the 15% level.

Talk to a tax advisor to help you crunch the numbers before you do the conversion. That's because tax regulations are always changing. But get the ball rolling on transferring your cash balance account to an IRA. The deadline for the conversion is December 31, and companies seem to have two speeds on this: slow and slower. They have been known to take weeks processing a rollover request.

Roth IRA or 401(k)?

Daniel and Patty have heard these spiels myriad times. Now they're ready to do something, but they're not sure what. You see, they both have 401(k) plans at their jobs, but their employers don't match their contributions.

Now they want to know which they should choose: set up a Roth IRA or make maximum contributions to their 401(k) plans at work.

They should use both plans. They should diversify their tax strategies in the same way they should diversify their investments.

The nice thing about the 401(k) is the forced savings. Their contributions are sucked out of their paychecks before they have the chance to spend the money. They get the current tax deduction, but they'll be stuck paying income taxes when they spend the money.

The beauty of the Roth IRA is the tax-free retirement income. You don't receive any tax deduction up front. Still, money grows tax deferred and comes out tax-free at retirement. Having money that one can access without taxes is a big benefit to retirees.

Daniel and Patty can put half of the savings into the Roth IRA and half into the 401(k). No one knows what the tax system will look like 30 years from now, but spreading their tax risks is bound to help.

A Lost Pension?

Jeff believes that he earned a pension some years ago. He worked for the company for 10 years, then moved on to several other jobs. Now, many jobs later, the 55-year-old Jeff wants to obtain what he believes is his small pension.

The Pension Benefit Guarantee Corp. (PBGC) is likely the best place to search. The PBGC is a government-backed agency. It insures private pensions and maintains information on thousands of pensions.

The best way to contact the PBGC is through its Web site, www.pbgc.gov.

IRAs Are Better Tax Shelter for Bonds than for Stocks

Howie, who is retired, wanted some advice on the best way to set up his portfolio. He thought it made sense to have long-term investments (such as stocks) in his IRA and bond investments held separately. But with the lower tax rates put in place by the Bush administration, Howie was wondering if this still makes sense.

Based on the current tax law, investments that produce income should be held in tax-deferred vehicles. Investments that provide potential long-term gains should be held outside tax-deferred accounts. The reason? Tax rates. Capital gains and most corporate dividends are taxed at a maximum rate of 15%. Income from bonds, savings accounts, and most REITs are taxed as ordinary income. And this can run as high as 35%. All income from IRAs, 401(k)s, and the like is taxed as ordinary income. And that's regardless of what type of investment produced the income.

For long-term investors like Howie, the most tax-efficient strategy is having bonds and other income producing investments inside a retirement account. Stocks should be held outside of retirement accounts. The main drawback is that withdrawals from IRAs are fully taxable. If the stock market is in the tank and Howie needs to pull some income from his investments, he would have to withdraw from his IRA. And that could trigger a big tax bill.

Many others have the same situation as Howie. They should have a large percentage of their investment assets outside of their IRA because they are not currently requiring income from their investments.

Retirement Plan Conversions

Lena is 35 years old and recently changed jobs. With Lena's previous employer, she had approximately $100,000 in a 401(k). Because Lena likes the investments she has in the account with her previous employer, she was looking to convert the 401(k) to an IRA account and keep the same investments option. She didn't see any problem in using this retirement planning strategy.

There is no reason that Lena couldn't roll the money from her previous employer's 401(k) to an IRA and acquire investments similar to what was held in the 401(k). However, she simply cannot transfer the securities.

Most 401(k) providers will sell whatever is held in the account before the funds are released. The exception to this is the employer's stock. Lena's employer would like employees to keep the stock and never sell it, so the company is more than happy to issue a stock certificate for its shares.

Occasionally, funds can be wired, but, more often than not, the 401(k) will send a check via snail mail.

Before you initiate a rollover, make sure the IRA custodian will allow you to purchase all of the securities you would like to own. Once funds are transferred to the IRA, you can then purchase whatever you wish. The only risk that Lena faces during the rollover is having her funds on the sidelines during the week or two it takes to complete the transfer.

IRAs are not covered under ERISA law (a law that covers company pension plans). This means Lena's money may be easier to access by creditors than if it the money were left in the 401(k).

Roth Tax Deductions

Doug was unlucky. In the spring of 2000, he finally decided to convert his traditional IRA to a Roth IRA, paying the taxes on the conversion. Doug also decided to switch these assets—about $36,000 in a bond fund—to a high-flying tech fund. Little did he know that tech stocks were about to crash.

By early 2003, after the debacle of a bear market, the value of Doug's Roth IRA had dropped to $9,000. Doug was upset, as were millions of other Americans who had put too much of their assets into one kind of investing, ignoring the common-sense advice that diversification is one of the keys of successful long-term investing.

Doug was looking to pick up the pieces. He was hoping to find some tax deductions to offset the disastrous 3 years of a stock market crackup.

The news wasn't good for Doug. He could deduct his Roth IRA losses, but only if he withdrew 100% of all his Roth IRA assets. Doug had a cost basis of his original $36,000 conversion in addition to any contributions he made. The loss can be claimed only if Doug itemizes deductions. Doug can only deduct those losses that exceed 2% of his adjusted gross income.

Taxing Situation—Lowdown on Roth IRA

Roth IRAs are fabulous retirement vehicles, but confusion about them abounds. For instance, Gary was puzzled by Roth information that he had read in a couple of personal finance magazines. Gary didn't understand whether he could redeem the principal in his Roth IRA without penalty for any reason. Gary had converted these shares from a regular IRA account several years ago.

Money that is deposited, but not converted, into a Roth IRA can be withdrawn for any reason without taxes or penalties. It is only the interest or gains that would be taxable. For example, if you deposited $4,000 into a Roth IRA and it grew to $5,000, then you could withdraw $4,000 without any tax consequences. If you withdrew the entire account balance, the $1,000 in gain would be taxed as ordinary income and early withdrawal penalties could apply.

Money that was converted to a Roth IRA is tied up for at least 5 years or until age 59½, whichever is longer. Converted dollars withdrawn before that date are not taxable, but they are subject to a 10% early withdrawal penalty.

Because of the tax-free nature of Roth IRA withdrawals, these accounts should be left alone for as long as possible. For most people, the Roth IRA should be the last money ever spent. Gary felt much better upon learning this.

Social Security Blues

Social Security can be confusing. Peter knew that he needed to have 10 years (40 quarters) of working to qualify for Social Security. But Peter wanted to know if he could pay himself, claim it legally, and pay into his Social Security fund to accumulate.

To receive Social Security retirement benefits, a person must have at least 40 Social Security credits. An individual can earn one credit for each $890 of earnings. Then the person can accumulate up to four credits per year. All four credits can be earned in one calendar quarter.

If Peter is short of the 40 credits, he'll need to have some type of employment that is subject to payroll or Social Security taxes. This can be accomplished by self-employment, but Peter must actually earn a profit. You cannot simply take money from your right hand and place it in the left hand and call it a profit.

Social Security Payments Are Taxable

What isn't taxable? Not much. However, there are various ways that one's income is treated if one is 62 years old, still works, and wants to start collecting Social Security.

Is there a limit on collecting Social Security because of wages from a job? Kathy will be 62 in August of this year. She made $11,640 last year in wages. She receives a pension each month from a former employer, a small income from a rental unit, and a portion from her 401(k). She expects to make another $11,640 this year from a job.

The earnings limit applies to wages and self-employment income. You can have an unlimited amount of income from pensions, interest, capital gains, IRAs, rentals, and so forth and collect your full Social Security benefits.

There is no limit on how much someone can earn once he or she reaches normal retirement age. The normal retirement age used to be 65, but it has been gradually increasing and will reach 67 for those born 1960 and later.

The annual earnings limit of $11,640 extends from age 62 until the start of the year individuals reach their normal retirement age. From then until their birthday that year, the limit jumps to $31,080. After their birthday, which marks their official retirement age, there is no limit on earnings.

The 401(k) Entrance Fee

Some companies view access to a 401(k) as a privilege. And they will confer it only after a new employee has met a certain standard. That's what Denise, a client, recently learned.

She joined a company that will not allow a new employee to take advantage of the company's 401(k) plan until serving 1 year of employment. That seemed a bit odd to Denise. That's because she just departed a company that had much easier 401(k) plan rules. She is unsure whether she should leave her money there.

Most companies require an employee to be on the payroll for a period of time before eligibility to enroll in the 401(k). This basically protects the employer from added hassles, should a new hire not last. There is typically nothing one can do about this. During the 1-year waiting period, Denise will have to fund her retirement through other vehicles during that waiting period.

Denise may want to consider the use of a contributory or Roth IRA.

With regard to Denise's previous employer's 401(k), most companies will allow a former employee to leave his or her funds in their plan even after one terminates employment. Denise should be able to leave the money in that plan until she can participate in the new plan. Then she can elect a "direct transfer" of her funds to the new plan and the transfer will be executed without any tax consequences

The Exception to the IRA Rule

When you are leaving a company, most times it makes sense to move your 401(k) plan assets to an IRA. Nine times out 10 it is the best move.

That's because an IRA provides much greater investment flexibility and control. However, there are a few notable differences between the 401(k) plan and the IRA. The major difference has to do with those 401(k) account holders who retire between the ages of 55 and 59½.

The tax law under IRC 72 states that all retirement plan withdrawals prior to age 59½ are subject to early withdrawal penalties. There is an exception for those age 55 or older. If individuals separate service from their employers in the year they reach age 55, there are no early withdrawal penalties from their employer-sponsored retirement plans.

That means those who quit or retire at age 55 or older can pull money from their employers' 401(k) plans without any penalties. There are no restrictions on the withdrawals. A retiree can pull $10,000 from the account this year, $20,000 the following, $2,000 the next year, and so forth. Unlike withdrawals from IRAs prior to age 59½, the withdrawals can be totally flexible.

The second difference has to do with creditor protection. Although money in IRAs is tougher for creditors to get at than cash in the bank, funds in a 401(k) are much harder. 401(k) plans are covered by ERISA rules, which provide protection in the event of bankruptcies, judgments, and so forth. IRAs do not receive ERISA protection.

If you are not between the ages of 55 and 59½ and are not worried about being sued or filing for bankruptcy, roll the money into an IRA. You'll have much greater control over your funds.

The Qualified Plan Withdrawal Mess

And you thought saving for retirement was the difficult part!

Most people are not saving enough for retirement. But there are people who are saving huge amounts. Some of them are going to have unexpected problems getting at their money. The mess will come from the different kinds of retirement accounts they have, the nature of their contributions, and Byzantine tax rules.

Tax rules usually change just as you have started to understand them. These rules have changed over the years so that some of IRA contributions were deductible and others were not.

As an example, Jim started multiple IRA accounts many years ago. At that time they were all tax deductible. Subsequently, Jim added money (non-tax-deductible) to the accounts as well as money from a 401(k) plan, which was rolled into several of the IRAs.

IRA contributions (both tax deductible and non-tax-deductible) were $23,500 between 1992 and 2002. Jim's 401(k) contribution was $700,000. Total value of IRA accounts is now $800,000. Now Jim is getting ready to withdraw some of this qualified money and is worried that he is about to venture into the Bermuda Triangle of qualified plan rules.

The news isn't good for Jim. Because the vast majority of his IRA is composed of tax-deductible contributions and tax-deferred earnings, his withdrawals will be almost entirely taxable. Only that portion of his IRA that was contributed with after-tax contributions will escape Uncle Whiskers.

The problem is Jim should have been filing IRS Form 8606 each year with his tax return to inform the IRS of the value of his after-tax contributions. However, Jim is like most people. He doesn't stay up to 3 o'clock in the morning going through obscure portions of the billion-page tax code. He doesn't memorize arcane decisions of the tax court to recite at parties. He doesn't live for heated discussions of little-known codicils of tax laws.

Because most people aren't tax experts, they don't know they have to file form 8606. Therefore, they have not been filing it. Therefore, they are likely going to pay more in taxes than they should. Therefore, they are consigned to the lowest reaches of the tax inferno.

Without that form, the IRS will do what it always does. It will assume the worst and try to collect as much as possible. The publicans will assume that 100% of Jim IRAs have yet to be taxed.

If you haven't filed that form in the past, be sure you do it this year.

All of your IRAs must be added together to determine what portion of a withdrawal is tax-free. You take the value of your after-tax contributions and divide it by the total balance of your IRAs to determine what percentage of a withdrawal will be tax-free.

For example, if you made $10,000 worth of after-tax contributions, you divide $10,000 by $800,000 to arrive at 1.25%. This means that any withdrawal will be 98.75% taxable and 1.25% tax-free.

The Retirement Plan that Can Help You Today

In general, you want to leave your retirement savings alone until age 59½ when you can start taking penalty-free withdrawals. You also want the money to compound for as many years as possible so you will have the best chance to accumulate the biggest nest egg.

However, there are cases when you can and may need to break into your 401(k) account and the taxing authorities will give you a break. Let's say that you were hurt on the job last year and forced to take out $12,000 from your 401(k). You had no other income. You spent about $12,000 in mortgage interest on your home. How much tax will you owe on the money withdrawn?

In these special circumstances you may not owe any taxes. In fact, you may be due a refund of the 20% that was withheld on the withdrawal from your 401(k). That's because the income tax due on retirement plan withdrawals is determined by your overall taxable income for the year. If you had no other taxable income and had itemized deductions that exceeded your withdrawal, your taxable income was zero. If so, your withdrawal was tax-free.

Depending on your age, you may get hit with an early withdrawal penalty when you file your taxes. Unless you are age 59½ or totally disabled, you'll have to pay a 10% federal and a 2.5% state early withdrawal penalty. You still want to avoid doing this, but sometimes it may be a necessary measure.

The Retirement Twilight Zone

There's a signpost up ahead. You've just turned age 59½. You've entered the Retirement Twilight Zone!

This can be a frightening place. You have spent 30 years building up assets in an IRA, or a SEP, or some other qualified retirement savings plan. Now you actually have some leeway in what you do with these assets.

Many people are confused. They feel that the government can wipe out huge amounts of these savings with outrageous and egregious penalties.

There are basically three stages in a person's life as it pertains to retirement plans: those years before age 59½, those years from 59½to 70½, and those years after age 70½.

When a person is under age 59½, there are a number of restrictions on pulling money from IRAs, 401(k)s, 403(b)s, and so forth. When a person reaches age 70½, there is a minimum amount that must be withdrawn from each retirement account.

But during the time in between those years you can do whatever you want.

Throughout your entire life you have just 11 years with which you have total control over your retirement accounts. You can choose to take a withdrawal, close out the account, or allow the money to continue to grow. The choice is yours. You need only to report any income that is withdrawn.

Finally, it always makes sense to go over this with your tax advisor. There are strategies that can reduce taxation. But these strategies sometimes change because the Solons on Capitol Hill and the taxing authorities who purport to carry out their wishes often change the rules just when everyone is close to understanding what they actually mean.

Are Your Retirement Savings Safe?

These days money-hungry states will do almost anything to separate you from more of your hard-earned money. Almost every state wants to hook you on their version of gambling (called lotteries). States also levy huge taxes on tourists through hotel taxes. And, in recent years, there has even been a move to start taxing the retirement proceeds of people who have come from other states.

Well, at least for the time being, the last one is not a problem. Indeed, state income taxes on pension income used to be a huge problem. Retirees who worked in several states had to pay state taxes in those states, even if they resided in a state with no income taxes during retirement.

The law changed in 1996 when President Clinton signed into law HR 394, now PL 104-95. This law prohibits states from taxing the pensions of non-residents. A retiree can receive pension income, including withdrawals from IRAs and other retirement accounts, without being taxed by their previous state of residence.

To avoid a big tax hit on your pension, transfer your lump sum to an IRA and wait until you are a resident of your state before you take a withdrawal. As long as you do that, you won't have to worry about your retirement state receiving a dime of your retirement savings. And look up the odds of winning a substantial prize before you play that state lottery.

Watch Out for Those 401(k) Transfers

You leave a job at age 54 with $55,000 in your 401(k). Without getting advice, you roll it into an IRA. Now you want to pull money out of your IRA without getting hit with federal and state penalties. You've likely made a very big mistake.

You should never have rolled your money to an IRA when you left your job. Your 401(k) plan provider, as well as your IRA custodian, should have warned you of the tax flexibility you were giving up when you transferred your money from the 401(k) to the IRA.

Withdrawals from an employer's retirement plan after leaving your employer can be done without penalties as long as you were age 55 or older when you left your job.

However, once the money is moved to an IRA, the penalty-free age moves up to 59½. Had you left your money in the 401(k), you could have taken a withdrawal of any amount and avoided the early withdrawal penalties.

But now that your money is in an IRA, you cannot take a lump-sum withdrawal before age 59½ without paying early withdrawal penalties.

Whenever you have access to any qualified money, be very careful what you do with it. Before you actually take it, consult with your advisor. And, if you have any doubts, leave it where it is before acting. Remember, Uncle Whiskers (in hock for trillions of dollars) is always in need of more of your money.

Borrowing on Your 401(k) Is Risky

Some assets you should leave alone and just let them grow. For example, it generally is a good idea not to break into the equity in your home. Let it grow. And some day you may be able to sell it for a big profit. And the assets in your retirement plan are the same. Let them be.

Young workers who want luxuries sometimes break into their 401(k) plans. This is a very bad move. However, there are exceptions to this rule. Sometimes you might tap the equity in these assets to invest in something like a small business that could help make you financially independent.

George was about to start a small home-based business with his wife, Debbie. They figured the total startup costs would be about $20,000. They didn't have a lot of money in the bank, so they wondered if they should borrow against either their house or their 401(k).

George and Debbie's 401(k) is one of the last places they should look for a loan. Although the interest paid goes directly to their account, there are several pitfalls with 401(k) loans.

Whenever you borrow from a 401(k), you have to sell investments you currently hold in the 401(k) to come up with the cash for the loan.

For example, if you have a balance of $50,000 invested in equities, $20,000 worth of equities would be sold to generate the cash for the loan.

When this happens, you no longer have that money working for you. You miss out on the opportunity for those dollars to grow.

Another setback with 401(k) loans is the repayment schedule. Most 401(k) loans must be paid back over 5 years. That might not be too bad, but a problem occurs if you leave your employer. Loans from 401(k)s typically need to be repaid within 30 to 90 days from the date of termination.

If the loan is not repaid, the loan is treated as a taxable distribution. In that case, George and Debbie would have to include the outstanding loan balance on their income tax return. And if George and Debbie were not of retirement age, they would be hit with early withdrawal penalties in addition to ordinary income taxes.

Too many people either lose their jobs or move on to better ones while there is a loan balance on their 401(k). If they have any equity in their home, a home equity loan would be a better alternative for George and Debbie.

What Happens When the 401(k) Plan Changes

Qualified plans are great for saving retirement and lowering tax bills, but they can sometimes be headaches.

Another company recently purchased Susan's company, and the 401(k) program is being "merged" with the new company's plan. However, the selections of funds are entirely different than the options Susan had.

The acquiring company has told Susan that she cannot roll her money over into an IRA, citing a "Same Seat Policy."

A company's 401(k) plan may go through many changes throughout a person's time on the job. And it is common for a company to change investment options every few years. When a company merges with another one, often the old plan is dissolved into a new plan.

The Same Seat Policy is part of the guidelines that direct the employer's 401(k). It provides for the plan to be transferred into a new 401(k). Law drives some of the guidelines; others are driven by an employer's desires. It is not tax law that is prohibiting Susan from transferring funds to an IRA; it is the employer.

If Susan has a strong desire to transfer her funds into an IRA, she should discuss it with her company's human resources department. If the company will not allow the transfer, then Susan should research the new plan and make the best of the new choices.

Which Qualified Plan Is Better?

It is the classic problem of those who have just started saving for retirement, but then change jobs.

To port or not to port? Should you take your retirement assets to another job or leave them where they are? Complicating the problem is another issue: Different employers have different kinds of plans. Some have 401(k) plans. Others have 457 plans, and there is a considerable list of kinds of retirement plans so that an employee can accumulate assets over 20 years or so in many different places.

Brian has about $13,000 in his 401(k). Now he wants to transfer the money to his 457 plan. First, the good news. Tax law allows individuals to transfer just about any retirement account to any other. One can move money from an IRA to a 401(k) to a 457 to a Keogh to an IRA to a 457, and so forth. There are very few restrictions.

However, whether or not you can transfer your 401(k) to your 457 depends on your employer. If your employer allows it, you can. But if your employer prohibits the transaction, you're stuck with two plans. Brian's former employer permitted the transfer, but it is not always a happy ending.

Nevertheless, it really doesn't matter how many retirement plans you have. The key is how much you have saved: $10,000 invested in ten 401(k)s should not perform any differently from $100,000 in one 401(k).

How Does One Treat a Settlement?

Tomas will receive a legal settlement from a class-action lawsuit filed against a former employer. The thrust of the suit was that Health Trust

Inc., a spin-off from the Health Care Agency (HCA), created an Employee Stock Ownership Plan (ESOP) in the late 1980s that provided employees with company stock in place of the existent retirement plan. His former employer also altered the vesting provisions, and it is this alternation that was the basis of the suit. Bottom line: Tomas will receive about $30,000.

Tomas is wondering whether this money has to be placed in one of his existing retirement accounts to avoid a legal penalty. Tomas already has a 403(b) and IRAs to avoid penalty. As a legal judgment, Tomas asked, is it tax-free? Tomas is 55 years old and no longer employed at that hospital.

Odds are the money Tomas is receiving will be considered "qualified dollars" and will be treated as a retirement distribution. Tomas can either have the money transferred to one of his retirement accounts or have it paid directly to himself.

If Tomas were under age 55 when he left the hospital, any money he received would be fully taxable and subject to early withdrawal penalties. If Tomas were 55 years old in the year he left the hospital, the money would still be taxable. However, Tomas could avoid the early withdrawal penalties.

If, in the unlikely event the settlement is not considered retirement dollars, Tomas will not have the ability to roll the money to a retirement account. Any money Tomas receives will be taxable, but early withdrawal penalties won't apply.

Chapter 10
Transfer Your Wealth Strategically

When people inherit money, they tend to spend it differently than if they earn it. People make totally different decisions on inherited money than on dollars that they've earned. A lot of times the largest estates are those that have been very frugal over the years. The typical millionaire is not someone who's been making millions of dollars as a corporate CEO. Those people exist, but the average millionaire is the small business owner who's worked his tail off his whole life and has been very frugal. When they pass on, unfortunately, 9 times out of 10, the kids are no longer frugal.

If you have any assets at all and you do no estate planning, it's cruel to your children. All it's going to do is cause fighting and bickering for most families. Taking the time to spell it all out beforehand avoids problems.

A Confusing Gift

Over the next few years, billions (possibly trillions) of dollars of wealth are going to pass from one generation to another. The Greatest Generation, the generation that fought and won World War II, is dying off, and the baby boomers will be inheriting huge amounts of money. Inheriting money can be a happy or a sad thing. It can also be a confusing thing. For many boomers, it will be the first—and possibly the last—time that they will have significant assets. The best advice is to take your time. Many brokers and financial planners will want to rush you into making an investment decision. You should be in no hurry to get these dollars invested. And you should avoid any advisers who, 5 minutes after they meet you, say they immediately have the best investment for you. Good advisers will want several sessions before they make any recommendations. Good advisers, no matter how smart, have a sense of modesty. It takes time to know someone and what is best for that person.

If you are like most people, inheritances come with some emotional ties. Many people feel guilty about receiving money from a loved one and have trouble spending the money. Typically, it takes several months after a death before the beneficiary can think clearly about any investment decisions.

Before you make any investments with your inheritance, you need to determine what you want these dollars to do for you. Do you want to use some of the money to buy a new home? A new car? Do you want to pay down your house? Pay off bills? Will some go to help pay for college costs for a child? Or will most of it be used for your retirement?

I encourage you to visit a qualified financial planner to help you develop an investment strategy based on your goals. You are about to receive an amount that can make a big difference in your life, and you don't want to make any major investment mistakes. This may be the most important chance you have to reach financial independence.

How to Pass on Property

Shawn's grandfather recently passed away and left his house to Shawn and his other three kids. All four are now adults and are financially well off. Shawn's three brothers have said they would make a deal on the house with Shawn that he couldn't refuse. Shawn says they have a very close family and that they aim to keep this house in the family for now. Shawn asked me how to best conduct (i.e., the least cost) this transaction. Shawn's relatives will pay him whatever price on which they all agree. Shawn, who has never owned a home, wanted to find the best way to avoid certain taxes and any buying or selling costs.

I told Shawn that he appears to have an excellent opportunity to purchase his first home. With interest rates still relatively low right now, buying a home at a reduced price seems like a can't-lose situation. This transaction need not be too complex. Depending on what kind of "deal" the family is willing to make, there may not be any tax considerations. Each family member can give Shawn up to $11,000 without any gift tax consequences, and as long as the "discount" is not greater than $33,000, no one needs to worry about gift taxes. If Shawn's three brothers sell him the home for a discount of greater than $33,000, they'll need to account for the gift when they file their income taxes. There will be no capital gains or losses to report on the transaction. Because the grandfather's death was recent, there probably hasn't been any significant change in the property value since the time of his death. Even if the home is sold below fair market value, Shawn's family will not be able to take a capital loss. That's because any reduced sales price is obviously a gift. I reminded Shawn that there is no reason to get into a sales contract with a real estate agent to complete this transaction because the buyer and seller are already lined up. However, unless someone in Shawn's family knows the ins and outs of selling a home, he still may want to consult with a real estate professional. He or she can help Shawn to complete all the necessary steps to transfer the home successfully.

Does Drafting Your Own Trust Make Sense?

Probably not! That's what I told Catherine and Larry, who were advised by their planner to draw up a living trust.

An attorney will do it for some $1,300. But, the couple told me, they could buy a software program and write the trust themselves.

The thing to remember about wills, trusts, and other estate planning devices is this: You'll never know if they work well or not. Your estate plan won't be tested until you're 6 feet under and unable to offer any additional input.

I hate dealing with attorneys as much as the next guy (No, more than the next guy!). A simple problem always seems to need a complex solution. But, because Catherine and Larry are not experts in estate law, I believe they need an attorney to draw up effective estate documents.

Catherine and Larry may think they know all you need to about trusts. But they don't know what they don't know. In other words, what you don't know can hurt you.

Leaving It to Your Children

Monique and Gregory are a low-income, very senior couple. They cannot afford a living trust. Nine months ago, Monique and Gregory paid $80,000 for a new mobile home. They put the title under their names and those of their three children. Thus, after they die, they reasoned, their children will some day avoid probate. Big mistake, I told them.

Monique and Gregory, by having their children listed on their property, are taking a risk. They could have their home taken from them by their children's creditors. And this applies not just to Monique and Gregory. If someone's child has financial problems or has a financial judgment against him or her, the parents' home could be seized. Monique and Gregory might think it couldn't be possible. I know better. I've seen it happen. For example, what if one of Monique and Gregory's children was in a bad auto accident where the medical damages surpassed the insurance limits? Monique and Gregory shouldn't have worried about probate. That's because, typically, probate isn't a problem for estates valued under $100,000. Even if one's estate were greater than $100,000, it would probably be better for one's children to deal with probate than for you to risk your home. If I were in your shoes, I advised Monique and Gregory, I'd take the children off the title of my home.

Estate Problems for Your Children

You could unwittingly be setting up your favored child for an estate-planning nightmare, giving the child an impossible task.

Marcia, a friend of mine, was named the executor of her mother's estate. Her mother passed away recently and now Marcia, who has two sisters and a brother, is facing an estate-planning problem that would have taxed the wisdom of Solomon.

The mother passed two IRAs to Marcia. She is named as sole beneficiary. But her mother wanted her to ensure that everything would be divided equally. But because the assets are in Marcia's name, and only her name, she is the one saddled with the tax bills.

Now Marcia wants to have the money put in a floating IRA. Then she could distribute money to her siblings from there. She has been told by friends to hold back about 40% in taxes because that is about what she will have to pay next year.

Still, that advice worries her. She fears that, if she transfers her part back into an IRA, that part of the estate will be taxed. Marcia, understandably, wants the tax burden apportioned among the family members.

Marcia's problem probably is a common one. Her mother made a costly error when she listed only Marcia as the beneficiary of her IRA. If her goal was to divide the money among her children, she should have listed all four children as beneficiaries.

Now Marcia has two problems that require attention. First, there's the matter of the income tax. Because she is listed as primary beneficiary, all withdrawals will be taxable to Marcia. She cannot transfer the tax liability to her siblings.

Unfortunately, there is no way for Marcia to get the money back into an IRA. Non-spouse beneficiaries do not have the ability to do a 60-day rollover.

Once the money is out of the IRA, it must stay out. She cannot set up a new IRA and deposit the funds there to avoid taxes.

The second problem Marcia faces is the potential gift tax consequence. She can give each sibling only $11,000 per year. Once she exceeds that limit, she reduces the amount she can pass on, free of estate taxes, upon death.

The best course of action may have been to leave the money in the IRA and draw it down over the next few years. This could have reduced the tax liability considerably. Regrettably, there is little that can be done at this time.

Getting Your Son Started Early on Retirement Planning

It's never too early to start retirement planning for someone, even if that someone is a teenager.

That's because it's not only how much money you put in a retirement account or what the investments earn that leads to wealth. Possibly, a bigger factor in creating wealth is how many years the money compounds. The more years, the better.

Recently Jan, a neighbor, asked me if she should help her teenage son set up an IRA. I said, absolutely, yes.

Jan's son just graduated from high school this spring and will heading off to college this fall. He is 18 years old and will be working as an intern during the summer months, but his pay will probably be less than $2,000 for the entire summer.

Yes, the boy isn't making much money. But Jan can, and should, deposit an amount equal to her son's income into a Roth IRA each year. If he earns $2,000 this summer, he can deposit that amount. But if he earns less, say $1,000, he'll be limited to that amount. But, even at the small amount, it still is a very good idea. Why?

Starting a Roth IRA at such a young age is a wonderful idea. If he could earn 10% per year, a $2,000 Roth IRA would be worth over $100,000 by the time Jan's son turns 60 years old, all of which could be tax-free. I encourage any young person to participate in the Roth IRA. I wish they had Roths when I was a teenager.

Going Half and Half with the Kids

The kids can't quite afford to buy a big new house on their own. You're in your 70s and want to go half and half with them on buying a lovely house that can be your dream retirement home.

Be careful! Be very careful. Money and property do strange things to people—especially family members. That's what I told my friend Phil. Yes, they're your children—who are now adults—but Phil could be walking into a minefield of economic, legal, and emotional landmines.

I told Phil that he has a number of questions that need to be answered before he can buy a house with his kids. And there is no perfect way for Phil to structure the transaction. If he titles the home jointly, he loses the ability to claim rent. If he titles the home in the kids' names only, he loses control.

Before Phil does anything, I advised him to meet with a real estate attorney who is well versed in estate planning to review all of his options.

I never recommend getting into any type of business relationship without having some type of legal agreement in place. And that also applies when the business is with family.

Helping Your Grandchildren Through College

College costs always seem to be going through the roof. That's because higher education inflation usually outstrips general inflation. But the value of a higher education is considerable. So it is inevitable that thoughtful grandparents want to help pay for those huge costs.

But remember, before you give, it is important to look at the tax implications of any help. Possibly, you should even talk things over with your advisor. Give too much, for example, to your grandson or granddaughter, and the gift tax can be triggered. And, by the way, the gift tax—like any other of the myriad, pesky taxes that infect our daily lives—can and has been changed. But, our taxing authorities say that the individual is entitled to give up to $10,000 per year to any person that individual chooses without incurring a gift tax (a tax on your generosity). However, the government doesn't want you to get carried away with the spirit of giving. So the giver does not receive a tax deduction on the gift of education, and the person receiving the gift does not receive a tax bill.

Nevertheless, there is a loophole in this maze of tax laws. If the grandson's college costs exceed $10,000 per year, one can write the checks directly to the school without incurring a gift tax. Education expenses paid directly to a qualified school are exempt from the $10,000 limit.

How Not to Help Your Daughter

Parents do the strangest things.

Take Bob, a client. His daughter and her family all live in his home. He was told that when he dies that this home would belong to his daughter, provided her name is on the deed. Putting her name on the deed, the daughter insists, will ensure that she will avoid a big tax bill after the death of the father. So, to help his daughter, he put her name on the deed.

In general, this is not a good move. It is typically inadvisable to put a child on a deed of a home for the purpose of estate planning. In most circumstances it will not eliminate taxes, but may cause a capital gains tax that would otherwise be avoidable.

Furthermore, if the daughter is listed on Bob's deed, the home may become part of the daughter's assets and could be subject to her creditors.

If Bob's goal is to have his home passed on to his daughter, his best bet is to list this wish in his will or living trust. Every person is entitled to pass along up to a large amount of assets without any estate taxes. So unless the estate is running into the millions of dollars, the daughter will not be assessed with any taxes.

Keeping Assets All in the Family

Most of the financial assets in this country are held by people age 55 or over.

They've had more time than the rest of us to accumulate assets. And it is also because they were raised in a culture that valued thrift more than ours does. However, sometimes success can result in tremendous problems. They want to ensure that their assets are passed on to family members, but the IRS is waiting just for those who haven't designed effective strategies to minimize taxes.

Some people have accumulated huge retirement amounts in their 457 plan. They decide to set up a living trust, which will be the beneficiary of this 457 plan upon death. They believe this will reduce taxes for their beneficiaries. However, a living trust can add a layer of complexity when it is named as a beneficiary of a 457 retirement plan. The living trust's potential disadvantages must be examined, especially in light of how and when one takes distributions. One must also consider other ways of protecting assets from the ubiquitous taxperson and his or her helpers.

Many living trusts are terminated after one's death. Living trusts are used to distribute assets without the hassle of probate. But once the assets are distributed, the trusts can be closed. The only time trusts continue is when they hold assets to be paid out at future dates.

When a trust is listed as a beneficiary of a retirement plan, the trust must continue in existence until the retirement plan has been fully distributed. Because withdrawals from retirement plans are taxable, deferring distributions well into the future can be a great strategy. However, this often forces the trustee to keep the trust open for years, having to deal with administering and filing tax returns for the trust.

The most tax-advantageous way of passing on your 457 plan is to roll the plan into an IRA and name your heir as the beneficiary. When you die, your heir can keep your IRA intact and defer a good portion of the taxes for the remainder of his or her life.

The Bypass Trust—Another Mixed Blessing

The government gives tax breaks. And it also taketh away. This is another reason why you need a good tax adviser. The breaks and the penalties change practically every year. And the ways these rules are interpreted and used change endlessly.

Take the Bypass Trust, also known as the A/B bypass. It can also be another way of avoiding, or reducing, estate taxes. But the downside is that it can also lead to potential capital gains.

Let's say a husband and wife bought a home in 1977 and lived in it until each of them died. They had created an A/B bypass trust in 1990 and put the house in Dad's side when he died in 1991. Mom continued to live there until her death in 2002.

When the house is sold, the heirs (the children) hope to use Mom's $250,000 tax exemption against any capital gains. Sorry. Can't do. The heirs are stuck in a place where it will be very difficult to avoid paying capital gains taxes when the home is sold.

A/B trusts, sometimes known as bypass trusts, can be effective in reducing estate taxes, but they can create other tax problems down the road. These trusts are used when a couple's estate is worth more than what one person can pass on without estate taxes.

When Dad died, the home was not transferred to Mom but was instead put in a bypass trust. Mom had the right to live in the home the rest of her life, but the home was not part of Mom's estate. She had no ownership interest in the home.

Now that Mom has died, the heirs will pay capital gains taxes on whatever they net from the home above the home's cost basis. The cost basis of the home is most likely not what Mom and Dad paid for the house, but what the home was worth when Dad died.

Typically, when a person inherits an asset, the asset's cost basis is stepped-up to the current market value, thus eliminating any capital gains. But when an asset transfers years after a person's death, as in this situation, the stepped-up cost basis reverts to the time when the individual died, not when the asset was transferred.

For families with estates greater than $1.5 million, it makes sense to use an A/B trust to reduce estate taxes. However, keep in mind that the portion that remains from the one who died will not receive a second stepped-up basis when the surviving spouse dies.

The government gave you a break. Now it wants that break back.

Family Peace

You want to provide something for your children when you die but there are good ways and bad ways of going about it.

The good way is to provide assets or cash in a clear undisputed manner. You don't want your children sharing assets after you're gone because money tends to cause people to act strangely.

Let's say we have two brothers in their 50s. They equally inherit a modest little house in a rotten neighborhood. The younger brother will continue to live in the house, paying the property taxes, utilities, general upkeep expenses, and so forth. He will not be paying rent to the older brother. Both brothers would pay any large expense, such as a new roof.

If the younger brother cannot or will not take care of the home, it will be sold and the proceeds split. A trust will be drawn up so that when one brother passes away, his share of the house will pass to the son of the older brother. The younger brother has no offspring and has never been married.

The older brother is preparing for retirement from a longtime government job with a good retirement package, several savings/investment accounts. He has his own house. The younger brother has a spotty employment history with little savings and no retirement package. Here's a recipe for disaster.

Why? Inheriting a home with a family member is often complicated, particularly if the home came from Mom and Dad. Not only are there the financial issues to think about, but also there is the emotional baggage that can come with siblings.

I see nothing but troubles down the road for both brothers if the younger one moves in. The older brother may have the best of intentions. But the odds are the younger brother will run into financial problems in the future. He always has in the past, and unless there has been a monumental change in his life, he'll continue to struggle with his finances in the future.

From my experience in dealing with inheritances, it is usually best to sell the family home and split the proceeds. It is the most equitable way. It also eliminates the heartache and pain that can come when family members start fighting over who deserves what.

The brothers should sell the home, and each one can make his own investment decisions. The younger brother can use the cash to help him meet his financial expenses and won't feel like he's accepting a handout from his older brother each month.

Living Trust Should Have Included House

When Peter's mother passed away, she had a living trust dividing everything between Peter and his sister, Jean. The mother's net worth was approximately $500,000 minus her home, which had all three of the names on the title.

After her death the home was sold and the proceeds were split in half, approximately $41,500 each. Peter came to me worried about his tax liability.

I asked him why wasn't his mother's home in a trust? Far too often I see people take the time and money to establish a living trust, but fail to transfer the home into the trust. Peter's mother received some bad advice. She never should have listed Peter and Jean on the home title. This can create a problem. The estate of Peter's mother was relatively small, so there will be no estate taxes due. However, when Peter sells the home, there may be capital gains due on the sale of the home. Had Peter inherited the home, either through a living trust or through probate, Peter would have received the home with a cost basis stepped-up to the fair market value, thereby eliminating any capital gains. Still, Peter did not inherit the home. That is unfortunate. Peter and his sister were given a portion of the home when their mother listed their names on the home. Because of this, Peter only received his portion with a stepped-up basis. The other two-thirds of the home carry over the mother's cost basis. That could cause Peter to pay capital gains tax on the sale. What a shame. Once again, Uncle Whiskers get a bigger slice of the property it took a person a lifetime to accumulate.

There still might be something that could remedy or mitigate the situation. Peter should contact an estate-planning attorney or CPA who specializes in estate taxes to see whether anything can be done at this point.

Looking at the Revocable Trust

Tom has several IRA-type retirement accounts. He was recently thinking of setting up a revocable trust. But he was worried that, if these accounts were to be transferred to this new trust, the taxing authorities might view the transfer as a total distribution that would be taxable in that year.

I told Tom that there is confusion regarding retirement plans when establishing revocable and/or living trusts. A trust cannot own an IRA, 401(k), or other type of retirement plan. If you transferred one of these accounts into a trust, it would be treated as a total distribution, fully taxable in the year in which the transfer took place.

Most revocable trusts are established for the purpose of estate planning in order to designate beneficiaries of one's estate and avoid probate. IRAs, 401(k)s, and other types of retirement plans already have those characteristics (namely, listing beneficiaries and avoiding probate). So there would be little need for a trust owning those assets.

I told Tom to think twice about what he was considering. That's because transferring ownership of IRAs to a trust would simply create an unnecessary tax bill.

Love, American Style

To watch the tube today, one would think that marriage is an impossible institution. However, marriage, in the right circumstance, can actually be a very effective estate-planning tool. I'm not saying that people should get hitched just to save a buck, but there are financial advantages to a legally recognized marriage.

Say a California woman has been engaged to a man in Nevada for 8 years. His net worth is over the $1.5 million estate tax exclusion. In the event of his death, he would like to leave the house to his Californian fiancée. In fact, he said so in his living trust.

If the Nevada man dies prematurely, then his Californian fiancée would not be responsible for any gift for inheritance tax. However, she would not receive his home until the estate has paid any federal estate taxes due. Depending on the size of his estate, the estate tax bill could cause a home or other asset to be sold in order to come up with the cash to pay the tax bill. As a fiancée, she has no marital rights. If she had been married, anything she would have received from him at his death would avoid estate taxes. Although each person is limited to a $1.5 million exclusion, spouses can receive an unlimited amount without triggering estate taxes.

I don't want to turn this into an Oprah or Dr. Phil book. I don't have any advice for singles. Certainly, having an 8-year engagement is entirely this woman's business. But—like it or not—there are tax consequences. Indeed, getting married is an excellent estate-planning technique. I wouldn't recommend marrying just to save on taxes. Nevertheless, if marriage is already in the plans, it certainly provides a reason to speed things up.

Mutual Fund Inheritance

All over America people are inheriting stock. But this inheritance can trigger all sorts of tax, investment, and emotional questions.

Far too often people are reluctant to sell securities that they have inherited. Many times people think that if the investment was good enough for Mom, Dad, or Uncle Charlie, then it must be good enough for them as well. But any investment held should reflect the individual investor's goals and risk tolerances—which may or may not be consistent with the inherited investment.

It can be an emotional issue. People get attached to certain companies. But sometimes they are not attached to the company, but to the memory of what the company once was. Maybe dad held a certain company for many years. It was a great investment in his time. But we're no longer in his time. And today the company has been overtaken by the competition. It is no longer a good investment. Or maybe the company was perfect for what your father was trying to accomplish, but it no longer fits into your portfolio philosophy.

These are issues you must resolve. And, because it can be an emotional issue, you may need an independent third party (a trusted adviser) to help you reach the correct conclusion.

As with any investment, you should always ask yourself this question: Would you buy it today? If you would, then keep the investment. But if you would not, get rid of it (or at least part of it). You'll be better off by paying a small capital gains tax today so you can build a portfolio that is best suited for your goals and objectives.

Providing Maximum Help for a Charity

Donating an appreciated stock, instead of a check, to a charity is good for you as well as good for the cause you want to help. I tell everyone to consider doing it.

The main advantage of "gifting" an appreciated asset is the avoidance of a potential capital gains tax. For example, let's say Raul purchased a stock for $10 and that stock is now worth $50. Raul would realize a $40 capital gain if he sold the stock. However, if Raul gifted the stock to a charity, he would avoid realizing a capital gain and the taxes associated with that gain.

And there is a further tax benefit for Raul. If he itemizes his deductions, he would be able to include the fair market value of his gift in his itemized deductions.

Gifting appreciated assets is almost always more advantageous than gifting cash or a check. Anyone who is currently gifting cash should seriously consider ceasing the cash gifts and gifting stock or other appreciated assets instead.

Chapter 11
Thrive after Retirement

Success will come to those people who are prepared.

You've reached a place in your life of reflection: There's nobody telling you what you have to do next. You no longer have to jump out of bed to fight your way to work on crowded freeways. You can shelve those uncomfortable suits. This chapter presents you with a guideline for building a new future and life, a life designed by you.

You may discover that managing your own life is very exciting. But the absence of discipline or a guiding hand can wreak havoc. Many people simply can't function unless someone else is calling the shots or establishing the framework; you will have to come to terms, perhaps for the first time, with excess time and space.

A recent study points out that baby boomers expect to retire from their current jobs, but many desire to launch into an entirely new endeavor by starting a new business or career.

Millions of baby boomers have a date with destiny, specifically their last day of work. The question isn't whether they'll retire; it's a matter of when and in what circumstances. The challenges of dealing with the largest generation in human history, the generation that has the longest projected life expectancy, is about to erupt.

Boomers reject a life of either full-time work or full-time leisure. When probed about their ideal work arrangement in retirement, the most common choice among boomers would be to repeatedly cycle between periods of work and leisure (42%), followed by part-time work (16%), start their own business (13%), and full–time work (6%). Only 17% hope to never work for pay again.

It's not just about the money either. Although 37% of boomers indicate that continued earnings is a very important part of the reason they plan to keep working, 67% listed mental stimulation and challenge as their motivation.

From "me" to "we." Boomers are now 10 times more likely to "put others first" (43%) than "put themselves first" (4%).

They are three times more worried about a major illness (48%), their ability to pay for health care (53%), or winding up in a nursing home (48%), than about dying (17%).

Boomer women are better educated and more independent, are simultaneously juggling more work and family responsibilities, and are more financially engaged than any generation in history. In fact, they are more than six times more likely to share responsibility for savings and investments compared to their mothers' generation (33% now, 5% then). They also view the dual liberations of empty nesting and retirement as providing new opportunities for career development, community involvement, and continued personal growth.

Get Ready for Changes

Ken Dychtwald, demographer and author of *Age Wave*, says companies are heading off a demographic cliff over the next decade. "There aren't enough people in the baby-bust cohort to replace all the aging boomers. The 35- to 44-year-old in the labor force will decline by 3.8 million, as the number of available 55- to 64-year-olds will increase by 8.3 million. If you were to visualize what is happening as boomers retire from their jobs, what follows behind us is a cliff.

How do you prepare yourself for your next stage of life? Why not take all those years of experience, knowledge, and know-how and become an entrepreneur.

You can ask yourself the question: What do I love to do most of all in my life? Use your gift of expertise or look at the convergence of two demographic trends: the increasing number of aging baby boomers and the more limited number of potential employees in the following generations, Generation X and Generation Y. Generation X—now ages 27 to 40—will provide a shrinking pool of prime-time workers. Many also predict that Generation Y—now ages 18 to 26—will simply not supply enough young workers to fill the void that will be left. The Employment Policy Foundation of Washington concluded that demand for labor in the United States would outstrip supply by 22% over the next 30 years.

Of course, the overall increase in the labor force wouldn't mean there is a sufficient supply of workers with the skills needed to handle those highly paid professional jobs in the financial services industry, but it does show that the widespread shortages that are being predicted may not occur.

Retiring boomers will leave a huge void in the workforce, so start a business that provides services for people in their retirement years. Before you open that sport shop you've dreamed about, stop, and consider this decision carefully.

Look at the Demographics

Before you buy that fast-food franchise, you might want to consider starting a wheelchair-manufacturing business. It is a matter of looking at the demographics and planning ahead. Becoming successful in business will depend on the changes and challenges in our population.

Small Business, the Heart of the American Economy

It's the American Dream. Start a small business, become your own boss, and make a million dollars. But many, many small businesses fail and turn into the American nightmare.

How does one achieve the former and avoid the latter? What you need is dependent on what type of business you plan to start and who will be involved in the business. Are you acting alone? Will you have partners? Do you need to protect yourself from future liabilities?

The best place for you to start is with the trade association in your industry. All industries have some type of trade association—from florists and chefs to computer and auto repair. Contact your association to learn what types of licenses are required. There are also numerous regulatory and tax requirements.

Depending on your requirements, you may find you need only a local business license and a doing-business-as (DBA) filing with the state. You can complete the necessary forms by contacting the various agencies yourself, or you can hire an attorney, CPA, or other business professional to help you.

Regarding tax filings, it all depends on how your business is organized. If you're operating as a sole proprietor, you don't need a new tax ID, and you simply file an additional form (schedule C) with your income taxes. If you operate as a partnership or corporation, you will need a tax ID, and the company will have to file its own tax returns.

You will be required to pay quarterly tax estimates when your business generates a profit. The tax rate will be based on your other income, but you'll have to pay FICA taxes as well. Quarterly estimates can easily run 30% to 50% of the profit.

Don't let the bureaucracy intimidate you. It might seem like a daunting process to get the business going, but the rewards could be well worth it.

RESOURCES

SMART Recovery®

SMART Recovery® offers free face-to-face and online mutual help groups. SMART (Self-Management and Recovery Training) helps people recover from many types of addictive behaviors. SMART sponsors an online message board, more than 300 face-to-face meetings around the world, and 13 online meetings per week. Their Web site is www.smartrecovery.org.

Debtors Anonymous

If you find you need a lifeline to help you from sinking in debt, contact Debtors Anonymous.

Debtors Anonymous (DA) assists people in recovering from debt problems. Visit their Web site to take a quick quiz to decide if you have such a problem. What are the signs of compulsive spending? To get started, visit the following: www.debtorsanonymous.org.

There are no dues or fees for DA membership; they are self-supporting through their own contributions. DA is not allied with any sect, religious denomination, political party, organization, or institution; it does not wish to engage in any controversy. DA neither endorses nor opposes any causes. Their primary purpose is to stop "debting" (1 day at a time) and to help other compulsive debtors to stop incurring unsecured debt.

If this sounds like a group that would be helpful to you, find a DA meeting.

Please Note: The Web site links and phone numbers below are provided to facilitate information about local DA activities. Providing this information does not constitute or indicate review, endorsement, or approval by the author or publisher of this book.

The following is a list of local phone numbers that provide information about DA meetings in your area. Visit the regional Web sites for detailed meeting information.

Albany-Kingston-Woodstock, NY, 888-344-1990 - www.empirestateda.org

Albuquerque, NM, 505-798-9025

Atlanta, GA, 770-662-6060

Austin, TX, 512-320-7678 - www.main.org/debtorsanonymous

Baltimore, MD - www.midatlanticda.org,

Boise, ID, 208-562-8288 - www.geocities.com/idaho_da

Boulder, CO, 303-430-2811

Chicago, IL, area; WI & IL Information, 312-409-2222 - www.glada.org

Cincinnati, OH, 513-403-7957 - DACincinnati@hotmail.com

Columbus, OH 614-470-2243 - www.dacentralohio.org

Dallas, TX, 972-504-6332 - www.dfwda.org

Dayton, OH, 937-640-2750

DELAWARE information - www.delawareda.org

Denver, CO, 303-430-2811

Detroit, MI, 734-489-0252

Dublin, Ireland, 087-121-5540 - www.debtorsanonymous.info

E. Pennsylvania, 877-717-3328 - www.njpada.org

Gainesville, FL, 352-332-4636

Greensboro, NC, 336-917-0901

Hartford, CT, 860-793-3766

Houston, TX, 281-470-8868 - www.dahouston.org

Indianapolis, IN, 317-731-3728

Jacksonville, FL, 904-269-8010

London, England, and U.K. Information, 0207-644-5070 - www.debtorsanonymous.info

Los Angeles, CA, 310-855-8752 - www.socalda.org

Milwaukee, WI, 866-331-7881

Minneapolis, MN, 952-953-8438

Nashville, TN, 615-269-3628

New England, 617-728-1426 - www.danewengland.org

New Jersey, 877-717-3328 - www.njpada.org

New Orleans, LA, 504-363-1132 - steps2debtfree@cox.net; steps2debtfree@aol.com

New York, NY, 212-969-8111 - www.danyc.org

North Carolina - www.dartnc.homestead.com

Northern California, 415-522-9099 - www.ncdaweb.org

Northeast Ohio, 330-327-3562 - home.neo.rr.com/dacanton/index.htm

Orlando, FL, 407-263-4243

Paris, France, 01-48-22-16-58 - www.debiteursanonymes.org

Philadelphia, PA, 877-717-3328

Phoenix, AZ, 602-234-6566

Portland, OR, 503-972-8576 - www.oregondebtorsanonymous.org

Richmond, VA, 804-254-2371

Sacramento, CA, 916-349-7093

Salt Lake City, UT, 801-359-4325 - www.utin.org

San Diego, CA, 619-525-3065 - www.dasandiego.org

San Francisco, CA, 415-522-9099 - ww.ncdaweb.org

Santa Fe and Taos, NM, 505-798-9025

Seattle, WA, 206-903-9463 - www.dawashstate.org

St Louis, MO, 314-851-0915

Southern California, 310-855-8752 - www.socalda.org

Toronto, Canada, 416-207-1077 -mywebpage.netscape.com/torontoda/
Meetings.html

Tucson, AZ, 520-570-7990

Vancouver, British Columbia, 604-878-DEBT

Washington, DC, 202-319-0229 - www.capitalareadebtors.org

Washington State, 206-903-9463 - www.dawashstate.org

Wisconsin - www.glada.org

Free 2 Week Trial Offer for U.S. Residents From Investor's Business Daily:

INVESTOR'S BUSINESS DAILY will provide you with the facts, figures, and objective news analysis you need to succeed.

Investor's Business Daily is formatted for a quick and concise read to help you make informed and profitable decisions.

This book, along with other books, is available at discounts that make it realistic to provide it as a gift to your customers, clients, and staff. For more information on these long lasting, cost effective premiums, please call us at (800) 272-2855 or you may email us at sales@fpbooks.com.